✤

CONFLICTS OF THE CLERGY

A Psychodynamic Study with Case Histories

✤

Conflicts of the Clergy

A Psychodynamic Study with Case Histories

BY

MARGARETTA K. BOWERS, M.D.

THOMAS NELSON & SONS

Edinburgh   NEW YORK   *Toronto*

DESIGN BY FRANK KARPELES

TO MY DAUGHTERS

Foreword

I

Clergymen are people and, as such, they deserve that care and devotion from the psychotherapist that the rest of the human community needs when troubles of psychological nature develop. But there are several reasons for making clergymen the object of special concern. In their role they must not only help preserve the spiritual values of the past, but have a molding influence on the innovating forces of the present time. Similarly to psychoanalysts, they must find a solution to their conflicts before they can affect people favorably; but, whereas psychoanalysts affect a relatively small number of people, clergymen can affect masses.

In reading *Conflicts of the Clergy*, in fact, one discovers this important and frequent similarity between clergymen and psychoanalysts; in both groups there is quite a number of persons who were consciously or unconsciously directed by their inner conflicts to select their profession. That this is not necessarily an unfortunate origin, but one which through various vicissitudes may lead to healthy channels and to enriching sublimations is amply demonstrated in the second part of the book. Some of Dr. Bowers' patients went into the ministry in search of love, having never experienced human love; others in search of a good father; others as a reaction to an early death or abandonment by a parental figure. Dr. Bowers' vivid reports of specific case histories portrays the anguish which, in some instances, led to the first childhood encounter with the Divinity, later to the selection of a pastoral vocation and finally to the therapeutic solution of the conflicts. This book teaches how to separate and treat differently those conflicts which lead to an intuition of the divine, which is helpful and meaningful, from the distortions which may affect adversely the future ministers and their parishioners.

In the first part of the book a theoretical background is offered which prepares for the full understanding of the second, clinical part. The intimate connections between what in psychoanalysis is called the primary process and the mystical experience are clearly revealed. Some Christian Sacraments, like that of the Communion, are analyzed from many psychoanalytic angles. Here again it is demonstrated how the unconscious symbolism does not necessarily detract but may actually widen the religious meaning.

Dr. Bowers' book is the result of many factors which blend in harmonious fusion: first, her diversified human experiences as a country doctor in the deep South for several years; second, an excellent psychiatric and psychoanalytic training; third, an uncommon experience in treating ministers and rabbis with psychotherapy; fourth, an unusual knowledge of both the Jewish and Christian theologies. This combination of attributes puts Dr. Bowers, I would say, not in a rare but in a unique position, which commands our respect and careful consideration.

Before closing these brief remarks I would like to comment on another characteristic of this book: its style. Quite often the author does not make her point directly, in a streamlined, mechanical, or logical approach, as it is usually done in scientific presentations. At the very first her style may even evoke a feeling of impatience in the reader who would like to grasp the meaning immediately. But soon enough this particular style catches you. You come to understand that this is the author's way, inherently congruous with the content of the book. The round-about style and the analogic thinking create an atmosphere of closeness to the religious spirit, in which relations between psychoanalytic and theological concepts are more easily felt and recognized and better studied. At times the reader can even ask himself whether some of the chapters are psychiatric presentations or sermons, and the answer is that they are both. They are answers to a religious need and to a psychiatric inquiry.

It is wtih great pleasure that I introduce Dr. Margaretta Bowers' book.

SILVANO ARIETI, M.D.

New York
April 28, 1963

Foreword

II

Conflicts of the Clergy is a very special book and Margaretta Bowers is a very special person.

She is a therapist who has undergone analysis of her own religious attitudes. She has had thorough training in the technique of the psychotherapy of religious conflicts. And she has acquainted herself with the theology of the Roman Catholic, the Jew, and all manner of Protestants.

This I learned some years ago when I sent patients to her and I can vouch for her success with psychiatry and religious counseling.

Now comes this book which is bound to stimulate the interest of ecclesiastical authorities, who face difficult situations they themselves cannot meet.

There are men who think they are called to the Sacred Ministry, but who are not always truly and immediately fit for the vocation they would choose. There are others who are admitted yet break down after their ordination though they have made their required promises to frame and fashion their own lives and the lives of their families according to the Doctrine of Christ, and to make themselves wholesome examples and patterns to the flock of Christ.

Dr. Bowers summarizes such problems as may be met in clerical psychotherapy, for example, the loneliness of many patients who must learn to find compensation in the warmth of human relations with people. Sometimes the problem is the suffering of clergy because of their need really to be what they feel they ought to be and what their congregation expect them to be. They know that they are expected to be devout, but devotion eludes them. As they continue to feel their lack they become more and more angry. They find it difficult to pray. They feel completely hopeless and despondent, with no depth of emotion. Try as hard as they will, they find it impossible to meet the demands of their ideal self-image. Or it may be that they have had traumatic childhood experiences, perhaps with death, which have been carried over into adulthood, with the result that there is a loss of trust in human relationships. How these and many other problems can be successfully met in clerical psychotherapy are to be found in the case histories.

For the time and work involved in the preparation of *Conflicts of the Clergy* I would ask to be numbered among many readers who will have reason to be grateful to its author.

BENJAMIN M. WASHBURN

Ridgefield, Connecticut
April 1, 1963

Foreword

III

Every clergyman deals with emotionally unhealthy as well as emotionally healthy congregants. He knows, too, that he meets and lives with unhealthy as well as healthy clergymen. If he is honest with himself and has deep feelings about his calling and the destiny of religion in human society, he is concerned with the emotional capacity and stability of the clergy.

There has long been a real need for basic studies of the motives which send young men into the priesthood, ministry, and rabbinate, of the unique emotional stresses they face in the course of their complex and difficult work, of the approaches which can be used in psychotherapy to help them regain full mental health when disabling disturbances occur within them.

We know of no one better qualified to have undertaken this study than Dr. Margaretta Bowers. As a psychiatrist, she combines many years of intensive work with sick clergymen and a breadth and depth of understanding of religious systems and religious values.

We hope that Jewish readers of Dr. Bowers' book will not find it difficult to transpose the nomenclature and concepts of Christianity used here into their own framework. Rabbis and Jewish laymen alike can learn much from this book, even though Dr. Bowers obviously writes as a committed and devoted Christian.

Protestant and Catholic clergy as well as laymen can learn much from the chapters of this book devoted to problems of Jews and to concepts of Judaism. The same kind of transposition suggested to Jewish readers should not be difficult for Christians. Nor should Christians of other persuasions than Dr. Bowers' Episcopalian affiliation find difficulty in making her ideas relevant to their own denominations.

Finally, it is to be hoped that psychiatrists, whether or not they are personally religiously committed, will be willing to study the unique combination of clinical competence and religious understanding Dr. Bowers has brought to this work. There is much to be learned here which can be of benefit to therapists, not only when they treat clergy patients, but in the treatment of all patients whose lives include religious problems—and so many do.

Conflicts of the Clergy is a superb symbol of the merging of psychiatric discipline with the compassion and devotion religion at its best tries to instill in men.

MAURICE N. EISENDRATH

New York
April 15, 1963

Preface

During the years of my psychiatric residency I had, at the suggestion of Dr. Smiley Blanton, begun to lecture to Episcopal clergy on the subject of psychiatry and religious counseling and put in a year of part-time work at the Marble Collegiate Clinic. My first seminarian patient was referred to me by the Reverend Thomas Bigham shortly after I entered private practice. Later, when another case presented disciplinary problems, Father Bigham advised me to call on the Right Reverend Benjamin Washburn. Bishop Washburn apparently approved my work in that particular case, for more referrals followed. Clergymen and seminarians began to come to me voluntarily, and a few came under discipline. For many years I followed the custom of calling on Father Bigham and Bishop Washburn for theological clarification when problems emerged both in the treatment of patients and in the writing of my papers on the psychological problems of the clergy. Later, when I began working with rabbis, I found similar generous assistance on the part of Rabbis Eugene Lipman and Samuel Glasner.

For many years I was quite unaware that clerical psychotherapy was of special interest to many professionals both in the field of psychotherapy and the field of religion. Only after my papers had been well received did I realize that the field was relatively unexplored and that publishing my findings in book form would be of value.

This study is the result of fifteen years of work with clerical patients and religiously dedicated persons in psychoanalytically oriented psychotherapy and group therapy. The patient body consists of 37 ordained clergymen, 28 seminarians, missionaries, and dedicated men and women—a classification that includes those who studied for the ministry but did not go on to ordination, wives of clergy, and those who failed in their novitiate as monks or nuns.

Among the many to whom I am indebted for advice and encouragement the following names stand out: Silvano Arieti, M.D.; Harold Rosen, M.D.; Mortimer Ostow, M.D.; Benjamin Nelson, Ph.D.; the Reverend Alden Sears, Ph.D.; the Reverend André Godin, S.J.; and Sylvia Brecher-Marer, Ph.D., for her psychological studies and insight; and the Bishops' Committee on Pastoral Counselling of the House of Bishops of the Protestant Episcopal Church.

The designations "priest," "minister," and "clergyman" are not meant to refer to denominational differences in this book. They are used strictly in the primary, spiritual sense.

New York   MARGARETTA K. BOWERS
October, 1962

Contents

PART ONE

A Survey of the Problem   1

PART TWO

Case Histories 77

PART THREE

Conclusion 227

PART ONE

A Survey of the Problem

I. Introduction

The clergy are lonely, set-apart people. Even the healthy, fulfilled, successful ones remember the loneliness of their childhood. The sick clergy—who are the concern of this book—were even more lonely. They were frequently only children. Often, they were culturally isolated, or thought they were. The interesting thing is that in working with a patient population of seriously sick people this same quality of a lonely isolated childhood is very common. I can, therefore, only pose the question: Is there something in the religious vocation that makes it possible for these lonely ones to compensate for their loneliness in their vocation so that they make a better working adjustment in the world than those with the same problem who have not made religion their life work? These clergy were very, very lonely ones, watchful ones, interested in what was going on around them but set apart from it. Why was it that they went into religion instead of going into the other set-apart types of vocation? The sea captain is equally set apart. He is equally lonely on the bridge of his ship. He is equally a person who carries the dreadful weight of authority. The ship's captain learns to endure and seeks out a life when for days, weeks, months, or in the olden days, years, he is master of all he surveys. He has no confidants, no consultants. His ship's officers can only advise him of the conditions of the ship, of the wind, and of the storm. His is the decision to go into the storm or around it, to go into battle or to run from it. If the ship goes down, he goes down with it, because if he is rescued, he faces a trial so severe and so condemnatory that few men survive to be given another command.

And yet, the sea captain of old, alone on his bridge, with only an occasional citing of the North Star, was relying more on the sturdiness of his ship and the loyalty of his men, more on the predictability of outer reality and the essential value of human relationships, than does the religionist. Somehow the religionist is even more lonely because he charts a course in inner reality where there are no beacon lights, where there are no proper charts and soundings of the depths unexplored and fathomless. He carries out of his own needs the command of the ship of the church, of the whole of humanity into these unfathomed, uncharted depths of the human soul, seeking a safe harbor in life after death, seeking to break through the sound barrier like a jet pilot without even the jet pilot's reliance on familiar instruments, and dies. He explores an unknown of which reasonable people doubt the existence. Columbus sailing westward seeking to find China knew more precisely where he was going than do these men.

Somehow in childhood they had in their loneliness, in the remnants of childhood omnipotence, the need to carry the awesome authority of the divine. And now they dare to interpret the divine, to pronounce to the people an ethical system of right and wrong; they dare to say which is good and which is not good; they dare to carry the keys of heaven and hell, ordained with the absolute authority: "whatever you bind on earth shall be bound in heaven, and whatever you loose on earth shall be loosed in heaven." They have sought to determine what is best for the multitude, as Moses high in the mists of Mount Sinai spoke with his God, and coming down translated for the people the words which they heard only as the voice of rushing waters, as the noise of a great wind.

The responsibility of the country doctor is a heavy one. He also has no one to turn to in consultation. There are those times in midwinter when the snows are heavy on the ground, or in the spring when the ice is thawing, when he must make his calls before the sun has risen high in the sky, for otherwise, the roads are impassable. He learns to treasure the icy ruts because at least he can get through them. He may have a dozen people critically ill with pneumonia in a dozen scattered locations. He spends night after night on his rounds, making the travail of women in childbirth more secure, snatching a bit of sleep now and again. But his responsibilities lie within his human skill. Even in the worst of his fatigue, he knows his competence and he can live within his ability.

The religionist carries what for him is the awful responsibility of the eternal welfare of his people, not just this life, but the next. If only the religionist could somehow permit himself to share his burden with the others who carry the set-apartness, the terrible responsibilities of human judgment; if he could know somehow his own humanity as a judge who passes the sentence of execution or grants a pardon. For his confidence is solely in the divine when he counsels the doctor and the lawyer, the judge and the sea captain.

It is said of Rabbi Akiba that of the four who entered the Parde—the exploration of the mysteries of the law—only Rabbi Akiba returned as he had entered, unharmed. One went into that delirium which we call insanity; one committed suicide; and one became a heretic. But Rabbi Akiba returned as he had entered, in peace. Now, when Rabbi Akiba was asked to describe the palaces of God, which he had explored in the divine chariot-throne mysticism of that time, he said, "In one palace I contemplated the everloving kindness of God. In another palace I contemplated His stern justice. In another palace I contemplated His mercy." And so it went. He used the discipline of the divine chariot type of intense and lofty seeking-after-God as a means of understanding God; yet, he did not cease to be human. He could remain a human being. He could contemplate God, in His attributes, and he could, undoubtedly, like Maimonides who came after him, realize that His rule is not our rule. Rabbi Akiba did not seek to lay down absolutes, and yet when he died, he died the death of a martyr who, accepting the inevitable, uses every bit of the cunning which has been given man to handle the pain of physical suffering and death. He was accused of being a sorcerer because of this. His answer was that he knew the pain, but he was able to set this aside in his intense concentration upon the love of God. This concentration, this discipline, was probably also present with St. Stephen whose face was that of an angel when he was stoned. We have other words by which we try in this generation to understand this type of discipline of the mind, body, and soul; but that is another book.

What happens in the lonely lives of these priestly children that makes it necessary for them to want positions of such dreadful authority, of such consuming responsibility, of such lonely set-apartness? What made it necessary for them to give the whole of their energies to the service of the Divine Presence as they proceeded? Why do they need to perform their rituals? Why do they need their special garb, their special set-apartness in dress? Why do they need this type of authority with which to clothe their very natural need to be the center of attention, not just of the whole family, but of the whole community? Why do they need to have the power to sway the people with honeyed words or make them tremble in the fear of their damnation? Why do they need these compensations for their loneliness? Do they find compensation in the warmth of human relationships with their people? Do they find some sublimation in helping their people at the time they most desperately need help, when the death angel has been among them? What is happening inside them? Why is it that no one dares study them, that no one dares pin them down under a microscope and watch them? Is it that we are too fearful that they may have answers which we do not? That there may be a power with which they are in touch but with which we have no communication except through them? And yet, it seems to me that if we, as physicians, have the right to try to heal their mental ills, to do so we have to study them; we have to do autopsies; we have to do exploratory operations. How can we find what religion is except by finding out what motivates these people?

Ezekiel speaks of the vision of the glory of God as the color of *hashmal,* which means lightning. It is usually tranlated into almost nonsense syllables meaning electrum. In modern Hebrew, *hashmal* means electricity and is used in works on electronics as signifying electronic energy. Now we would never know anything about electronic energy if we had not sought to study lightning. It was not many years ago that Benjamin Franklin tried to catch some lightning with a kite. It was a rather crude way of trying to get a little of the unknown into a bottle where it could be smelled and tasted, or felt, or seen. And so I have tried to send up a kite and catch a little *hashmal*. I think we need to spend an equally serious amount of effort trying to understand that driving force which we call religion, just as we have done with that force in outer reality which we call electricity. We still do not understand but we know very much more about how to use electrical energy safely and skillfully than we did a couple of hundred years ago.

I think, too, that the great admirals of that fleet of ships we call the Church have to face a new and stern responsibility. In the past, there was no way for navies to avoid sending their sea captains out to sea in what might turn out to be leaky, rat-infested ships. They had no way to prevent the plague of scurvy. Now, things are a bit different in the ships that plough the ocean waves in outer reality, or in the planes that fly through the air ocean of outer reality. We know that probably nothing requires more of a man in sturdiness of judgment, physique, moral fiber, self-confidence, and split-second timing than going through the sound barrier and flying beyond the speed of sound. I do not know whether the men who dare to do such explorations are given all of the available safeguards of modern medicine and science, but I think they are given a vastly greater amount than are our clergy. Our clergy are asked to do the same thing. But they are still using the same antiquated set of navigational instruments they used hundreds of years ago. They are told that no new methods of navigation are available to them. They are still sent out in worm-eaten, rat-infested, rusty ships with a scurvy-ridden crew. And they are told they should pray and everything will be all right. But how can a man pray when his ship is in such desperate plight? How can a man pray when day after day he is never able to get a set on the sun and find his course, when night after night he is unable to find the North Star and get a set for his course by celestial navigation? How can the man be asked to get his ship into port when his crew becomes mutinous because of the bad conditions?

It seems to me that the very least we can do for these men is to give them the mental and psychological health, the emotional health and maturity so that they are not weak, scurvy-ridden ships. If this *hashmal* which we call the divine revelation in religion is so precious to us all, it would seem as though it were worthy to be put in new, strong, and sturdy vessels. And we can make it possible with those tools which we now have to give these men the best of navigation equipment. We can give them good ships. We can give them charts. Granted that we may have many years before us in careful study before we are able to tell them what their course is. Perhaps we can never tell them. Perhaps we can only be navigation officers and ships' surgeons. But if they would only take us on board to help them in their lonely watch as captains of the ship of God, then we might be of assistance.

II. The Self-Image

All of us have an ideal of ourselves. To the extent that we are able to fulfill our ideal self-image we are healthy or sick.

The clergy suffer terribly from this need to be what they feel they should be, that they know their congregations expect them to be and what they know or feel themselves to be. They know their people expect them to be devout. They know they should be, and yet no matter how hard they try to find that inner sense of faith and security we call devotion, it eludes them. As they continue to fail they become more and more angry. They become fearful that they will be found out, that no matter how skillful their pretense someone with a keen awareness will sense them out. That is why we need devout lay people in the group therapy situation. That is why we need therapists who can look with compassion beneath the façade.

All through the ages the clergy have suffered from the insurmountable contrasts between their very real humanity and the transcendent requirements of their symbolic representation as *the priest*, the Incarnate Christ. In Reformation times, the glaring contrasts between the evils of the Church and the demands made on the priest, who in his lonely sanctuary brought down God to his people in the Elements of the Bread and Wine, became too much to endure. Reformers such as Martin Luther rebelled and, out of their own needs, developed the doctrine of the Priesthood of All Believers; this sharing of the responsibility of the act of bringing down the Divine Presence among the congregation lessened the magical set-apartness of the Divine Liturgy. But no matter how the understanding of the Sacraments has changed,

9

the tension between the mystical and the reasoned theology remains, and even the healthiest, most devout clergy feel a very
real anxiety at the moment the Service begins. The clergy whose
anxieties were increased by their own psychopathology relive in
their struggles the conflicts of all the ages gone before and seldom can feel the comfort of present-day liberal Protestantism to
which they usually belong intellectually and ecclesiastically.

Some years ago I found a book which expresses this self-image
in a manner that staggers the imagination. When one realizes that
this is soberly written, one sees the despondency of the religionist who in his heart and conscience feels he should fulfill these
demands which cannot be met except by cutting all ties with
sanity.

> For a priest is a miracle of God's love to us; a man who,
> through His Sacrament of Ordination becomes *another* Christ
> with powers that beggar human imagination. . . . Nothing can
> be greater in this world of ours than a priest. Nothing but God
> Himself.
>
> A priest is a holy man because he walks before the Face of
> the All Holy.
>
> A priest understands all things.
>
> A priest forgives all things.
>
> A priest is a man who lives to serve.
>
> A priest is a man who has crucified himself, so that he too
> may be lifted up and draw all things to Christ.
>
> A priest is a symbol of the Word made flesh.
>
> A priest is the naked sword of God's justice.
>
> A priest is the hand of God's mercy.
>
> A priest is the reflection of God's love.
>
> He teaches God to us. . . . He brings God to us. . . . He
> represents God to us.[1]

This statement on the nature of priesthood, though put in ex-
alted terms, reflects in a very real sense the clergyman's ideal
self-image, and at the same time intimates the staggering demands on his heart and conscience if he is to fulfill it.

All religions of Judeo-Christian origin place fearsome demands

[1] Catherine de Hueck, *Dear Seminarian* (Milwaukee: Bruce Publishing
Co., 1950), pp. 85–87. Used by permission.

on the minister; the burden of the ideal self-image recognizes no denominational differences. In the Sacrament of Holy Communion, the priest symbolizes the people, the congregation in relation to God; to the people, he is in communication and in direct relationship with God. He represents God, he may even become God. At the moment of the consecration of the Host, this feeling is most intense for at that moment the physical elements of the bread and the wine become the body and blood of Our Lord. This is accepted by Catholics as a literal actuality in the doctrine of transubstantiation and as a symbolic reality by Protestants. The inadequate self-image represents a perpetual source of agony as each ritual is performed. Although the Catholic believes that the Sacraments are grace of themselves and the properly ordained priest knows the Sacraments he performs are valid for his people no matter how inadequate he may be, his inadequacy intensifies his own sense of damnation. The rabbi is in an even more difficult position for he knows that according to his tradition the prayers of his congregation will not be heard unless he is worthy and devout. In Jewish theology, the entire hope of efficacy of ritual or of prayer is wholly dependent on the person's achieving a proper state of concentration and devotion called "Kavanah." Bachya denied all value to the outward acts of religion if devoid of Kavanah, and Maimonides declared that a prayer without Kavanah is no prayer at all. As staggering as the awareness of inadequate self-image is to the Christian, it is vastly more so to the Orthodox Jew. The Jew lacking in ideal devotion as rabbi would be guilty of a conscious crime against his people while the Christian priest is hurting only himself.

As we have said, the burden of the ideal self-image recognizes no denominational differences, although for the Christian ministry it is a matter of individual conscience whereas for the rabbi it has firm historical and theological definition. On the Day of Atonement when the high priest prayed that the sins of Israel be forgiven for that year, he went into the inner sanctuary alone, with a rope tied around his ankle, so that if God be displeased and strike him dead, his body could be removed from the inner sanctuary without desecration and without endangering other people who might also be subject to God's wrath if His sanctuary was needlessly violated. If the prayer of the high priest was accepted by God, the scarlet thread that was woven into the cord around his ankle would turn white, and then the people would know that the sins of the past year were forgiven. The privilege of being a hereditary priest, a *kohane,* was thus a heavy burden and a dangerous duty.

The nature of the ministry with the awesome demands it places on the self-image of the individual minister constitutes the most formidable obstacle in the path of clerical psychotherapy. It is an integral part of the priestly self-image that if the minister is sick in his religious life, he should be able to cure himself. And when he finds that the Sacraments do not heal him, and that all of the beneficent services of the Church do not heal him, when he finds himself unable to pray, he feels that this means only one thing— he is bad. He cannot believe that it may just mean that he needs a doctor. It is very, very difficult for the clergy to realize that their religious life can be healthy or sick, and that if sick, it can be exposed to therapeutic intervention in the same way that their bodies can. The idea that if they prayed their spiritual disturbances would disappear is deeply rooted not only in their minds, but in the minds of their congregations. Psychotherapy is accepted for the clergy in some sophisticated parishes in metropolitan areas; but in general, the immediate reaction to such an idea is that if they only prayed, they would be all right. They should shut themselves in a closet and pray and God will take care of them. And the clergy do pray. They pray long and earnestly, and the sweat rolls down their foreheads and drips on the ground.

Then the time comes when a man cannot pray any longer. Many of the great saints have lived through what is called the "dark night of the soul." Many of the great religious mystics have written about their personal experience of such a time in their lives. These were uncommonly gifted, devout people who suddenly were no longer able to feel the comfort and the fulfillment of their devotion. They were suddenly shut away from God, their prayers empty. Service to their religion was an empty discipline. Life was empty. The sun did not shine as brightly, the spring was not as beautiful, nothing had the meaning, nothing had the intensity, nothing had the beauty it should have. What emerges from their accounts with great clarity is in actuality the picture of the classic depression. They felt depressed; they hated themselves; they shut themselves away from God. They felt completely hopeless and despondent, bad, useless, wasted.

I feel that there are many clergymen like these. I have the feeling that I cause many such people discomfort when I speak to them because I probe too deeply. They have the same discomfort with the devout of their cloth, but their defenses are better in relation to their own profession, where they know better how to appear in the semblance of piety. It seems to me that, of all the clergymen I have treated, it is these men who are the most worth while for society. These are the solid reasonable men and women who are concerned with making religion function for the good of society. If they were aware that they could be relieved of their inner humiliation and shame, a great burden could be taken from them. They feel that they are phonies, that they are whited sepulchres. They never have the satisfaction and the joy in the value of the work which they perform. Only in the moment of doing are they happy and fulfilled. As soon as the job is completed, they are once more empty and dead. They try to find a surcease in human love, and here too they fail. They cannot feel any depth of emotion, be it love or tenderness or sadness. They are cut off from the wellsprings of their emotional life.

The well-organized, well-oriented person in outer reality may keep his outer reality reasonable and logical at the expense of sacrificing his inner devotion, his inner awareness of his creative unconscious. He is like the captain of a ship who in the midst of a storm battens down the hatches and when the storm is over finds that one of the hatches is jammed. He can no longer open it. Unfortunately it covers the compartment where the engineering devices that control his radar equipment and his gyrocompass are located, and so in time these valuable aids to his navigation are cut off. He is no longer able to sense his way through fog and murk. He is no longer able to rely on the automatic setting of his compass. He has to resort to primitive methods of steering his ship by the devices of outer logical, understandable reality;

and after a time he forgets that he has lost the means by which he could unerringly plot his course or, more tragically, he feels cheated because other ship captains have this equipment and his ship is deprived. He does a good job, and he gets his ship into port, but it is hard work, tedious work and the old deep upsurge of happiness and fulfillment in being a ship captain seems to be gone.

It is generally at this point that the psychotherapist sees the clerical patient for the first time. Prayer has already failed him. He feels unable to live up to his self-perceived image. He is unable to fulfill his priestly functions without suffering unbearable agony. He is likely to have developed psychosomatic disturbances. It is at this point that the subjective elements that went into the composition of his self-image begin to unfold. (See the case of Jacob whom we have named after the patriarch who struggled, as did our Jacob, with the Angel of the Lord.)

III. Primary-Process Thinking

Symbols are the language of the normal thought processes of
children, of the creative mentation of artists, poets, and mystics.
It is the picture language which Freud called the primary
process, and Arieti has named as characteristic of the paleological
or prelogical mind. As Bleuler pointed out, so many years ago,
it is only when this primary-process thinking becomes distorted
that we have the condition which we call schizophrenia. It is,
perhaps, more useful to apply the term "prelogical" because the
laws of logical thinking are not available to the prelogical mind.
Although we have learned much about the process of distortion
of prelogical thinking, we have not learned enough of the laws
or yardsticks by which we can determine readily what is rational
and irrational in undistorted prelogical thinking.

The myths, the rituals, and the creeds that make up what we
call religion are like the manifest content of a dream which, while
using common symbols, expresses for the individual his own personal feelings, attitudes, relationships, needs, symptoms, and
defenses. Always the analyst must seek to know the hidden meaning underlying whatever a patient says, does, or dreams. The
signs and symbols, the language of religion, have unique personal
meaning for each person. The unknown in the God-idea is a
powerful projective stimulus to which we each respond according
to our own individual personality patterns. The literal-minded
analyst is already lost before he begins. It is only the analyst who
has the freedom to fantasy such things as a means of communication with porpoises or the B.E.M.'s from Mars who will also
understand personal meaning of religion for his patient.

15

I remember the first staff meeting I ever attended as a young psychiatric resident. I listened wide-eyed to the most fantastic conversation I had ever heard. Dr. Nolan D. C. Lewis was talking, before all of us, with a patient who had a doctorate in philosophy. They were discussing philosophy, yet they did not make sense. Dr. Lewis called on me first to give an opinion, inasmuch as he knew it was my first day on duty.

I said, "I didn't understand what was being said." But, I went on, I realized that Dr. Lewis did understand what the patient was saying and what he himself was saying. They were using philosophical words and English words, but the language they were speaking was obviously not philosophy and not English. I suspected, but I could not say why I suspected, that they were talking in the patient's personal schizophrenic language. This was exactly what had taken place.

In time I, too, learned to speak in my patient's personal schizophrenic language, and I, too, learned to talk with a philosopher in philosophical English, which was neither philosophy nor English, but which was his own personal delusionary language.

While my professionally religious patient will probably not be schizophrenic, some of his theological talk may make him sound as though he is. So I have remembered this experience of communication and have gone on the premise that theology ought to make sense, when explained in ordinary English.

The analyst who undertakes to study the problem of religious conflict needs to have a broad and deep experience in the whole range of human psychology. He needs to know the primitive, the child, the neurotic, the schizophrenic, the psychopath, with all their complexities as well as their symptom formations, defenses, and resistances. He needs to have a very sure knowledge of the endless means by which the inaccuracies and distortions of thinking result in obscuring the idea of God within his patient as well as within his culture. He needs to remember that the neurotic does not always think clearly. Although his reality testing is excellent, the patient may not have developed sufficient maturity to analyze and criticize what he is taught in Sunday school or seminary. A common fallacy often suits his unconscious needs. The neurotic may think quite logically until his emotions overwhelm him and he is pushed back to the level of primitive or primary-process thinking, where mistakes are much easier to make and much harder to correct by logical methods.

Even the religionist's logical arguments may be contradictory if one listens carefully and long enough. Although at first his rationalizations may seem quite reasonable, questioning brings out other rationalizations, and the contradictions indicate that something is not as it should be. Rationalization is after all our defense against that which we do not understand and for which we must somehow find an explanation if we are to be comfortable. If the erroneous explanation satisfies the analyst, then the conflict can continue undisturbed. Since the religionist is usually highly intelligent and gifted in the use of words, his rationalizations are better than those of the average patient. He also has the bearing of authority and frequently the scholarship that makes his explanation more readily accepted. This failing, he has a well-trained voice and will shout to lend further weight to his arguments. The schizophrenic rationalization is less well thought out and frequently easier to recognize.

The analyst must have the sureness to sense at once when the usually logical, well-trained religionist suddenly no longer makes sense. This often happens when, after speaking quite logically about Old Testament theology, the religionist begins to talk of New Testament. The former has its framework grounded in the law and in the history of a people and is, of its very nature, more logical and rational. In the New Testament, the mystical, the symbolic, the miraculous, the emotional elements require unusual clarity of primary-process thinking to be understandable. "For the law was given through Moses; grace and truth came through Jesus Christ" (John 1.17).

Primary-process or prelogical thinking is the picture language of the primitive, of preverbal and early childhood. It is the mentation of dreams, of all the creative arts in the moment of conception. It has a logic of its own which, when clear, very easily moves into Aristotelian or ordinary logic. It is the language of all emotional response including, of course, devotion, love, and hate. Only when this primary-process thinking becomes distorted is it schizophrenia. In schizophrenia as Bleuler pointed out in

1911, there are: (1) a specific loosening of the associations so that the expected orderly path of one thought leading to another is disturbed; (2) disturbances in the emotional response so that the effect may be inadequate or overly intense and inappropriate to the occasion; (3) autism—that is, the extreme self-centeredness in which the patient lives in his inner world, ignoring all outside reality, where everything has only personal meaning and all fantasy becomes reality. This is a normal state of being only in the first weeks of infancy, but traces of it persist throughout the childhood of the individual and the mythology of his culture.

The schizophrenic clings to his ideals, to all that he feels is true in his inner world. To that end he sacrifices the outer world of reality and even life itself. He is the religious martyr, saint, and genius. The neurotic holds onto outer-world reality and will sacrifice his devotion and his convictions. He never chooses to be a martyr and rarely becomes a saint.

It cannot be too strongly emphasized that all mistakes in paleological thinking are not necessarily schizophrenic. Unfortunately, psychiatrists pay too little attention to the thinking difficulties of their reasonably well-adjusted, neurotic patients, just because these patients happen not to be locked in the back wards. Yet the difficulty caused by these mistakes in paleological thinking has been of concern to religious leaders for a very long time.

In 1150 one of the great physicians of his age, Moses Maimonides, wrote *The Guide for the Perplexed*. In this book the renowned rabbinical scholar discussed the thinking difficulties that caused the devout to be troubled by doubts and misunderstandings. Few books have had the intellectual impact of this one. He was accused of manifold heresy; and when the *Guide* was translated into Hebrew, the Jewish leaders of Europe issued a ban on secular learning in order to protect their young students from the noxious influence of "Aristotelian philosophy." This was the beginning of the restriction of cultural freedom (1300 to 1800) for the Jewish communities huddling in their ghettos while the Renaissance unfolded, so that when the Jewish breakthrough came, there was the necessity of rebelling against all their religious and scholarly tradition and basing everything on "science."

Quite a different reaction followed the translation of the *Guide* into Latin.

Here it became a part of the intellectual stimulus of the Renaissance. St. Thomas Aquinas, among others, not only studied it carefully but used Maimonides' methods of thinking and reasoning in the writing of his *Summa Theologica*. This work continues to have a profound influence on theological thinking today among all Christian churches who accept the ameliorating effects of tradition and scholarship.

Anyone who has come to appreciate the importance of clarity in theological thinking will understand this disgression. The analyst, confused by his patient's Christian mysticism will learn, if he asks his patient, to explain the traditional, theological views on the subject. He may at this point learn of the compartmentation in his patient's mind between his personal theology and that which he was taught in seminary. He will then realize his task lies in building a bridge so that his patient can develop communication within himself between his inner and outer reality thinking, between primary-process thinking, whether repressed or conscious, and his logical thinking.

Freud, in our time, made possible the logical understanding of primary-process thinking so that this picture language of dreams, of sign and symbol, can be translated into the language of logical and, hopefully, of scientific thought. This is the bridge that permits communication between the symbolic understanding of mystical theology and logical theology, between psychoanalysis and the study of religion, between poetry and prose. The poet, the musician, the painter have each in their way transliterated the unrational primary-process picture language of inner reality into the language of outer reality. But of all who built those bridges that span these two worlds, none was as masterful an architect, none taught others so well how to design a mass of bolts and nuts, of steel and concrete, that when these materials were put together they might serve as a master pattern of the bridge that permits a steady stream of communication between the unconscious and the language of logic, than Freud.

The bridgehead won, it was possible for others to explore the unknown land beyond—the world of inner reality with its sunny fields, its dark forests, and its miasmic swamps with lofty snow-covered mountains beyond. This inner world, it must always be remembered, is a mirage, a reflection of outer-world reality. Sometimes the mirror reflects with unbelievable clarity, and the creative artist senses out and integrates an understanding of that essence of outer-reality experience which makes it possible for him to paint a great painting. Sometimes the mirror becomes clouded and bent in the desperate need to screen out of inner reality an outer reality which is too terrible to endure. When the creative artist can put outer reality back into his painting, he, as it were, cleanses and heals himself. The devout use the same mechanism of putting back into outer reality, in the guise of religion, what they have brought into inner reality from the outside world and its varied human experiences. Unlike the artist, they forget that the contents of their conflicts, their methods of resisting change, were derived from the real world. They insist it all came from God. The creative artist has more humility and more devotion. He knows that in his moment of creating, he is in contact with that deepest essence of life, that essential ground of his being which in the religious language is called the Indwellingness of the Divine Presence. He knows that somehow for that moment of creation, as for the moment of true devotion, he is in rapport with the Divine Analyst.

The analyst in his study of religious conflict must have a thorough knowledge of all the laws of primary-process thinking. He must know all the varied ways that mistakes occur. Then he can understand and make use of the fluidity, the creativeness, the healthy vitality of primitive thinking, yet at all times keep in mind that, in its very nature, it is more susceptible to distortion. The difficulty of translation into logical thought forms is almost insurmountable otherwise. Poetry is the natural language of prelogical thinking when words are the medium of communication, but poetry is not an acceptable means of communication to the precise logical, scientific mind of our generation. Still less acceptable are the languages of painting, of sculpture, of architecture, and of music. There is also the gesture, the body posture, the special vestments, the utensils and furnishings of the altar and sanctuary. There is the intonation, the special language of ritual and liturgy, not only in the common language of today and of medieval and Renaissance usage, but also the secret mystery of ancient Hebrew, Greek, and Latin, which permits an endless and infinite possibility of personalized meanings.

So the creative religious geniuses have built up for themselves a special language, out of the symbols representing their ideation and imagery, expressing the accepted religious concepts and ideation of their community, which differ only in usage from one group to another. Like analysts, they too feel that the truth is made more true and infallible if it cannot be understood by other groups. As with analysts who have created their own special lingo, many religious people have developed their own personal symbols and cease to be understood even by others of their own group. Thus the psychiatrist who studies religious ideation, whether in his patient or in the literature and ritual, needs to be a gifted linguist to understand what is being said when he reads, for example, "What is in Heaven is on Earth." He needs to be a gifted translator to put this understanding into the symbols of a common language so that everyone can read it.

If one looks at the development of the use of imagery in the child, one sees the loved child change his personal imagery with his personal symbols, which are his first words, into the language of his mother, his playmates, and his culture. The unloved child in reaction to feeling rejected puts back into his environment the rejecting images and shelters himself behind a barrier of impoverished thought. In therapy the warmth of rapport with an accepting parent substitute permits this process of increasing impoverishment of thought to change. The patient begins to want to communicate; he begins to learn his therapist's language and the therapist no longer needs to try to communicate in the special secret language of the patient.

It is the same with his misconceptions of religious ideas as with other ideas. In a group it is relatively easy for the whole group to develop the emotional intensity that throws them back into prelogical thinking where the distorted idea can come more freely to consciousness with full emotional impact and then more easily be changed into the healthy imagery of the group. At this level of common participation in prelogical thinking, these changes occur more rapidly and with less difficulty than by attacking them directly with logical criticism. The logical observing ego can thus function more easily because the whole climate contains more acceptance. Therefore less resistance due to guilt and humiliation occurs. The same easy change also illustrates the dangers of prelogical thinking when there is no observing logical ego, such as found in the group leader.

The same fluidity of prelogical thinking occurs in worship services or political meetings. The group regresses to prelogical thinking, finds a commonness of thought and feeling, expresses this in commonly accepted symbols, and emerges with greater strength and vitality for good or for bad, according to the leadership.

Religious ideation, always having its roots in prelogical thinking and feeling, is most easily expressed in imagery, hence the use of the simile, the allegory, the metaphor, the parable, the midrash.

In the parable a story is told in common language which permits a religious concept to exist on many levels of meaning at one time. Some are so clearly couched in common symbol language that the varied meanings are as easily understood today as they were thousands of years ago. The ignorant man understands correctly the message he was then, and is now, intended to receive. The scholar may, with his greater understanding of all of the connotations of the thought forms of the age in which it was first told, sense out a secret meaning. Then, by studying a number of similar uses of such imagery and words, he will make certain that he has correctly caught the trend of this secret concept through successive generations of religious teaching. This is especially true in a language such as Hebrew where the same word changes meaning as the vowel points are added to the original letters, which are consonants. Thus a traditional reading assumes a quite different meaning if the vowel points are changed or the letters transposed.

Sometimes a thought form has changed because the imagery referred not to a common symbol but instead to a denotative word-symbol which was clearly understood in the generation in which it was used. Two thousand years later the meaning is quite different, and the ignorant man is hopelessly confused.

It is written that "it is easier for a camel to go through the eye of a needle than for a rich man to enter the kingdom of God." In Jerusalem in the time of Jesus the most ignorant understood the "eye of a needle" to mean a small gate in the wall of the city. The metaphor meant only that it was as hard for a wealthy man to be righteous as it was for a camel to squeeze through a narrow gate—but if one thinks in literal English, the eye of a needle is the eye of a sewing needle. So it is obviously impossible for a wealthy man to get through the Pearly Gates. This and many other religious references to the dangers of wealth have led to an idea that only the poor can be good, and so the ramifications of the so-called virtues of poverty. Yet the imagery of the poor man is as a man aware of his need of help, food, and shelter. Thus the poor man is also one cognizant of his need of spiritual grace, and so he is a man seeking the love of God and therefore is more certain to find Him.

This is an example of the mistakes made by the denotation imposed by too literal an interpretation of word and phrase, with the resulting impoverishment of ideation, simile, or metaphor. Always it is necessary to associate with the word until the wealth of connotation becomes apparent. This same restrictive impoverishment occurs when only the traditional religious associations are related to the imagery to be understood. Often in reading mystical religious literature the essential meaning is quite clear if one reads with relaxed attention as in listening to a patient rather than as a learned scholar caught in the rigidly transmitted mistakes made by a previous generation of scholars.

The Jew has difficulty in understanding the Christian extravagance in the use of anthropomorphisms, especially in the Roman, Greek, and Anglo-Catholic tradition. The Reform Jewish and Protestant groups suffer from sterility because of being too logical and abstract.

In the many excellent manuals on prayer, both Jewish and Christian, the use of imagery is considered a part of the beginner's method of finding his devotion; later he can find the more abstract otherness of God if he is mature and healthy enough to do so.

When two objects or concepts are compared, they may be found to have similar qualities or attributes. The quality is part of the whole of the characteristics of the object or concept. When the part assumes the significance of the whole, mistakes are easy. The characteristic may be physical:

Oranges are round.
Apples are round.
Therefore oranges are apples.

Deer run swiftly.
Indians run swiftly.
Therefore Indians are deer.

Or emotional:

I want to be a Christian.
The cross is the symbol of Christianity.
Christ suffered on the cross.
Therefore I must suffer.

This syllogistic thinking excludes the whole of the meaning of Christianity and the cross. The Crucifixion is only one of the many events in the life of Jesus and His suffering on the cross is only one of the many meanings of His death. Yet this thinking led the patient to seek suffering without questioning the life of martyrdom his mother had taught him. (See the case of Stephen.)

A more simple syllogism might be:

My father is angry.
God is a Father.
Therefore God is an angry Father.

In dreams we make use of this device in order to get our meaning across. The various qualities of the dreamer may be shown in the guise of the representations of several people who, by association, have the quality the dreamer wants to discuss in his dream. But understanding of the dream is by association and not by identity.

Another way in which similarities lead to mistakes is in contiguity, that is, in nearness of time and space relationship. If two objects or concepts are spoken of together, occur at the same time, or are geographically close, they are the same. For instance:

"In the beginning was the Word,
and the Word was with God,
and the Word was God" (John 1.1).
Therefore every word in the Bible is divinely inspired.

Thus the sacredness of the Logos was established. Words have always had more magical significance than thoughts.

For that reason a patient can spell out a Yiddish curse, but he cannot bring himself to say it for fear it would happen. The name has the same magic power. Since the name of an object is an attribute of the object, a part of a whole, it becomes the object. The name of God is God and must never be pronounced. The Logos is the Word of God and, both by contiguity in the above example and as an expression of God's revelation, is a part or attribute of God, and therefore is God.

The ancient Hebrew tradition is the same. The alphabet was created before the beginning of the world, and all the letters are sacred. The whole of the Torah (the Five Books of Moses) spell out one great name of God.

In the first chapter of John the word "Logos" becomes a personalized attribute of God.

"And the Word became flesh
and dwelt among us" (John 1.14).

Thus the mediator, Christ, was prelogically developed out of the older Jewish mystical wisdom literature where wisdom was an almost personalized attribute of God. This developed later in the Cabbala as the ten sephiroth, or the ten attributes or qualities of God.

Most of the use of magic in religion hinges on the use of similarities—like will produce like. The primitive and prelogical mind understands that in Communion we, in partaking of His body and His blood, become like Him, become a part of Him, and too often the distortion occurs, and we become Him. This cannibalistic mystery becomes quite a problem to the rational scientifically minded amateur anthropologist who realizes that in Christianity we have glorified an ancient primitive ritual. One must really be able to think prelogically to understand and enjoy a ritual practice that, on the basis of reality, one is so thoroughly conditioned against.

Fetishes, too, derive in the same way—a part taking the place of the whole. The priest's stole, the prayer shawl, the cross, the Torah pointer, in fact all of the vestments and utensils of altar and sanctuary are blessed, sacred, a part of God in our primitive thinking. These fetishes enable the religionist to dare to represent (or be) God to his congregation and in his humility to represent (or be) his congregation before God. He can preach in surplice or robe for then his words are God's, not his own. As the pathological identification continues, "The feeling of unity with an object which results in reassurance against the anxiety of being abandoned is achieved in extreme submissiveness by the idea of being, a small part of the partner's huge body." [1] This results in what is called *unio Christi*.

Past, present, and future merge, and there is only the present. Hence, what happened in the past is also happening in the present. What is expected to happen in the future is also experienced or expected in the present. As a result, we have the generalizations that are commonly heard each Easter. For example: Since a few Jews under threat of Roman persecution betrayed a man whose doctrines threatened the peace of the administration, we have the premise that Jews killed Christ, becoming, 2,000 years later, *all Jews kill Christ*.

This is quite the same as my schizophrenic patient whose eyes glazed as he went out of contact, saying, "Doctors killed Joe, you're a doctor, doctors killed Joe, you'll kill me." This is also an illustration of causality, the problem of cause and effect. In ordinary logic we have a mechanical progression of ideas, such as: if the temperature goes down, water freezes into ice; or, if we go into the rain, we are apt to get wet. But in prelogical thought the psychologic motivation replaces the mechanical and "every act, every event, occurs because it is willed or wanted,

[1] Otto Fenichel, M.D., *The Psychoanalytic Theory of Neurosis* (New York: W. W. Norton & Company, Inc., 1945), p. 356.

either by another person, or by something that becomes personified." [2]

Even today among a great proportion of our population, times of drought or overmuch rain come as God's punishing the individual or the community. When the death of a loved one occurs the response is, "Why did God do this to me?" If a serious illness develops, the question is, "What sin have I committed, what have I done to deserve this?" Or, as the Book of Common Prayer puts it, ". . . whatsoever hath been decayed by the fraud and malice of the devil." [3] But the intuitive religionist who composed the prayer does not linger over the convenient scapegoat, the personalization of the death drive; he continues, "or by *his* [the patient's] own carnal will and frailness." [4]

In our scientific enthusiasm for mechanical rather than teleological causes of illness, the physician is trained to look for such physical causes as germs and viruses rather than for the psychological causes. If a disease cannot be found to have an organic cause and thus a specific treatment, such as quinine for malaria, the word *functional* is used to describe the illness. The patient is told he is, in effect, bad. The physician may become quite angry with him as he would with a recalcitrant naughty child.

Thus the treatment of a psychosomatic or *functional* illness is made difficult because the scientist has been forbidden by his training to think prelogically in terms of psychological intention and symbolism. It is not logical and scientific to think that a pregnant woman is vomiting because she wants to get rid of her baby. But according to prelogical thinking, it is not only accurate but effective. When the woman is given appropriate interpretation and help in accepting her child, her vomiting stops. If we do not stumble over the denotative meaning of the word "sin," there is the inherent wisdom of the ages in:

"O Blessed Redeemer, relieve, we beseech thee, by thy indwelling power, the distress of this thy servant; release *him* [the patient] from sin, and drive away all pain of soul and body,

---

[2] Silvano Arieti, M.D., *Interpretation of Schizophrenia* (New York: Robert Brunner, 1955), p. 219.
[3] Book of Common Prayer, p. 314.
[4] *Ibid.*, p. 314.

that being restored to soundness of health, *he* [the patient] may offer thee praise and thanksgiving." [5]

> . . . man living in a primitive culture is entirely satisfied when he can think that some person, or a personified entity, is responsible for an event. The moral point is not more important than the causal link; it is the only aspect taken into consideration: *to be responsible for an event means to be the cause of the event.* The concept of impersonal force is a scientific abstraction which requires a much higher level of thinking.[6]

God is the great scapegoat, He alone is responsible. Therefore, if we learn His wishes and abide by them, all will be well (if it isn't, it's His fault). So a vast number of intelligent people look for signs to point the way for them. They will open the Bible with eyes shut, put a finger on a page, and read the verse. This tells them the will of God. Yet all through the ages the more reasonable religionists have insisted that we ourselves must take responsibility for our actions, do the best we can, and only by observation afterward can we hope to find out if what we did was probably God's will, using as a rule of thumb that that which turns out well and is beneficial to the individual and his community is probably His will according to His natural laws. For instance, if a man has a religious *vocation,* he has the aptitude, the intelligence, the unconscious motivation that makes it possible for him to be a healthy fulfilled minister who is good for his community. Thus we can interpret psychological and psychiatric screening of postulants as our latest scientific method of searching out God's will.

Since so many of our people believe in "signs" and "calls" as actual directives of the divine will for them, such signs and calls are frequently found as a cultural phenomenon rather than indicating personal pathology. In many of the Protestant churches an emotional experience of being called is required of a man who wishes to go into the ministry. In a more liberal group what would be a time of conscious realization of the decision to go into the work of the religionist may still be said to be a "call."

---

[5] *Ibid.,* p. 320.
[6] Silvano Arieti, M.D., *Interpretation of Schizophrenia* (New York: Robert Brunner, 1955), p. 221. Used by permission of Basic Books.

Sometimes the dream is the vehicle for a "call." As the manifest content is taken literally, the devout are often misled. For example, a young man who had been severely reprimanded by his fundamentalist minister-father had a dream of nightmare intensity in which he heard a voice telling him to be a missionary. According to his cultural milieu, this was a "call" from God, and the boy went to seminary, was ordained, and became a most unhappy minister. He finally got into psychotherapy and realized that the dream was only telling him that it was his biological father who wanted him to follow in his footsteps, not his divine Father, asking him for martyrdom (his personal association with missionary work).

Another such mistake in prelogical sign-hunting was a young man's repetitious answer to his prayer for guidance in the question of marriage. The answering thought was always celibacy. Yet his culture not only did not require celibacy of its clergy, but really did not approve of it. Here too, later in psychotherapy, the thought was found not to come from God, the Father, but from the sensing in his 4-year-old mind that his Oedipal wish to marry his mother was forbidden by his dying father. The interpretation that God is actually represented in the dream should, I feel, be made with great caution and only when, by the patient's associations, it becomes clearly evident.

In this way the neurotic may be so cut off from his inner world that his loss of feeling makes it impossible to know love or devotion. This shutting off of inner reality may come at such an early age that we are startled to find all the magic and omnipotence of a small child playing "make believe" in the repressed but operative unconscious of the apparently logical religionist celebrating Holy Communion or conducting services in the sanctuary. For example, at thirteen, when he was confirmed or became a Bar Mitzvah, his "make believe" ordination was with such emotional intensity, such magical intention and dedication, that this was no longer "make believe" but reality and continued to be real until the experience was uncovered in the course of therapy. So the boy of thirteen was able to fulfill and fixate the needs of his childhood. (See the case of Peter.)

Thus the analyst needs to understand primary-process thinking so clearly that he can distinguish between the healthy, normal prelogical or paleological thinking of the primitive, the child, the creative artist, and these same processes as they become distorted.

Only with this background can the analyst understand religious ideation and conflict so that he will recognize the distorted ideation of his patient. If the analyst is free of personal blindspots and has done a workmanlike job of analysis, he can rest assured that psychological truth, as found in his patient, and theological truth, as found in the teachings of the most enlightened religionists of his patient's group, will coincide when both are translated into a common language. He then can concern himself with his patient's resistance to finding out about theological truth and why the patient defends himself against the awareness of this knowledge.

The writer can say this with certainty now after many years of checking his patients' findings with clear-minded scholarly theologians whose devotion was healthy and deep. (See the cases of Stephen, Martin, and Isaac.)

IV. The Role of Unconscious Motivations

A. *Death*

Having recognized the importance of an understanding of primary-process thinking it now becomes the major task of clerical psychotherapy to uncover the unconscious motivations that have led the patient to the choice of pursuing a professional religious career. The case histories presented in this volume make it singularly clear that one of the keys to the failure of clerical patients to fulfill their consciously perceived ministry lies in the distortion of a traumatic childhood experience. This distortion is encapsulated and carried into adulthood, thus affecting their conscious motivations. The uncovering of the distortion is an absolute prerequisite to successful therapy. In turn, the successful outcome of therapy invariably demonstrates that distorted theology is rooted in distorted subjective psychological truth. The successful, well-functioning clergyman is one for whom *theological truth and psychological truth coincide.*

The major unconscious psychodynamics that have been found to play a determining role in the choice of professional work will be briefly discussed in this section; their full import, their manifold theoretical implications, will unfold in the case material.

An early experience with *death* is a frequently occurring motivational dynamic among clerical patients. The loss of parents, grandparents, even great-grandparents, and also of nursemaids, siblings, or playmates is acutely traumatic in childhood. The bereaved one experiences his grief reaction in accordance to the degree of his psychological maturity and according to the intensity of his love and his hate for the lost one. The child's choice of vocation, whether it developed before or in response to the

31

death experience, is caught and fixated at that level of psychological development. The vocation is, as it were, encapsulated or
imprisoned. Although operative, it is unintegrated with growth
so that the whole of the personality development is stunted and
thwarted. The child turns to his idea of God. He regresses from
his intellectual stand and cries out, in his hurt, "Why hast thou
abandoned me?" And here lies the Christian's need for the Christ
figure, for the belief that He is the beloved Son and that He
endured the trials and tribulations of the insecurity which we call
life, and that He died. He faced this terrible ultimate insecurity
which we cannot tolerate facing, which is too terrible for us to
face. And in His being the Son of God and surviving the ordeal
of death, He gives us assurance that we too will be cared for
through the ordeal of the final terrible separation anxiety which
has haunted us from the moment of birth. For birth was the first
moment in which we tasted the fear of being separate, isolated
individuals, of being out of communication, out of reach, out of
touch with every other human being in the world, which is the
ultimate meaning of death.

When the devout say with certainty, "I know that my Redeemer lives," they really are saying, "I know someone loves me.
I know that I am not alone. I have not been alone, and I will
never be abandoned or left alone." I feel that the most wonderful
moment of the whole drama of the death of Jesus was that He
explicitly endured this moment when He felt abandoned by His
Father, God the eternal. In His agony He cried out, "My God,
my God, why hast thou forsaken me?" and expressed most mean-
ingfully His humanity. This is the voicing of the fear that everyone has, that everyone needs help against. This is the reason that
we want someone to hold our hand when we are enduring pain
or anxiety. This is why we call Christ Savior; He has gone through
the valley of death, and will be with us when we go through.

The subject of death constitutes a crucial point in the therapeutic process. The therapist must examine himself at this point. Can
he work with the naked reality of the unknown as experienced
by all of us in the death experience without the defenses he has
acquired in the anatomy laboratory, the morgue, the operating

room, and the delivery room? If he does not practice the most astute self-observation, he will join in the defenses of his clerical patient who has also developed a special callousness in visiting the sick and the dying, and in conducting funeral services. The medical profession jokes obscenely and laughs; the clergyman may be more guarded in his language, but he also jokes and laughs.

When a patient speaks of his fear of imminent death, the therapist must concern himself as to whether he is speaking of his suicidal intention or of his psychological withdrawal into out-of-contact oblivion. There is a specific difference between the symbolic use of death as an expression of anxiety and the literal anticipation of the moment of actual extinction. Psychologically, the very sick and very abandoned patient will speak of his death as that moment when he withdrew from all communication with outside reality, when the inner core of his being, his "little-me" self, retreated into the depths of his body, leaving the physical mind and body to blunder through a senseless, meaningless existence. In actually attempting suicide, on the other hand, the patient seeks the sleep of forgetfulness. He expects to awaken from his sleep to live again in this reality. He is attempting to produce or reproduce the death feint of the possum. His reality testing is faulty; he does not realize the finality of his action.

Those who have experienced the loss of consciousness in a suicide attempt and have been overjoyed and surprised to find themselves alive, as well as those who have lost consciousness in in a near-death experience in sickness or in accident, and have in losing consciousness expected to die and then awakened realizing that they had not died, can truly understand the meaning of rebirth, of resurrection. It is not unusual in psychotherapy to hear a patient say at a turning point in therapy that he has the feeling of rebirth, of having been born again. The same meaning is symbolized and ritualized in the Christian Sacraments: in baptism, we are born into this physical existence imbued with the love of God; in confirmation, we are accepted as adults in the religious community; in marriage, we are given the right to bring new life into the religious community; and in the last rites, the dying are given the symbolic reassurance that they are passing from one state to another.

In man's dream of immortality, in his concept of the resurrection, we have a most beautiful example of symbolic primary-process thought.

I am loved—I love.
I am loved; therefore I live.
I have lived; therefore I will live.

In this concept there is a mystical identification with the God who was and is and ever shall be, the Ancient of ancients, the Eternal of eternals. God has existed; God is; and God will always exist. Rudolph Otto, writing more than fifty years ago, spoke of the beauty of the idea of the resurrection, insisting that no one who clung to facts could have a realization of the meaning of this mystical, symbolic expression of man's eternal need and longing. Albert Schweitzer, in the greatness of his devotion and dedication, expressed the simple belief that we don't need to seek a historical Jesus. Christ's whole life may be understood as a vision of God more perfect and more meaningful than man has yet experienced.

In summary, the implications of a childhood experience with death are far-reaching and complex. While our interest lies mainly in the importance of the death experience in the unconscious choice of the religious life, it is evident that all areas of religious belief are intricately connected with it. The concept of God, of immortality, of time, of various ritual symbolizations, all have clear, as well as still unexplored, networks of interconnection with death. The crucial importance of its role in psychotherapy in general, and in clerical psychotherapy in particular, will require much intensive study. For the purpose of this exploration, it can be stated with sufficient assurance that a death experience in childhood tends to bring on a loss of trust in human relationships by the child, causing him to seek magical identification with God and the Christ figure, and that its presence in the history of a clergyman is an important indication in favor of therapeutic intervention. (See the cases of Peter and James.)

B. Exhibitionism

Another significant motivational dynamic lies in the sexual area. A full discussion of this area would, of course, require a separate work. I have selected exhibitionism, which is perhaps more characteristic of the clergy than of any other professional group, for brief discussion. Other equally important sexual dynamics will emerge vividly from the clinical material.

Exhibitionism may, when sublimated, become a source of deep fulfillment for the clergy, but it is likely to cause conflicts when sublimation has not taken place. In wearing his vestments the clergyman can indulge to an extraordinary degree in his exhibitionistic tendencies. While the round collar gives him a set-apartness—a distinction similar to an officer's insignia or a policeman's nightstick—it is in the use of vestments that these tendencies can be given full vent. The ostentatious enjoyment of rich apparel, offering a glorious, otherworldly type of superiority, and the covert pleasure in "drag," are often met with. There is a definite insistence in our culture that the enjoyment of walking in the rustlings of silk and satins, lace petticoats, and magnificent cloth of gold, is an expression of femininity. The fact that men throughout the ages, throughout the world, have enjoyed these luxuries and considered them masculine, seems to have little weight in the argument. In our culture, a man in a cassock is wearing a skirt, and therefore is getting away with something which he could not do in civilian clothes. There is a certain pleasure in the flaunting of a special privilege; there is a special conceit in doing what the ordinary man cannot do.

This sanctioned manifestation of exhibitionistic needs contributes to the congregation's enjoyment of a devotional service that is well put together, well thought out, well timed, and planned. All the creative arts were utilized in creating the setting for the drama of life and death, of love and hate, upon the altar. Architecture made possible the great cathedrals with their glorious stained-glass windows; the walls were decorated by the greatest painters of the age; the carvings, the statuary were the works of master craftsmen. The goldsmith made the chalice; and the peasant wove the linen that was embroidered and decorated for the altar that was laid as was no other table in the world. The setting for the drama of Holy Communion is more beautiful than any stage setting could hope to be, with music, with choirs, with instruments, with poetry, with the clergyman making use of these necessary adjuncts with skilled showmanship and walking in procession, with incense, with the cross, and with the altar boys, with the choir, and with inspiring and exciting delight. One cannot help but wonder about many of the Protestant clergy who have been deprived by the reaction formations of the Protestant Reformation of so many of these marvelous delights in stage setting, in rich clothing, in the beauty of wearing rich and sumptuous garments to enhance their otherworldly dignity. One wonders at their reaction to the deprivation of the set-apartness of the round collar, of being reduced to the courtesy titles of ordinary men, or in some of the fundamentalist churches being called "Brother," instead of "Father" or "Pastor." It would be extremely worth while to look into the matter of the possible relationship between the freedom to wear vestments and clerical garb and the contrasting prohibition of such, and examine the effects of the relationship on the degree of exhibitionism.

The clergyman's need to be the center of attention makes it imperative that he have an audience; and having an audience, he must lead them and sway them. He sways them by means of his stagemanship, his showmanship, his timing, his organization of the service. In his sermon he really lets go. He speaks not only with his own authority but with the authority of his cloth, and he works hard to think out the type of sermon which appeals to his creative need of the moment, to reach his people, to instruct them, to impress them, to deepen their devotion, to chasten them, to vent his spleen upon them, or whatever his need may be.

In psychoanalytic terminology coprolalia means the enjoyment of the use of words to paint pictures, to move a person or an audience to the desired emotional state. Coprolalia, according to Fenichel, does not necessarily mean the use of obscene sexual language. Since cursing is the opposite of blessing and the sacred is close to the obscene, we feel that stretching the meaning to include the use of a sonorous voice, the rolling of syllables upon the tongue to move people to a state of devotion is not unreasonable. We doubt if it matters much whether the subjecting of the audience to a direct sexual enjoyment, or to an indirect one, is important. What is important is that these men are masters at shouting down other people. They have trained powerful voices. They are trained to think and talk on their feet and have had a great deal of experience in this. They are especially trained in dialectic thinking, so that in a therapy group they can with great ease, and usually quite unconsciously, direct the course of discussion into a sidetrack, so that the group finds itself talking about something quite different than what they intended to talk about or were talking about. They are monologists and will talk interminably. The very quality of their proficiency can be a most disturbing element in a group setting.

One of the side effects of the exhibitionistic needs of the clergy has been the unexpected enjoyment that my patients have had in finding themselves in my papers, and in the manuscript of this book. It was easy for them to see through the necessary disguise and symbolic confabulation with which I have attempted to maintain the appropriate secrecy required by the principle of medical confidence. One would expect these people to be most terribly concerned lest it be known that they were in therapy at all; and much less would it be expected that they would enjoy seeing their case histories in print. And yet this has been my experience. There is a feeling of relief when they find that they have "made the grade," as one might put it, or have revealed an interesting picture that might be useful. As a matter of fact, one has to be watchful of the accuracy of material, because an exhibitionist will stretch more than one point if he finds it necessary to gain attention. I remember a psychiatric resident who spent many hours reading psychopathology in order to get some sort of a reaction out of me. Each day he would come in with a new grotesque or gory symptom. His descriptions of his fantasies of necrophilia, of his fantasies of cohabitation with the dead were fascinating, but they did not have the ring of authenticity. Having worked for many years with lay people, whose need to shock and to flaunt and to confabulate was so striking and so overwhelming,

I find that the clergy of my experience actually have a much more modest range of exhibitionistic needs. There appears to be a correlation between their acting out of these needs within their profession and the relative absence of acting out in their private lives. (See the cases of Peter, James, and Samson.)

Summary of Chapters I-IV

This study has been based on the following premises:

(1) The decision to enter religious life professionally is based on the desire to fulfill unconscious needs.

(2) The choice is explicable in terms of conscious motivation but can be understood only on the level of primary-process thinking.

(3) The choice may be healthy or pathological in its genesis as well as in its expression. Consequently, there is a direct correlation between a given individual's self-success image and the pathological content, or its absence, of his vocational choice.

(4) Pathological unconscious dynamics underlying the choice of professional religious life can be exposed in psychotherapy, and the insight gained in the therapeutic process may help clerical patients toward undistorted self-perception and greater professional effectiveness.

(5) Clerical psychotherapy, in addition to benefiting individual patients, can be of great value to seminary authorities, denominational leaders, and individual clergymen in establishing seminary admission policies, and in administering churches and clerical personnel.

Documentation for these premises is provided by the clinical material which constitutes the major part of this study. As a result of lengthy and careful deliberation and extensive discussions with professional persons actively concerned with the problems of the clergy, it was decided to give prominence to the presentation of clinical material in preference to an extended theoretical analysis. It was felt that reporting a number of individual case histories would not only lay the groundwork for future theoretical formulations by this author and, it is hoped, by others, but serve to stimulate interest in the area of clerical psychotherapy on the part of ecclestiastical authorities as well as practicing psychotherapists. While the introductory part of the study surveyed the salient problems encountered in clerical psychotherapy, it is the presentation of the clinical material which is intended to be of primary significance.

V. Psychodynamic Implications Underlying Holy Communion

A. Holy Communion as Communion and Blessing

Probably no other Christian Sacrament has lent itself to such a wide variety of psychological interpretations, as well as distortions, as that of Communion. In my experience no other Sacrament has as many levels of understanding and of illogical meaning. Probably no Sacrament brings greater comfort to more people and, simultaneously, such doubts and sufferings to still another equally large proportion of Christians. No other ritual has had as many differing interpretations by anthropologists and psychiatrists.

Those who have not had the Sacrament of Holy Communion in their personal background are often bewildered in trying to understand its subtleties and intensities of meaning. One has to study the Sacrament in all of its various psychobiological, psychological, and theological interpretations. The inherent varieties of meaning make possible the utilization of the symbolism of the crystal which breaks up pure white light into the spectrum of the rainbow. Each of the colors of the rainbow reflects separately, and somehow differently, the intricate meaning of the white light. If one carries the analogy to the rainbow which Ezekiel saw reflecting the glory of God in the cloud on the day of rain, one can understand that the religious sense of different people on different levels of understanding sees, feels, and perceives the meaning and the message of a religious concept differently. Yet all together, these different perceptions make up the whole of a religious concept. The sacrifice can be understood as a sharing of food with God, making communion and communication possible between God and man, man and his group, man and his

environment, and as a means of covenant. The sacrifice might or
might not be a totem animal. The goal was communion, kinship,
togetherness, oneness.[1]

The attention of the god or gods was attracted by the smoke
of the burning sacrifice, by the smell of the roasting meat, for
which incense was later substituted. The smoke of the incense
was a bridge on which the presence of the god was brought down
among the people so that they could establish communication
to learn his will, to appease his wrath, and assure his good
intentions toward his people. The sharing of food and drink
with the god was a communion between him and the people.
The god, being the projection of their fears and wishes, extended
into their perception of their environment—the mountains, the
rivers, the land, and the sea—and the fantasies of the spirits of
the dead, the ancestors. Because of their teleological thinking,
these projected wishes and fears were spirits who controlled the
weather, the crops, the success of hunting and of war. Since
these forces were projections of omnipotent magical thinking
they could be understood and appeased or controlled by magical
thinking. The essence was in finding a means of communication
with the god by a gathering in of their projections. This is done
in Haitian voodoo [2] and among the Balinese [3] by hypnotic trance
induction. The hypnotically induced secondary personality is
interpreted as the god who "enters" or "rides" the entranced person and speaks through his mouth and acts with his body, and
in so doing makes possible the assurance that the god's presence
is known and his wishes manifest. He accepts the offerings and
thus shares the food and the life of the community. The oneness
of the infant with his environment is reestablished, and the
anxiety of the people is reassured as the infant is reassured when
in answer to his cry the mother's breast appears and he is nursed.

I am reminded of one of the spontaneous examples in which
this occurred once in group therapy. It was a time when Job was

[1] W. Robertson Smith, *The Religion of the Semites* (first published in
1889; New York: Meridian Books, 1956).
[2] Alfred Metraux, *Voodoo in Haiti* (New York: Oxford University Press,
1959).
[3] Jane Belo, *Trance in Bali* (New York: Columbia University Press, 1960).

very anxious and was beginning to be disruptive on a very infantile level. The group was not inclined to pamper him in his baby acting out; and Thomas, sensing Job's need for help, and yet not knowing what to say, got up and went over to the table, picked up a piece of cake, poured out a glass of milk, and took this to Job. Job responded with the beatific smile that only a happy, understood, loved infant knows how to give. Later he said to Thomas, "You were never so much a priest as you were for me tonight. You have never given such meaningful love and comfort and reassurance to anyone at the altar rail as you did to me when you gave me the cake and milk." Thomas modestly shrugged it off, saying, "I couldn't think of what to say to you." And I explained that the symbolic realization of being understood, of having his needs met, was more wonderful to Job than any words could have been. In his overwhelming anxiety, Job had regressed momentarily to that level of infancy when words had no meaning. I, too, felt that Thomas would never be more a priest in his vestments than he was at that moment in the simple informality of the group.

The sharing of the food, the sharing of the sacrificial food by the priest and the people with God, was a part of Hebrew custom. The fat of the animal was burned, the blood was drained from the altars into underground cisterns, and the roasted meat was shared among the people. The same was true with the first fruits; and to this day, when the Orthodox Jewish housewife bakes bread, she tosses a bit of the dough into the fire with a blessing, or puts it in the corner of the oven to char to a cinder, thus consecrating the whole of her baking and blessing it.

We can understand the mystery of Communion in the terms of oral incorporation, of taking something into our bodies through the token of food and drink which would give us a strengthening of our human dignity and the beauty of our humanity, of our physical being, as the valuable, meaningful, and necessary garment of the soul. This symbol of becoming like the object which we eat and drink tells in a very beautiful sense that we, in partaking of this meal, are being blessed in our humanity, are being fed in our humanity, and the community of people is being brought closer together. We are all fed at one table. It is said of

Sarah, when she and Abraham fed the great company of the chosen people in commemoration of their being one family and one tribe dedicated to the one God, that she gave suck to all the babies that were brought to the feast. There are so many instances indicating that because of the sharing of food and drink we have the deep awareness that we are loved and accepted and that we have become and remain a part of the community.

We are reminded of the manna which was fed to the chosen people in the wilderness. Actually, the bread is more than manna, since it combines not only the idea of food, but of everlasting sustenance and life. On this level we are given a token, but a very tangible token, of food and drink. We have the feeling of being fed. At this level the Sacrament could truly be milk and bread because it is God's feeding us as little children, reminding us that we are His created children, feeding our souls in memory of the time when we were fed as little children. It is a reminder of God's concern for our welfare as human beings, of the incarnate Christ who lived and suffered as we live and suffer. It is the symbol of God's concern for our earthly humanity, of His feeding us in our human needs. This interpretation gives a feeling of the dignity and beauty of our humanity, of our physical being. This element in the meaning of the Eucharist is emphasized in a symbol which is being used on an experimental basis in some churches in England. It is a revival of the ancient early Christian custom of offering as the Host a whole loaf of bread, which then is broken and divided into portions for each of the communicants. In using the loaf of bread on the altar, we are reminded that we are all one family partaking of one Sacrament, so that the feeling of being one of a group is strengthened. The custom of having this loaf of bread baked by successive women in the congregation brings a quality of earthy reality that is lost, I believe, in the more symbolic use of the traditional wafer. When the loaf of bread is baked one week by Mrs. Jones, the next week by Mrs. Smith, and the following week by Mrs. Brown, there is a greater feeling of the true meaning of the sacrifice; for a sacrifice is something which we offer to God and receive back blessed so that we are strengthened, comforted, encouraged, knowing that we are good. When the loaf is baked by women in the parish, some of the magical supernatural quality is hopefully lessened, and more of a feeling of the value and worth of our humanity is realized. It brings us back to the Jewish concept of sacrifice, where, as in all ancient religions, something of value was offered to God in atonement and as a communication which was the beginning of prayer; for as the smoke of the sacrifice rose into heaven, God would be reminded of our piety, and hopefully would be pleased, come down, and dwell among us.

The anxiety of the separateness, of the aloneness of the individual is lessened as he enters into the ritual—dancing, singing, moving together, sharing food and drink. He loses his sense of differentness and becomes one with the common identity of the group. He emerges from the ritual more comfortable in his security as a member of his group, sharing common symbols, common customs, a common god; and he rebounds from the regressive experience with greater maturity, with that courage called faith which gives a sense of purpose and goal, with that sense of self and of being which makes life worth while.[4]

Patience's comment in response to the emotional experience of Andrew's consecration was that she had been most responsive to the group's cohesiveness. For her the community sharing the experience of devotion in groups of people, of corporate Communion where a group of specially identified people are communing together, gave her a feeling of relief and warmth in contrast to the stern, fundamentalist isolation in which she had been brought up. She felt it was so lonely to have one's devotion solely between oneself and one's God when it could be shared with a group of people. The communing group could act as a mediator in helping one find the love of God when one was lost as we had helped Andrew.

The minister in practice needs his congregation, just as the members of the congregation need each other and their leader. There is a custom of saying that when it is necessary for a priest to celebrate Holy Communion alone, he says Mass with the angels, that is, with the angels as his congregation. In the Episcopal Church where it is not obligatory for the priest to celebrate

[4] Samuel Z. Klausner, *Worship* (Worship Research Conference of the Union of American Hebrew Congregations, March, 1959).

the Eucharist but where, at his discretion, he may substitute
Morning Prayer, it is not considered wise or prudent to celebrate
the Eucharist alone. It was Thomas who finally helped me to understand this because in trying to help him with the discipline of
saying his offices, the ritual prayers which a priest is required to
say each day, I began to find out that this was a great pleasure
for him when he had someone for his congregation. He was always
so happy when anyone would join him for his offices, which he
would read aloud in a beautiful voice, projecting his very real
devotion. But when he was alone and tried to say the offices, he
never knew whether he was praying in his good personality or in
his bad one, that is, in the good identification with his beloved
minister father, or in the bad identification with his hated real
father. If he had a congregation, then he knew who he was because then he could be good and do all that was possible to bring
the love of God to the people on the other side of the altar rail
who represented his bad self. How much more dreadful this would
have been for Thomas if he had been required to celebrate Holy
Communion alone, because he was one of this group who had the
whole range of psychopathological investment obscuring and perverting the deep beauty and intensity of his devotion.

During the Babylonian Exile the Hebrew people discovered
that by ritual, the reading of the Sacred Scriptures, and prayer
they could establish communication with their God. "Let my
prayer be counted as incense before thee, and the lifting up of
my hands as an evening sacrifice!" (Psalm 141.2). They no longer
needed animal sacrifice, though when they returned to Jerusalem
it was resumed and continued until the destruction of the Second
Temple. The ability to communicate with God in prayer, in-
dividually and in groups, made it possible for them to develop a
deconcretized, deanthropomorphized God-Idea and thus come to
a mature and lofty concept of religon. The sharing of food with
God continued in the family religious observances such as Pass-
over.

When we can in prayer find communication with a basic almost protoplasmic security, which Freud called the "oceanic
bliss" but did not himself realize, we have the possibility of the

development of a mature religion. In another place I have written:

> During the first to the fourth centuries the understanding of penetrating inner world reality when one went into a deep state of devotion in prayer was well understood. (4) There is according to Scholem (5) the use of the words "*Yorde Merkabah*," "descenders of the divine chariot." Ordinarily, we think in terms of heaven being in the sky, so that one ascends to heaven, but the awareness that one related to God within the depth of one's mind, heart and soul was very clear at this time and has been very clear in the writings of Jewish mystics. It is very clear throughout the Zohar and in the writings of Ezekiel, where he speaks of digging through a wall and seeing the false priest worshipping false idols in the "chambers of his imagery." Ezek. 8:12
>
> It seems as if Ezekiel knew that it is within the depths of one's mind that the distortion of a sick, heretical, religious devotion would occur. But it is also true that within the depths of our minds we have the possibility of a good healthy and true religious devotion. Within us we have a personal god and a personal relationship with our personal, unique, experiencing of our god. This has nothing to do with the God of theology, or outer world reality. We believe that all men, having been created alike in his image, experience the same god, within the depths of their soul. This belief is ordinarily projected outside one's self so that one feels that one's personal god is the same God who is known to other devout people. But we have a unique and separate and personal relationship, each one to himself, with his own unique awareness of God in inner reality. This is the doctrine of the indwellingness of the Divine Presence, the Shekinah, or the Holy Ghost.[5]

4. Bowers, Margaretta K., and Glasner, Rabbi Samuel, Autohypnotic aspects of the Jewish cabbalistic concept of Kavanah. J. Clin. Exp. Hyp., 6, pp. 50–70.

5. Scholem, G. G., Major trends in Jewish mysticism, Jerusalem: 1941, pp. 140f.

[5] "Friend or Traitor? Hypnosis in the Service of Religion," by Margaretta K. Bowers, M.D. Reprinted from *International Journal of Clinical and Experimental Hypnosis*, Vol. VII, No. 4, October, 1959, pp. 206–207. Used by permission.

When this deep security is lacking or unavailable because of traumatic fixations, we have to search for communication in the patterns of later development. The oneness of "oceanic bliss" needs a mature psychosexual development for its full utilization in an adult mature religious development. Freud, as much of the human race, was not able to communicate with his roots in the time before his fixation on the "Angry Father of the Primal Horde myth" explanation of religion to which we now turn. Among a people whose livelihood was its herds or its hunting, the shared food was naturally an animal, just as among an agricultural people it would be fruit, grain, or flowers. Among some people the sacrifice was personified and concretized as the god himself. The god was then eaten to bring him inside the worshiper. The purpose was the same as the trance induction, to bring the god down among the people to establish communion. And this gives a feeling of courage and dignity to our humanity and reminds us that God created us in human form and endowed us with souls, because of His creative purpose for us. As the poem of Solomon Ibn Gabirol says:

> Who can comprehend thy power, when thou didst create from the splendor of thy glory a pure lustre? From the rock of rocks was it hewn, and dug from the hollow of the cave. Thou also did bestow on it the spirit of wisdom, and didst call it soul. Thou didst form it hewn from the flames of intellectual fire, so that its spirit burneth as fire within it. Thou didst send it forth to the body, to serve and guard it, it is as fire in the midst of it, and yet does not consume it; *for from the fire of the soul the body was created,* and called into existence from nothing because the Lord descended thereto in fire.[6]

This is the truth and beauty of the mystical theology of sacrifice, in which we find the concept of bringing something, anything, to God and receiving it back from Him enriched with His blessing. We present our prayers and the meditations of our hearts upon the altars of our minds, as it were, and we receive back the blessing, the comfort, the enriching emotional fulfill-

---

[6] Isaac Husik, *A History of Mediaeval Jewish Philosophy* (New York: Meridian Books, Inc., 1958), p. 77. Used by permission.

ment of being loved, being cared for, and being understood. "With a freewill offering I will sacrifice to thee; I will give thanks to thy name, O Lord, for it is good" (Ps. 54.6). (See the case of Patience.)

B. Holy Communion as Covenant and Conditional Curse

All Sacraments, therefore, can be properly and simply understood as blessings, as symbolic realizations of God's love and providence extending to all mankind. The Sacrament of Holy Communion has many origins, Jewish, Greek, and pagan, as would be expected in such an important focal point of devotional ritual. Among many Protestant groups it is celebrated as a ritual meal, where the religious community sits down at one table and eats together, in memory of the Last Supper which Jesus celebrated in the upper room the night before His death. This has behind it the tradition of all Jewish ritual meals where, after the blessings, the wine and the bread are distributed to the family group.

Within this is the idea of a covenant, a contract among ourselves and between ourselves and God. We give something and expect something in return. Karl Menninger [7] has written of the psychoanalytic treatment situation as a contract between patient and analyst.

In the beginning of treatment the patient agrees to pay a certain sum for the analyst's time for an indefinite period of time. The patient agrees to try to be honest and to say what comes to mind and the analyst agrees to be awake, skillful, and interested in helping the patient understand himself. Yet within the continuing relationship unconscious motivations, transferences and counter-transferences, concerns, and feelings develop and are hopefully resolved.

Just so we have formal religious structure and setting, yet within each person there is a personal unique contractual rela-

[7] Karl Menninger, M.D., *Theory of Psychoanalytic Technique* (New York: Basic Books, 1958).

tionship with God that is expressed in his personal and group concepts of God which change with his growth or his fixations and are reflected in the formal, good or heretical, theology of the group.

The simple child prays and magically expects mother to get well. He makes a bargain with God. He will be good or he will perform a ritual. His mother dies and in his anger he cries out, "Why did God do this to me?" As the child grows he develops more complicated or mature covenants.

A covenant requires the exchange of something tangible. In our present legal system money and the exchange of services or goods is required to seal a contract. A handshake seals a verbal contract. The conditional curse is the penalty for not fulfilling the contract. This may be bilateral or unilateral. In religious ritual it is sacrifice, blood, bodily contact, and the sharing of a meal which bind the covenant and transfer the curse or the blessing. The blessing is the opposite of the curse and is the hoped-for fulfillment of the contract.

The Judeo-Christian religion has been a progression of covenants between God and His people. With Noah, God made a promise never again to destroy the world—the rainbow is the symbol of this promise. Even if the people disobeyed the seven laws which God gave Noah, He would punish them, but He would not fully annihilate the world.

At Mount Sinai God and the Hebrews made a more specific covenant. God would bless, love, and cherish the Hebrews as His special people, and they in turn would be faithful to Him and obey His laws. From that time they began to attribute any failure in war to punishment and looked into themselves to discover in what way they had failed to live up to that part of their contract.

According to Rudolph Otto, Jesus originally made a covenant of unconditional blessing, a b'rit to His disciples which Otto paraphrases as, "This I am *and as such* (viz. broken and shared out for partaking) I bequeath unto you the Kingdom." [8]

[8] Rudolph Otto, *The Kingdom of God and the Son of Man* (Boston: Starr King Press, 1943), p. 290.

The tangible symbols were the bread and wine shared together. The blessing was the Kingdom, the living experiencing of a growing relationship with God within themselves which was present and timeless in its continuity.

But with the passage of time the blessing was brought back to the pathological regressive covenant with the conditional curse. Jesus died in atonement for our sins against the Angry Father, and in the First Letter of Paul to the Corinthians are the following words: "Whoever, therefore, eats the bread or drinks the cup of the Lord in an unworthy manner will be guilty of profaning the body and blood of the Lord" (11.27).

The curse is then that the "unworthy" participant is guilty of the death of Christ. Paul and Freud agree and share the same mythology. To the medieval Christian the meaning of the words "my body," in the literal sense, was "flesh and blood"; only to the scholar was the more accurate meaning, "I, myself," known. The ritual was developed so that the wafer was placed on the tongue. It must not be chewed. The wine, the blood, was too precious, so that it was reserved for the priest until the Reformation restored it to the people.

This is illustrated in the widespread belief in legends of ritual murder. The accusation of desecration of the Bread is described as "impiercing" or "stabbing it until it bled" or "the crime of pounding a sacred wafer in a mortar until the blood flowed forth profusely." [9] When the mind of the educated as well as the common people so believe in this type of ritual murder that for over a thousand years we have historical and court records of trials, tortures, burnings, and widespread massacres of Jews, we are less shocked that the same fantasy comes from the unconscious of a few sick clergy—for they, like the medieval mob, are able to project their anger onto the scapegoat and then destroy in righteous wrath the helpless minority. Our sick clergy endeavor to contain this aggression in being the sacrificed or the sacrificer within themselves, yet quite too much wrath is spilled out on their congregations. As Róheim shows, all taboos against aggres-

[9] Max Margolis and Alexander Marx, *History of the Jewish People* (New York: Jewish Publication Society and Meridian Books, 1958).

sion fail and the aggression is turned inward. "Such a Father God or superego was too severe to be endured. An attempt was made to make a covenant; to regress to the oral stage, the dual unity of the mother-child stage."[10]

Under this impact the ego may regress to the pathological oneness of infantile reunion with the mother where the sense of self is lost. As Paul says, "It is not I, but Christ" in me that speaks. This is not the splitting off of a secondary personality but the death of the self—in the hope of rebirth as a "new man." Adult Baptism by immersion is spoken of as "a watery grave."

Such a loss of self results in the phenomenon of post-devotional emptiness and depression and is not uncommon in devout laity and clergy. One such unusually gifted and dedicated Episcopal priest wrote of his experience in the following words:

> "I do believe most of my masses are offered in something of an hypnotic state; the voice—my voice; and yet not entirely mine—moves me into the inner world of reality, and I see *identification* at first with both the Liturgy and the reality behind the words and the rite, and then more gradually a very strong and at times almost complete *incorporation* into the words, into the voice, into the Body of the Lord in the whole action, words and movement, as it conveys me to the point of the actual Holy Communion itself, at which time, and on some occasions considerably before that point, my own perception of myself seems not to be my own but *another's* perception of me, which Perception then becomes mine by adoption and Grace, as it were."

He is one of a number of such devout priests who experience a sense of emptiness, of being drained, following a religious service of great devotion. This is similar to the descriptions of post-orgiastic emptiness which are found in the psychiatric literature. These men complain of great fatigue, of loss of a sense of self, of inability and unwillingness to be with people or to relate to them. This is followed by a depression which may last for hours or days until gradually the sense of self returns, only to be lost at the next service in which deep religious devotion is

[10] Géza Róheim, ed., *Psychoanalysis and the Social Sciences*, vol. IV (New York: International Universities Press, 1955), p. 208.

felt. This accounts for the sorrowful mien of these devout and unhappy clergy.[11]

This is the state of surrender to what Róheim calls the covenant and the conditional curse in which we must completely give up all sense of self or be bad. (See the cases of Abel and John.)

C. The Element of Sacrifice in Holy Communion

Thus, when man's picture, when man's concept of his God as presented by certain of his omniscient all-knowing interpreters is so cruel, so heartlessly and uncontrollably, unpredictably wrathful, man's sacrifice and atonement are equal to the insecurity and self-degradation he feels as a result of this concept. When the religionist insists that God's glory is enhanced by man's utter dependence, or when man is described as a horrid nothing, man must resort to the most bloody of atonements to appease this terrible wrath; and in trying to appease this wrath, the Christian community has developed many patterns of denying the essential dignity and value of human existence. There have been those who have spent their lives in magnificent atonement in identification with the great atonement which was made in the beginning of the Christian era. The necessity for this atonement is clearly understandable in view of the background of hell and preaching of the damnation and wrath of God which is all too operative in our generation. The drive toward atonement is equally operative. The atonement is typified or is most beautifully demonstrated from a pathological standpoint in the sacrifice of the Eucharist. And the whole doctrine of the atonement through the sacrifice of Jesus hinges on this point.

In Jewish theology, as Maimonides has so beautifully presented it, God led the Jewish people through the years of their childish

[11] Margaretta K. Bowers, M.D., "Friend or Traitor? Hypnosis in the Service of Religion," *International Journal of Clinical and Experimental Hypnosis*, Vol. VII, No. 4, October, 1959, p. 214. Used by permission.

religion from the human sacrifice of their neighbors to the more civilized animal sacrifice. He patiently taught them in visions and in dreams and in parables that no further sacrifice of human life was needed. This is the meaning of the great story, parable, vision, or historical fact—whatever you wish to call it—of Abraham's sacrifice of his beloved Isaac. Now this is the story of a man who was willing to sacrifice the only son of his only beloved wife. He had other sons and other daughters of other wives, but only one son of his beloved wife. When the boy was but a lad, Abraham received the command to sacrifice Isaac. He went out into the wilderness with the young boy, he set up an altar, and he prayed. He bound the child upon the altar, and as he was about to strike the child with a knife, his hand was stayed, and the voice of an angel, whose restraining hand he felt about his wrist, told him to listen; for in the bushes there was a ram caught which God had given to him and to his people and to all generations to come as a substitute for human sacrifice. In being willing to give his son upon the altar, he had fulfilled God's intention. He so loved God that he was willing to give his only beloved son, but God could not permit him to make such a costly, bloody sacrifice.

For this reason the ram's horn, the shofar, is blown on Rosh Hashanah, the New Year, to remind God that a covenant was made with Abraham on that day that no human would any longer be needed to expiate the guilt of mankind.

When a Jewish convert to Christianity begins to talk about the fact that the sacrifice of God's only beloved Son Jesus was needed, it is necessary to look at the private and personal devotion of this man in relation to what sacrifice means to him. Occasionally one will find a Jewish convert to Christianity who feels that in the sacrifice of Jesus the previously rejected sacrifice of Abraham's only beloved son was accomplished, that tradition was fulfilled, and that God alone in giving His only begotten Son was able to make the perfect sacrifice—the sacrifice without blemish, the divine sacrifice which was necessary in order that the guilt of mankind be atoned and that mankind be free of the stain of the guilt of Adam. This need to pervert Jewish theology in order to rationalize one's Christian conversion is one of the many ways in which these converts frequently show their intense religious conflicts.

To the learned Jew throughout the ages, the sacrifice offered by Abraham was the perfect sacrifice. No further sacrifice was needed or wanted. There are many who feel that the Suffering Servant of Isaiah, when interpreted to mean the whole of the Jewish people, is already becoming a gentile perversion of the need for sacrifice. When we explore the meaning of sacrifice in mystical theology, it becomes all the more evident that we have to inquire into every patient who presents any clues in the area of sacrifice. I have come to question, probe, and watch my clergy very carefully for evidence of pathology in the area of sacrifice.

Throughout his long life Freud reiterated his belief that the origin of religion was in the reaction of the child to his father in response to his Oedipal conflicts. In both *Totem and Taboo* written in 1913 and *Moses and Monotheism* published in 1939 Freud writes of his myth of the "Killing of the Father of the Primal Horde" by a band of angry brothers because they were deprived of their mothers and sisters by the Jealous Father. In reenactment of this, the Father was eaten in the symbol of the Totem animal, and thus the brothers could identify with the Father by the process of becoming the Father through injestion of his body and thus acquire his strength. Out of the guilt of the murder of the Father the stern superego of the Hebrews developed. In atonement one of the brothers was sacrificed and eaten, so that in Christian communion we have the symbolic reenactment of human sacrifice in the symbolic cannibalistic rite of the Eucharist, or Holy Communion.

The level of the human sacrifice of Jesus was perhaps intensified when the Christian missionaries evangelized the Celts, because the Druids [12] in their priesthood had the sacrifice of a man who was crucified on an oak tree, the top of which was lopped off and used to make the beginning of the funeral pyre. The extensive use of the sacrifice of the priest-king in so many pagan religions, which were still extant when these people were converted to Christianity, as a rule by force of arms, may account

[12] Margaret Murray, *The God of the Witches* (New York: Doubleday & Co., 1960).

for the ever-increasing insistence on the Eucharist as a sacrifice of Jesus to atone for the sins of mankind. In a sense, Jesus has symbolized very many of the ancient pagan gods who were sacrificed and resurrected at the spring equinox, Tammuz, Balder, and Adonis, among many others.

That the atonement was necessary is the crux of the problem of rationalizing the meaning of the sacrifice. If we accept Judaic tradition, no human sacrifice was needed. Therefore, to some it was necessary to postulate original sin and then to say that the sacrifice of Jesus alone could atone for the sins of Adam. In one sense, this can be understood as a symbolic reassurance of man's triumph over death. In Jewish theology, the change that came over Adam when he partook of the forbidden fruit was that he would die. At this moment death became the expected end of mankind. His immortality was lost. According to this interpretation, all that is sinful is that which is destructive or self-destructive and therefore leads to death, whether it be death of the body or death of the soul. In the resurrection, Christ symbolized mankind's being reminded again of the eternal soul, which essentially is its immortal life.

Thus, in partaking of the death and resurrection of Christ, we are assured that we, like Jesus, will die in our human bodies, and that our souls will live in the eternal glory of His presence. Underlying this is the sympathetic magic which is the mystical meaning of the ancient human practice of cannibalism. Probably at this level of understanding we have the greatest revulsion and the greatest misunderstanding of Holy Communion. The deep psychological meaning and beauty of the theology of cannibalism, characteristic of a primitive stage of human development, is that, in the use of sympathetic magic, the cannibal hopes to acquire and expects to acquire the strength and courage of the man on whom he feeds. He does the same with the animals in which he has symbolized human virtues. He eats the heart of a lion to give him courage, and, in the same sense, we are fed the love of God in outward and visible tokens of the symbols of His humanity and of His eternity. The Host [13] symbolizes the bread which we need to sustain our human bodies; the wine, the blood,

[13] From the Latin, *hostia*, meaning victim.

is the life which courses through our human body and symbolizes the life to come. "Grant us therefore, gracious Lord, so to eat the flesh of thy dear Son Jesus Christ, and to drink his blood, that our sinful bodies may be made clean by his body, and our souls washed through his most precious blood, and that we may evermore dwell in him, and he in us." [14] By feeding on one who partakes of the dual nature of God and of man, we are strengthened in the knowledge that we, too, have a dual nature, our created bodies and our created souls.

In the trance-induced "possession," as in the devouring incorporation in the actual eating of the sacrifice, the worshiper or priest became God for the time. Blood was symbolically understood as life, and the blood or anything red was life giving to the people and the God who shared the sacrifices. Many people have been horrified by the killing and eating of the sacrifice and have developed taboos against the eating of the blood. Among the Hebrews the blood of the sacrifice and the wine were poured upon the ground or sprinkled on the altar and/or on the people.

One fundamental distinction between the Jew and the Christian exists here. The Jew has set up dietary laws forbidding the eating of blood. The Christian ritually drinks it in the wine or grape juice of the Holy Communion.

Freud seems fascinated and shocked by the cannibalistic devouring incorporation of the totem animal. He quotes at length from Robertson Smith the description of the orgiastic eating of a live camel by a medieval Arab tribe. He sees in this barbaric religious ritual the enactment of his myth—the killing of the angry Jealous Father by the equally angry sons. It is in his need of defense against his fear of his own death wishes that Freud reveals the intensity with which he cannot move beyond this point in his understanding of religion. Freud can speak of the identity of the mechanisms by which the phobic child projects his fear of his father onto an animal, or the savage, his Father-God onto the totem animal, but he cannot permit himself to consider the child's wishes to devour and so take into himself, to incorporate, to become his mother. Freud shares this use of the Father as a screen to protect himself from realizing his aggression toward

[14] Book of Common Prayer, p. 82.

the frustrating Mother with the Judeo-Christian world. How our Semetic ancestors changed from the worship of a Mother-God to a Father-God I do not know; but if we look into the personal unconscious religious life of our patients we find that their personal God is intrinsically Mother or Father according to their personal life experience and their psychosexual development. If the personal religious life of the individual is fixated in the stage of the need and defense against the devouring incorporation of the mother, where his unconscious fantasies are of biting and eating his mother's breasts, he would be expected to project this onto his unconscious understanding of his relationship with his God. I base my conclusions on clinical case histories and Róheim's psychoanalytic analysis of anthropological data. The answers are similar.

In the opinion of Róheim the eating of the totem animal is not the eating of the father but, "is really the eating of the mother." [15] He quotes his article on the subject [16] which is unavailable to the writer.

It has long been psychoanalytic custom, when lacking clinical, anthropological, or mythological evidence for a hypothesis, to permit ourselves to use the literature of prose or poetic fantasy to illustrate our point. The taboos against verbalizing the motherhood of God are very strong in modern Protestant Christianity. It was not always so, apparently in the imagery of the following:

> The knife which the priest thrusts obliquely thru the holy loaf to symbolize the soldier's lance which had been plunged in the side of the Savior.

> While the boy explained all these mysteries, the liturgist cut a second loaf which he turned into the "Body of the Virgin Mary," whose "physical presence" in these mysteries was believed in by the Eastern Church of that time [800 A.D.]—especially after the day when, while the priest was chanting the *Ave Maria*, the bread had turned into a visible virgin who appeared to all holding her Son in her arms. . . .

> The bread and wine are indeed the dead body of our Savior

[15] Róheim, *op. cit.*, p. 203.
[16] *Ibid.*, "Nach dem Tode des Urvaters. *Imago, 9.*"

and our stomachs is its grave in which it is interred by the
priest: and that shortly afterwards it rises as Christ did after
the Crucifixion.[17]

The understanding of what is expressed here in the terms of
killing and being killed is called in psychoanalytic jargon, anal
incorporation, as opposed to what we earlier described in the
mystery of the cannibalistic concept of the Eucharist, as oral incorporation. Oral incorporation is becoming that which we take
in through our mouths. This is a much less disturbing fantasy or
symbolic understanding, because we have long been prohibited
against the eating of live flesh by the seven laws of Noah. And
we are further protected by the fact that few of us have teeth of
sufficient strength to actually tear and devour live flesh. But the
enraged infant has such fantasies and has such fears that, having
nursed in anger, the milk he has swallowed has taken the mother's
breast and the mother into his stomach. The ease with which we
can spit this out, vomit this out, is a reassurance; and so we
blithely use the word "eat" in vulgar language to signify those
caresses of love, which are done with the lips, the mouth, the
tongue.

In the early infancy when sucking and eating and taking in
through our months was the all-important method of communicating, of receiving and giving love, we were relatively harmless,
except in fantasy. Bites of love, of lovemaking, may leave bruises,
but little more. However, with the development of our muscula-
ture, with the development of the awareness of our ability to use
our strength with our muscles, to use our extremities as weapons,
and to take weapons into our hands in order to make us more
powerful, we come simultaneously to that period of time when
we become aware of our ability to control our anal sphincters.
Thus, a great deal of confusion may set in because, in the distorted logic of primary-process thinking, two separate and dis-
tinct occurrences, which happen at the same time, are the same.
If we are angry, if we want to hit out and hurt, and this takes
place when we are having a bowel movement, then the idea of

[17] Emanuel Royidis, *Pope Joan*, revised edition translated from the Greek
by Lawrence Durrell (New York: E. P. Dutton & Co. Inc., 1960; London:
Andre Deutsch, Ltd., 1960), pp. 92, 99. Used by permission.

extending one's extremities or expelling and pushing out a part of one's self becomes a confused concept of destruction. At the same time, a taking in, a holding back, may be related to refusing to please mother by giving out with feces, and this may be related to a wish to keep, to hold onto, to retain, so that, in reaction to the enema, the helpless, passive infant feels that everything is being taken away from him, that he has no control over the insides of his body, that he is become nothing and is totally annihilated. This may go on to the point where he feels that an examination is like an enema, in which his knowledge is being torn out of him, as by an enema.

The result of all this is vulgar terms that connote this happy death in sexual orgasm. The fear of killing, of letting go, and killing during orgasm; the fear of being killed in being penetrated, such as occurs in some women who feel that everything is being taken over, that they are helpless and passive. Somehow, in Christian terms, we have the concept of dying unto sin and being reborn in Christ, so that we experience a death and a rebirth, a feeling such as has been a constant theme in all the fertility religions of the winter solstice as this time of death and rebirth. Christ is born at this time, at the time of the winter solstice and dies at the spring equinox, when the earth comes alive in the spring. Moreover, in the moment of dying, we know we are loved, or, in the moment of dying we will know that we are loved. When we feel the thrust of the knife, then we, the sacrificed, know and will know that the sacrificer loves us. And conversely, it is only in the moment of killing that the sacrificer will know that he is loved, that he will never be abandoned, that the beloved in death will always be his. And he makes her his in the moment of oneness, when his knife penetrates her body on the altar.

This fantasy is unfortunately acted out in its most horrible form with the woman who can only enjoy sex when she is beaten and raped, and so goes to her death at the hands of a man who kills her as he rapes her. This I only began to understand when I tried to do hypnosis with Job many years ago, while he was still psychologically a very, very angry little infant. I was concerned. I was not sure that this was the time in which to do it. I could not understand my hesitation and Job was most insistent. I tried a very light trance. And the second time a very moderate trance. The third time I sensed that something was very wrong. I didn't know what. And so, since Job was insistent that we begin, I began slowly, and as is too often my habit when I feel disturbed, I moved about the room, crossing over to the fireplace and arranging some flowers on the mantel. Job responded with an anger which frightened us both. He lay there with his hands clenched together, talking to himself as well as to me, telling me to stay very quiet, telling himself to get under control. He wanted to kill me so terribly; he wanted to strangle me so terribly; and he also did not want to. He wanted to hold on to me. He had been so terribly threatened by the abandonment of my crossing the room that he had been thrown into this terrible anger that impelled him and compelled him to kill me in order that I would get inside of him and stay with him, so that he would never be so terribly abandoned again. Now, four years later, we are doing hypnosis again; after Job is in a happy deep state of hypnotically induced prayer, I leave him with the tape recording, continuing the hypnotic vehicle in which he is finding his devotion. He is very proud that nowadays he does not notice when I leave. He is often amazed that he was unaware for hours afterward that my leaving was unnoticed. This is because he has come to know through the years that I am with him, that I have not abandoned him, and he is finding through this a depth of love in a profound and wonderful devotion so that he is now beginning to find the God that he has always searched for in human form. He knows now that people die. He knows that this could even happen to me. But he knows more than he has ever known, more than most people know, that no matter what happens, his God will be with him; he will never be abandoned again. (See the cases of Phillip and Jerome.)

D. Sexual Deviations Expressed in Holy Communion

Now if we can understand what happens in the perversions of love that are so frustrated by abandonment and loneliness that they become riddled with hate, and that cruelty which is compounded of distorted, soured aggression and love, if we can understand this in the light of the terrible fear of being abandoned, of the terrible need to hold one's loved ones, to hug that beloved in such a bear hug that the beloved is drawn in under one's skin and becomes a very final part of one's self, if we can understand this in terms of the desperately terrible need of the abandoned child, then we can begin to have compassion for those whose loneliness and crippled, unhappy devotion has been caught and symbolized in the sacrifice of the Eucharist. It may help at this point, to show how the Church has compounded this in some of the prayers, teachings, and practices that are advocated.

Some of the difficulty in understanding this perversion of devotion may be clarified by a quotation from the *People's Anglican Missal.*[18] On page 19 of the introduction, a prayer to the wounds of Christ:

> I pray thee, Lord Jesus, by thy sacred wounds which thou didst suffer on the cross for our salvation (whence flows thy precious blood, whereby we have obtained redemption), would this my sinful soul, for which thou hast vouchsafed even to suffer death, with the fiery dart of thy exceeding and unconquerable charity. Pierce my heart with the javelin of thy love, that my soul may say unto thee; I am sore smitten with thy love; that so from the very wounds of thy love my tears may flow without ceasing both day and night. Strike O Lord, I beseech thee, this my stony heart with the mighty spear of thy gracious loving kindness; and pierce it to the inmost depth of thy mighty power. Who livest and reignest forever and ever. Amen.

In the instructions for prayer and meditation there are frequent examples of the insistence on dwelling in meditation on the intense identification with the wounded and crucified Christ, so that one is able to experience in fantasy the penetrating wounds. This of course at times results in the hysterical stigmata, where a patient spontaneously develops bleeding wounds of the hands, feet, and the side during Easter week. The investment of the passion and death of our Lord with this full component of cruel

---

[18] American edition published by the Frank Gavin Liturgical Foundation, Inc., of Mount Sinai, Long Island, New York, by permission of the Society of Sts. Peter and Paul of London, England.

mistreatment and painful suffering increases the possibility of the sexual perversion of wounding and penetrating by means of the phallus, which is not at all disguised in the above quotation where it is called a spear or a javelin. Thus women experience this as a rape fantasy; men also experience it as a rape fantasy, but of necessity a sodomistic attack. According to their personalities they are passive or aggressive in relation to the Christ figure. It is thus not difficult to understand why in a case which a colleague has reported to me, a lay woman was unable to receive Communion because, in her delirium, she experienced the wine as menstrual blood and the wafer as semen. In this context it makes sense, but is often tragic in its effect on the person experiencing it. I have worked with many of the perversions of love and hate as they are manifested in the devotion of the individual.

The value of being able daringly and brutally to analyze the sacrifice in its literal terms in the group process is illustrated by the experience of another patient who did not have this therapeutic experience at the time when he needed it. This was a case in which a young seminarian just before ordination became extremely troubled in his spontaneous awareness that in the depths of his devotion erotic fantasies in relation to the crucified Christ had broken through to consciousness. He knew a little about psychology, just enough to make the picture seem pitch black to him. He went to a confessor who likewise knew enough about psychoanalysis to make the worst possible interpretation, and so the young man confessed that he had feelings of homosexual excitement and arousal in contemplating the crucified Christ during the celebration of the Eucharist. The confessor's horror was such that the young man refused ordination. He felt himself completely damned and worthless. He had a feeling that he was a Judas who had committed an even more unpardonable sin than Judas had. His family was heartbroken, so he felt completely martyred and self-righteous; and his family felt that he was doing a very cruel act in depriving them of their happiness in seeing him ordained, in having a priest as a son and as a brother. Having been accused and having accepted the accusation as true, he set about proving his damnation, and it was only after several years of frenetic, restless promiscuity, that he went to a wiser and more intuitive confessor, and there found his way into therapy, where he could cleanse himself of the sordidness of his driving need to prove himself damned, and where he was able to understand that we at times perceive the love of God in ways which are somewhat unconventional.

This leads into the perverted devotion which is in the terms of becoming one with the loved object through an act of sodomy. An example of this was a young deacon, Matthew, whose background was that of the unhappy youngster whose mother and sisters dominated the home environment so that he was unable to fully identify with his father for whom he had much love, but not enough respect. He had a mixture of Episcopalian and Methodist religious training. At about the age of thirteen, a young lad in his gang was wounded in a hunting accident. The boy lived for several months. Feeling that his life had been spared because of the many prayers of good and pious people, Matthew, our deacon, decided to dedicate himself to the service of this good God. When, some months later, the boy died a death which had only been delayed but which had been caused by the original accident, our fourteen-year-old suffered a great deal of religious doubt. How could God have permitted this accident to occur? How could a loving God let this young man be killed?

Feeling that he wanted no part of such an untrustworthy God, Matthew gave up his decision to go into the ministry. When he was nineteen, he met, in the course of his work as a cub reporter, an old friend, a member of the old gang in which the death had occurred. As they were talking and showing off, this newfound old friend showed him a new gun, which he had just bought. It was an automatic, and he very proudly showed him how it was loaded, and ejected the bullets, reloaded, and ejected what Matthew suspected was only five of the six bullets. Matthew had always known how to handle weapons. His father had been very strict in teaching the boy good gun manners, and his friends had often accused him of being a sissy because of his adherence to his father's strict rules. And so now when this lad was flourishing the gun around, pointing it in all directions, and frequently at Matthew, Matthew was uneasy because if he challenged him and the gun was really empty, he would be made a fool, and if the gun was loaded, he would be called a sissy. And suddenly the gun went off and the bullet almost creased his shoulder. He saw the look of terror on his friend's face. And looking out into the street where he pointed, he saw a crowd gather. He ran out. A young woman walking on the sidewalk had been innocently murdered. Matthew testified honestly and clearly what he knew, and the charge was dropped after due investigation as an accidental killing. But Matthew always felt that if he had had the courage to tell his friend to put that gun down and check whether or not it was loaded, that young woman would not have met her death. So Matthew carried this guilt away with him to college. That fall a friend persuaded him to go to a nearby convent school, where he was serving as acolyte, to attend Holy Communion and be roped in as an additional acolyte. Here he was so frightened by the austere purity of the nuns that he attended services several times before he dared approach the altar rail; and when he did, he had a feeling of absolution and forgiveness, and within a few months, he again knew that he wanted to go into the priesthood. He was accepted as a postulant and entered seminary. There, as his childish religion was confronted by form criticism and mature liberal theology, he became increasingly disturbed. He fell in love and when his wish to marry was reciprocated more frustration developed. According to seminary rules he could not marry until graduation; according to his bishop's personal wishes, not until his ordination. His normal masculine wishes surfaced and his guilt increased. The daily celebration of the Eucharist became an ordeal which he began evading by oversleeping. As his anger mounted, he became more passively identified with Christ crucified. Somehow his God had betrayed him once again. And so this boy whose screening psychologist found him immature on entering seminary was found sick and in difficulties psychologically when he graduated. He had hidden his illness from everyone until this time. He had tried to be the Rock of Gibraltar which he felt his young wife needed him to be. And gradually he had become more and more passive and long-suffering in his effort to hide and control his mounting seething anger. He was quiet and difficult to draw out in the group, but a few nights before he was ordained priest, he had suddenly been able to express some of the pent-up rage. He was saying Evening Prayer alone in the church, and the prayers, the psalms, the lessons seemed to fit his mood. "Ah, Assyria, the rod of my anger . . ." (Isaiah 10.5). He roared them out. He shouted them out with all the strength of his magnificent voice. And then he snuffed out the candles, took off his vestments, put on his overcoat and his hat, and stomped out. He stopped and deliberately did not reverence the high altar at the center aisle. He looked up angrily at the high altar, he was very angry with the angry God. And then he walked over to the side altar where the crucifix and the reserved Sacrament were kept, genuflected, and, still with his hat on, he said, "Well, cheer up, old boy, I'll get the shaft too in a few days."

A few nights later, he was telling us about it in the group. He had to explain what the term "get the shaft" or "shafted" had meant. It is a term used at the present time in adolescence and in the army servicemen's slang to express the meaning of being overridden on one's wishes, forced to undergo something one does not want to endure.

In Matthew's identification with the shafted God, the practical meaning was to be crucified, and symbolically in the crucifixion to undergo a cruel penetrating sodomistic attack. This would be to get the shaft with the purple barbs. This symbol was also found in the Rorschach protocol of James when he entered treatment. In this percept he saw a giant empaled on a spear.

The group discussion turned to a general speculation as to where, anatomically, the wound of Christ was located. A number of the men in the group whom we could expect to know the Gospels quite well, being either clergy or intelligent lay people, speculated about the exact translation of the word "side," or "the wounded side," and wondered if the wound actually had occurred in the groin, or perineum. They overlooked the functional reality of the problem of killing a man suspended overhead by spearing him, a method which would practically call for a thrust aiming at the heart through the abdominal wall, which is also the traditional and scriptural location, the wounded side.

As time went on, the occasions in which Matthew acted out his identification with his shafted God, through those periods of passive depression, of passive aggression, being so helpless, so unable to help himself, or to help us to help him, became gradually less and less, and he more and more found his identification with the angry Father-God. Almost a year later, he was able to realize that when he was saved, and the girl on the street sacrificed in his stead, he had to repay God for sparing his life. And so his priesthood was "to do God's dirty work for Him." He was the one who had to kill the innocent sacrificial lamb on the altar in the Eucharist. He was the one who had to carry out the angry Father-God's revenge. And this too yielded to therapy gradually so that there came a time when Matthew no longer had the need to project his own intolerable rage onto the transference symbol of his God; and as his God was cleansed of the anger, so too was Matthew.

In the infantile injestion type of reunion with the mother there is oneness but also the loss and death of either the mother or the self. In the passive sodomistic act the priest identifies with the sacrifice, the mother as Christ. In becoming his mother he hopes he will be loved by the father and he himself dies.

In a number of cases the pathology has been first found on the level of the enjoyment of pain through cruel sadistic attack, and in therapy proceeds to the devouring sadistic level. In other words, the identification with the sacrifice, if first found thus, is later reversed to the identification with the sacrific*er*.

Clergymen are often troubled by an awareness that "carnal thoughts" come to mind during Communion. Occasionally a devout and fulfilled minister will be troubled by the realization that he has an erection at the moment of greatest religious intensity.

Such a case was a devout and magnificent celibate priest, who, in a social situation, where I had the least possible opportunity of knowing exactly what he meant since he spoke in very guarded language, told me that at times he had been aware of sexual feelings in the celebration of the Divine Liturgy, and that this had bothered him and worried him, but it had never stopped him because his faith in the forgiveness of our Lord was such that he could endure the evidence of his frailty. I said to him, "Father, you're very much a man. You have a magnificent body. You have dedicated everything, mind, body, and soul to God. Why are you surprised that at the moment of the most perfect and complete rededication, in the moment of Holy Communion, you should be aware that you are offering to God your masculinity? You should be aware that God has accepted this and has given it back to you blessed and pure and strong, so that you are much more effective in your work because you are every inch a man." It seemed to give him a feeling of reassurance. I hope it did.

I have known other minsters who have worked out these same feelings in the course of long analysis and so not only have come to live with such expressions, such physical expressions of devotion, but have come to realize their deep and powerful significance. We cannot worship with a part of ourselves and be whole people. When we can accept our sexuality as a part of the wonder and strength and goodness of our humanity, then we can bring this as its rightful share of our offering of ourselves to God and our receiving back ourselves blessed from God.

In the mature sexual symbolism the adult phallic genital stage of the priest as a man and the sacrifice as a woman not his mother is achieved. This is the religious concept of the Zohar, the textbook of medieval sephardic cabbalistic mysticism, that only when a man enjoys a good sexual love relationship with his wife can he be truly righteous. The symbolic contract or covenant is found in maturity in the solution of the Oedipal situation. Unfortunately few Jews and Christians are permitted to know of such a God who relates to His Divine Presence as a man should have his wife.

This concept of the dual nature of God was also found in some of the Gnostic sects in early Christianity. This "heresy" was supposedly stamped out because of the sexual orgies which followed the communion love feasts or agapes. Other Gnostic sects were austerely ascetic. The characteristic in common was the belief that only in mystical or conversion experience could we come to know God.

One of my older ministers, a man whose devotion is exceedingly mature, and whose courage and imagination are strong and deep, can speak of a feeling of the Eucharist as an expression of the relationship between himself and his wife, so that the moment of total involvement in the consecration is equated with the human experience of total involvement in love with his wife. This would be the Zoharic understanding of the marriage relationship making it possible for a man to be truly able to experience righteousness; for only in the fulfillment of a good marriage can a man realize the comparable ecstasy of the unity of God in His union with His Divine Presence, the Shechinah.

A saintly and dedicated monk priest of the Episcopal Order of the Holy Cross has spoken of this relationship of the sexual fulfillment in a good marriage as a picture of heaven, as a fore-knowledge of the experiencing of the life to come, of experiencing the joy and wonder of the knowledge of God. One of the great difficulties for the immature priest, especially the immature celibate priest, is the increase in the sadism of his necessary sexual frustration, and this, of course, reveals itself in projection onto an angry God, so that the sacrifice becomes more the sacrifice and less the experiencing of a moment of total involvement. It is for this reason that the celibate priest needs such great maturity of personality in order that he may continue in his personality as representing God in His essential qualities of grace and justice combined with long-suffering and tender mercy; so that he can remember the triumph over death in the wonder of the joyous creative experience of the joy of total involvement in the creative love of God as symbolized in the Eucharist. (See the case of Andrew.)

VI. The Special Nature and Goals of Clerical Psychotherapy

What is the nature of the therapeutic process and what are the specific goals of clerical psychotherapy?

The conscientious therapist must decide either to work with people who have religious conflicts or to refrain from doing so. The conscientious therapist spends many years in his preparation for the analysis of sexual or aggressive conflicts. The conscientious therapist does not undertake the therapy of people whose political conflicts are a source of discomfort to himself. If he does not feel comfortable in trying to understand his patient's conflicts, he will refer that patient to someone who will enjoy working with him.

Too often in our profession there is the feeling that all religion is an illusion, "the opiate of the masses." A less dangerous but still unsatisfactory course is the attitude of assuming that if the rest of the patient's problems are resolved, the religious ones will take care of themselves. This occurs occasionally, especially among persons whose religious conflicts are not severe, or whose turn of mind is such that they themselves can carry on with the self-analysis of this area as the analyst helps them with other areas.

The religious life of an individual is a very precious and intimate area, about which one does not speak easily even to one's beloved. We have to open ourselves much more to the knowledge and awareness of our patient if we are to be given the precious inner confidence of the religious life. It is not easy to do. It is especially difficult for the therapist who has been brought up in the tradition of the intellectual agnosticism of recent generations.

70

Fortunately, the pendulum is swinging back, and the therapist who admits to personal religious devotion is in a much easier position with his colleagues than he was ten years ago.

But even those therapists who are unafraid to admit their devotion to their colleagues have revealed to me their squeamishness in talking of religion with patients. The fact that a therapist may be able to go to religious services, may be able to ally himself socially and professionally with religious groups of his denomination, does not seem to mean that he is free to discuss problems of religion with his patients.

When one accepts a patient into therapy, one undertakes to work within the framework of the patient's life. One has to accept certain preconditions as operative throughout the analysis. In working with professional religionists one can no more ignore or get rid of religion than overlook the need of human relationships. The therapist who is truly dedicated to his profession can only search for the means of helping his patient to a healthier and fuller life in the context of his patient's needs both within himself and within his community.

For a long time I have known that theological and psychological truth coincide. But only recently have I found that theologians have come to believe that theological doctrine is to be questioned whenever it is not conducive to mental health and well being. One of the cornerstones of Protestant religious ideation is the importance of the individual. The rights of the individual are conceived to be a freedom to think, to explore and to determine for one's self, one's own concept of the interpretation of God's will for him as revealed in scripture. The Protestant has no obligation to higher authority than himself, and no need of a mediator between himself and his God. This type of a value system offers a healthy mature individual an opportunity to find for himself a mature and good religion, but for the less fortunate immature person, it offers many pitfalls.

For the therapist who is faced by a patient who refuses treatment in part or wholly because of blind religious conviction, it offers at times tremendous obstructions. The unfortunate therapist who reacts badly may further increase the resistance by too vigorous an attack. Religion is a much more intimate area than either money or sex, and in discussing failure in the treatment of religious problems . . . with other therapists, I have found that their failures often stemmed from the fact that religion was for them a far too intimate subject about which they could speak comfortably. It would be rather difficult for analysts who had no sexual experience, or no personal analysis with sexual problems, to work with them with their patients. And yet the average analyst feels that he must never be guilty of any personal religion, and many report a supposedly completed personal analysis in which no mention had been made of any personal religion. I feel, personally, that it is possible for a person to have had such a secure and loved childhood, and such an utter lack of religious orientation in his community life that he has never felt a need to project what we call a personal devotion towards what we generally term God. But I think this is so rare that we would seldom find it among analysts, and never among patients.

Without a climate of comfortable acceptance of religion, of the same order we would ask for a discussion of the problems of sex or money, the utilization of specific techniques . . . is useless and without any value. Unless the patient can feel the therapist's respect for what is healthy in his religious life, just as in all other facets of his personality and of his ideals, he cannot permit his therapist to help him think through his sick and distorted self in a constructive and therapeutic fashion. In the absence of such a climate there is danger of self-destructive acting out, regression, intensification of the unhealthy religious attitudes with greater use of these attitudes as resistance. When there is established a basic security in the reality of the therapeutic relationship, the religious problems can be subjected to psychological scrutiny with the same penetrating skill as in every other facet of the human psyche. A true problem of heresy has never developed in the course of the analysis of religious problems in my experience, although I have had many patients dashing about seeking theological help because some new psychological insight was at first thought by the patient to be heresy. In every instance, with all of the creeds prominent in our western culture, the new psychological insight was found to coincide with the higher theology of the patient's religious group.

In the severely fundamentalist Protestant one may have the patient who has replaced the healthy independence of thought and action with a rigid prejudice against listening to anyone else's opinion about anything, but especially the Book. He may have been brought up in some of the more austere groups that permit none of the ameliorating effects of the tradition of a long established church and of the body of commentary of theologians and scholars within that tradition. He may, to make my example as severely defined as possible, belong to a group that is no longer interested in the Greek or Hebrew of the earliest available copies of scripture, who are equally oblivious to Latin translation, but who profoundly believe that the King James version is an inspired translation—that is to say, is accurately and clearly translated and that the English of several hundred years ago is as easily understood now as then. In this case, there is no possibility of asking the patient to search out other translations of the passage on which he anchors his distorted religious ideation. Because of the narrow focus of his authoritative transference attitudes upon the Book as opposed to the other variety of religious ideation where the authoritative transference is to the Church and its tradition, a great deal of time must be spent patiently and emphatically by the analyst in creating a sufficiently comfortable attitude so that a part of this transference is transferred to the analyst. As I have said before, this can only be done when the analyst is comfortable enough to work within a religious climate. . . .

In the course of working with religious patients one may be certain that no matter how much they preach a loving God, more often than not their own personal God is consciously or unconsciously an angry, punishing, cruel God. Thus, if the first phase of working with the religious is to share in the transference to the Book and to God, the second phase is to analyze both the transference to the analyst and to the Book and God.

The term transference is . . . seen to be those emotional attitudes which the patient projects onto important persons in the present out of his experiences with important persons in the past. Thus I do not restrict the term wholly to those focused on the therapist. I also feel that the reality of the therapist's own personal reactions when they enter into the therapeutic situation becomes part of the reality which the patient needs to define accurately. The reality of his God I accept . . . , but I treat as transference distortions of the divine reality everything which is noncompatible with psychological health, both individual and community. The reality of the therapist, being human, is, of necessity, more earthy and imperfect.[1]

At the present time, religious denominations have no standards for determining the outcome of therapy and thus have no guidelines for the selection of therapists. Churches have been discouraged about the use of psychotherapy owing to the large number of seminarians and ordained clergy who have left their vocation, apparently as a result of psychotherapy. In my opinion, the present high rate of therapeutic failure is due to the therapists' indifference toward the patients' religious conflicts. A pathogenic religion may be completely unconscious, and as the result of the therapist's failure to approach it analytically, the religious conflict remains encapsulated and compartmented but continues to be operative.

Success or failure of therapy can be determined by the application of a simple measuring device: Do the patients remain in their vocations or do they drop out? The characteristics of therapists with high failure rates can then be compared to those with low failure rates and, as the result of a significant number of comparisons, a profile of the successful therapist is expected to emerge. The bias of the survey must be unknown to those supplying data.

What, then, will be the profile of the successful therapist in the religious area? In the light of my experience I will advance four tentative propositions: (1), the therapist has undergone analysis of his own religious attitudes; (2), the therapist has had thorough training in the technique of the psychotherapy of religious conflicts; (3), the therapist has had orientation in the theology of the denomination of his patient, which means that the well-rounded therapist must acquaint himself with the theology of the Roman Catholic, the Jew, and the Protestant; (4), *he must regard the patient's religious conflict as a core problem and respect the patient as a religious person.* If we accept the premise that successful therapy of religious personnel consists in

[1] Reprinted from Annals of Psychotherapy Monograph #2, *J. Am. Academy of Psychotherapists* (New York, 1959), pp. 6–8, 11–12. Used by permission.

reconciling the patient's *unconscious religious attitudes* with his *conscious theological* attitude, achieving a state where *theological truth and psychological truth coincide*—and I believe we must— then, the successful therapist must definitely possess these four requirements.

The selection of therapists for work with religious personnel will become a relatively simple process if the suggested method of success rate versus failure rate is applied in the process. While I have advanced my personal expectations as to the outcome of such a study, a detailed and thorough examination of the problem is certain to bring about rich practical, as well as theoretical, results.

The specific goals of clerical psychotherapy are of special concern to church authorities of various denominations since a significant portion of religious personnel are converts from other denominations. A study of my patient sample shows that very few converts are able to discard teachings imposed on them by parents or their previous denomination. Earlier teachings are repressed and become unconscious but continue to operate. Even patients who were brought up in the church are subject to conflicts arising out of childhood distortions. The childhood religion is repressed and, while the individual tries to believe and teach what he has been taught in the seminary, childhood distortions continue to operate. Seminary education has failed to eliminate this source of potential conflict with the result that not only are these clergymen subject to personal conflict, but the Church itself is in danger of losing its traditional identity. Psychotherapeutic intervention in such cases acquires an importance that transcends the benefits of its individual successes.

A detailed and confidential study of the total seminary and clergy population of the various churches is needed to establish their requirements for rehabilitation. These requirements cannot be judged by the number of clergy who have come to the attention of their superiors to the point of requiring the disciplinary action of suspension or deposition. Therapy should be made available so as to be sought voluntarily by those whose physical or mental illness or conduct is as yet a matter of personal and not public concern. It is my firm, realistically grounded belief that the pastor who has had the privilege of personal psychotherapy should, as a result of successful therapy, not only be a happier and more fulfilled person but in every respect should be a better pastor and a wiser and more understanding leader in his community.

PART TWO

Case Histories

❧ STEPHEN ❧

Stephen [1] was compelled to enter into treatment "under discipline"; that is, he had been suspended from his professional duties and privileges. He was told by his bishop that he would be returned to his active priesthood if, as a result of successful therapy, the Church were no longer embarrassed by his sexual deviation (which was one of passive homosexual submission).[2] In the light of conventional and popular attitudes, this decision represented a progressive step that came about chiefly because of the intervention of a psychiatrically trained priest who had known Stephen in seminary and who was able to insist that the bishop consider his behavior a manifestation of psychiatric illness and not a case of moral turpitude.[3]

On preliminary examination, Stephen was found to be passive, reserved, confused, and bewildered. As a part of the testing, he

---

[1] From "The Cross as a Command to Suffer" by Margaretta K. Bowers, M.D., and Thomas J. Bigham, M.S., S.T.M., in the *International Record of Medicine*, Vol. 171, No. 12, Dec. 1958, pp. 753–760. Used by permission.

[2] As is quite common with the severely sexually inhibited clergy, Stephen's homosexuality had been due to a preponderance of guilt and a small degree of actual acting out. He had been so inhibited from any expression of heterosexual desire that as his relationship with his fiancée deepened his normal but unacceptable frustration caused repression so that he began to dwell on homosexual thoughts. He had had the usual prepuberty homosexual experience and now found himself in a situation where he was seduced by an aggressive homosexual with whom he had no emotional relationship. In fact, he had never had a homosexual relationship. He was confused and bewildered in the grips of his mental illness; he was lonely and frustrated in his longing for his fiancée; he was very angry with his father for this frustration and, under the influence of a few drinks, he could be seduced. When he was questioned, he was so overburdened by guilt that he confessed in such ambiguous terms that his bishop thought the situation far more serious than it really was.

[3] This attitude is prevalent in Stephen's church, the Protestant Episcopal Church, which has been utilizing psychotherapy in various ways for the past fifty years.

was asked to draw his most unpleasant concept. He drew a simple unadorned cross. His mask of passive submission and his acceptance of the therapeutic program covered a great deal of unhappiness and resentment at being forced into treatment which he neither understood nor wanted. He felt that, if the screening before entering the seminary and before ordination had been more thoroughgoing, if he had been ordered into treatment while he was in seminary, he would not now have been disgraced and humiliated. Although he had been more sympathetically and leniently treated, he still had much to be angry about; he had had little or no choice about anything, even the selection of his therapist. Still, Stephen needed a great deal of help in order to begin to feel and verbalize this anger. He consciously felt that he should, without question, submit passively to whatever happened, for it was the will of God. He had what one can call the usual Christian difficulty with the problem of anger; he felt that all anger was wrong and sinful, and needed a great deal of help and support to accept at first even the most justified resentment.[4]

He began to work slowly in treatment. He began to realize that, although I was obligated to make a report to his bishop at the end of treatment, I was essentially "on his side," and there was reason to believe that, if we worked together, the outcome of his treatment could be successful. With this attitude came the realization that he needed more hours of therapy than either one of us could afford. Since he wanted to get ahead more quickly, I suggested that we implement his two hours a week of personal therapy with seven hours a week during which he would write out his free associations and feelings.

With masochistic zeal, he undertook this discipline and continued to carry it out constructively during the two years of treatment.

His early writings as well as his therapy sessions were concerned with his difficulties about probing into anything; inhibition of curiosity was for a while the dominant focus of therapy. We worked through problem after problem, and it became very clear that he felt forbidden to inquire into anything. He had a

[4] The problem of the theology and the psychology of anger will be discussed elsewhere.

deep, uncontrollable prohibition of curiosity and was not permitted by his conscience to inquire into anything, to question or to consider anything, to be skeptical at all. He felt that I was always right, but, when I pointed out to him that this made him very angry, he admitted that deep underneath he had known all along that I was not always right, but was quite fallible.

He began to tell me about his life, to recall childhood and adolescent experiences. We finally went back to the day when he was told that the stork would bring his mother a baby. He was three and a half years old. It was a Sunday afternoon, his mother was in bed, and there was much coming and going. He was told to sit in the living room and look at the funny-paper, to stay there and be a good boy. The doctor came in with his little bag and went upstairs. He stayed a long time, and the little boy wondered what the doctor was doing there. Did the stork really bring the baby? Well, why did the doctor have to be there, and what was in his little black bag? But he did as he was told and never once did he permit himself to indulge his curiosity and look out the window to see if the stork did bring the little baby. No, he sat there for hours until finally there was more commotion and someone came down to tell him that the stork had brought him a little baby sister.

It was on this pattern that the rest of his life was based. He made the choice that he would not be curious and look into things, he would not venture to find out, or be skeptical. He made the choice at the age of three and a half years that he would believe any story, however absurd it may appear to be, that was told to him by authority. Later, the doctrine of the inscrutable will of God had, of course, readily appealed to him, especially when coupled with the suffering it entailed for the innocent Son. In the light of his history, it is no wonder that he had drawn as his most unpleasant concept what ought to be for any Christian the symbol of his deepest loyalties in the triumph of divine love.

When Stephen began to realize that he had abdicated his right to think, to feel, to inquire, to be curious, at the age of three and a half years, the anger that had accumulated over the twenty odd years since that momentous life decision had been made suddenly started to seethe and break through into his consciousness. Instead of just floating passively on the surface of life, he now began to question everything. From then on, my job became easier. I had only to point out various contradictions and to steer him toward another of his blind spots. Of course, he went through a great deal of the agony we call resistance. He would find all kinds of excuses for not facing these realities, but gradually he would dig in and realize that here was another area that had been closed off.

One day he came in unhappy and disturbed. For the first time he could remember, he had noticed a woman on the street to be most sexually attractive. He felt this was very bad. What was I doing to him? After all, he didn't know this woman, and one must not have such fantasies about strange women. It was all right for him to fantasy having such feelings about the woman he would marry some day, but not about a perfectly strange woman. This was very bad. I asked him why it was so bad, and we had a discussion about carnal thoughts. I said, "Yes, yes, but this doesn't add up. You're talking in contradictions. You're saying that you want to be a monk until you get married. Now make up your mind. If you want to go into the celibate life, we will consider that as the problem and recognize the fact that you should be able to give up sex, although not without some struggle because you are a man." I reminded him that, according to the theology he knew, spontaneous carnal thoughts and fantasies without any intention of fulfillment are not considered sins but temptations, and that even if he were considering becoming a monk-priest he would have to endure the discipline of such temptation in the world. All healthy men are inevitably aware at times of the sexual attraction of the opposite gender, and his church expected him to do no more than to discipline his acts and intentions. "But you intend to marry," I said. "You will not allow yourself to have such thoughts about women until you get married. Yet, you suddenly expect to turn on a switch and have the proper sexual feelings for your wife on your marriage bed."

The source of Stephen's confusion in this area began to emerge after this discussion. Stephen was the second son of a devout family which believed in passive submission to the will of God, especially in matters relating to bundles from heaven. This attitude resulted in seven children, far more than their financial circumstances should have allowed. The girls shared the same bathroom and bedroom with the boys. This was not only a matter of economics but of purity of thought. The family could not afford more bathrooms or bedrooms, so the boys worked hard to be unaware of their sisters as sexual, exciting females, and the girls were taught to be unaware of their brothers as sexually exciting males. The little boys and girls shared, in a very nude condition, the sleeping and bathroom arrangements until the girls began to menstruate. At that time their devout mother felt that the older boys should stop sleeping with their sisters, and a separate room was provided for them. By then Stephen had been taught an absolute discipline of ignoring sexual excitement. He had learned the lesson so well that he made all attractive women his sisters.

It took quite a while before Stephen was able to remember the times when his sisters had seemed to him to be very exciting and voluptuous, especially just before Mother decided that the chastity she was imposing may have been a little bit too much to obey.

The next area we explored was that of suffering. Stephen really had made a vocation of suffering. He had been brought up to suffer. He perceived his mother as one of those poor unfortunate women who marry men that are cruel, thoughtless, and who are called "brutes." She had suffered, and she was a good woman. She had always done her duty, had given her all to her family and church, had done everything for her husband and children. She had devoted herself, even on days when her headache was so terrible, had slaved away in a hot kitchen cooking so that her husband and children would have good hot meals.

Stephen remembered that his father had been a very difficult man. Stephen had always been very angry with him because his father had a terrible temper. He was always screaming and yelling and hitting. Although his father was devout, attending church regularly, seeing to it that the children always went to Sunday school, he had apparently identified himself with the angry God because he certainly showed that type of father-picture to his family. Stephen was scared to death of him. His older brother, the first child of the family, was the rebel. Stephen had suffered as he watched the older boy repeatedly beaten for his rebellion.

We were able to uncover an incident in which Stephen remembered choosing between Father and Mother. He wanted to run to meet his father; he felt that his father wanted him to come to him, wanted to pick him up in his huge arms, hold him up in the air, and hug him. This would have been fun. But he also had a feeling that his mother did not want him to. His mother wanted him to stay with her, and he did. He hung onto her skirts and sensed the fear in his mother's relationship with her husband. That was the last time he had a choice. After that, he was always with his mother. He never again was tempted to go to his father.

He always had to play in the back yard and was never allowed out of the yard to play with the boys in an unsupervised situation. He was never allowed to do anything that was strenuous or in the most remote way dangerous. Girls were preferred by his mother as his playmates since boys were too rough. He was never allowed to have a bike—it was too dangerous. He might fall and break his leg. This was all the more ridiculous because he lived in a country town where the roads were not dangerous or crowded with automobiles. He was never allowed to go off with his father to play golf as his older brother did. This brother, in spite of his rather tempestuous relationship with his father, was still permitted to go off to do these brutish things—playing golf or hunting. But Stephen was a good boy and stayed at home with his mother.

Stephen was beginning to tell me more and more in his effort to show me how black and bad and brutish his father had been. I merely listened and asked for more details. It seemed he never could have any fun on a family outing because Father always ended up in a temper tantrum. No matter what they did, Father always blew up. Here was a very devout family, which always said grace before meals, which read family prayers before the children went to bed at night, but which could never enjoy a family outing or a picnic because Father always had a temper tantrum. So we spent time trying to remember all the minutiae of how the plans were made and how the day was spent. Did Father make the plans? Did Mother? Did his sisters? Did he? How was it set up? Who wanted to have a picnic? Who wanted to go out to eat at a restaurant?

It finally developed that Mother could never make up her mind. Whenever Father wanted very much to celebrate a family occasion, a wedding anniversary, or Mother's birthday, he would ask Mother where she wanted to go and she, being a very noble, self-sacrificing woman, would say, "Anything you say is all right. Anything. I'll enjoy anything you suggest." But Father would insist that she tell what she wanted to do, and she would insist right back that anything was all right. Finally, he would make the decision. "Well then, we'll go to Lake Ommapassalong for a picnic." So Mother would pack a picnic lunch, and the seven children, Mother, and Father would all squeeze into the family car. Very soon after they got started, Mother would say, "Do you think it's wise for us to go so far? After all, it's threatening rain." Father would say, "Oh, it's not far. It's just two hours' driving, and it's only a little overcast. It's early in the morning; it will pass over." But Mother would say, "Well, don't you think we really ought to have gone to Lake Boomerang. I mean—after all—it's closer. Let's go there." Father would say, "Well, do you want to go to Lake Boomerang?" "No," she would reply, "I want to do anything you want to do. I was just saying, I was just wondering —anything you say is all right."

And so they would proceed a while further and finally reach Lake Ommapassalong. But Mother would be very unhappy about the number of people there. After all, it wasn't really quite the kind of place that she'd expected it to be. Wouldn't it have been better if they had gone to the so-and-so park. And Father would say, "Well, let's get back in the car and go to the so-and-so park." "Oh, no, no, no, I wouldn't dream of it." And Father would say, "Well, suppose we go down the road a bit until we find a nicer place." Eventually, they got down there and Mother would say, "But I think the other place was really very much nicer." And Father would say, "Well, shall we go back?" "Oh no, we shouldn't go back. I mean, after all. . . ."

And finally, after she found fault with every decision that she had refused to make herself, avoiding responsibility for anything, always finding fault and criticizing, never being happy or satisfied about anything, her husband would burst—blow his top. It was impossible to please her. But she was such a martyr, such a sweet, Christian woman, that all of her friends and neighbors and her children felt she was the most abused woman. But only an angel could have endured her many impossible demands. She had most successfully provoked her husband into such displays of temper that he was humiliated and damned.

Only after his father's death did Stephen begin to examine his family situation and particularly his mother's martyrdom. Finally, he had a chance to discover why he had drawn a cross. The cross was unpleasant because it was his life. He felt himself to be doomed, to be the martyr his mother had always been. There was no way out. He was confined within the narrow womb of his family with a mother who had never let him out of her sight.

He also began to realize that very little of his mother's suffering was necessary, that his mother had brought her troubles upon herself. In a community and in a church congregation where it was felt wise to limit one's family within one's economic needs, she had flaunted a pseudodevotion by having seven children and had insisted that the test of firm devotion was her submission to the will of God.

Yet, Stephen kept coming back and saying, "But we must suffer. Christ suffered. If it hadn't been for His glorious crucifixion, we would all be lost. We would have no hope of redemption."

I said, "Look, Stephen, you are supposed to know Christian theology. But I suggest that you go back and read the Scripture. I don't think that you have read the whole story of our Lord and His death. It's there for anyone who wants to hear it. I want you to read it all. I think you should study the Gospels, especially that portion which describes Christ's vigil in the Garden of Gethsemane the night before His death."

At his next hours, Stephen was shocked. For the first time he experienced a theological blackout, because this Jesus was someone he had never met before, nor read about. Stephen had never known such an experience. It was as if he had always lived in a

darkened room and suddenly I told him, "Stand up. Take hold
of that knob and pull." He had pulled away a heavy wooden
shutter—and the sunlight poured in. He read those wonderful
verses describing Jesus in the Garden of Gethsemane, how He
prayed in the garden that if it be God's will that His burden,
this suffering, be taken from Him, then let it be done. There he
found a human, warm person with whom he could identify; a
man who did not want to die or go through the suffering which
was to come within the next day; a man who accepted it only
because it was inevitable to His purposes, and there was no other
way out.

After having been thoroughly indoctrinated with the Christian
emphasis on suffering, Stephen was suddenly confronted with
evidence that our Lord did not agree at all. He did not want to
suffer. The essence of the suffering was in the agony of enduring
the abandonment in death itself, and not in the physical suffering which led up to His death. "My God, my God, why hast thou
forsaken me?" We arrived at a private conclusion that the experiencing of death itself was all-important and proved the
humanity of Jesus and His divinity. It was in His endurance of
the terror of the unknown, which each of us faces unwillingly,
that Jesus triumphed over death.

Thus Stephen had to answer the question: Is this suffering
necessary and unavoidable, or is this martyrdom avoidable?
Is this martyrdom efficient in terms of realizing a goal? He realized that his mother's life was most inefficient in these terms.
He realized his own life had been completely inefficient for he
had adopted his mother's pattern. Perhaps the most important
thing we had got out of the treatment, he thought, was the
realization that, when he clung to his mother's skirts and did not
yield to his desire to run to his father and welcome him, he had
displayed the suffering martyrdom which he had been told was
the Christian way of life.

Stephen was engaged to a girl he had fallen in love with in
high school, but his father had forbidden him to marry until after
his sisters were educated. But then his father died and left the
whole family without adequate finances. So it looked as if it
would be forever before Stephen could marry Rebecca. He was

taking care of his mother, and was devoting himself to the care
and education of his younger sisters. His older brother had refused
to participate in this responsibility. He was married and had
young children. Besides, his brother had worked his way through
school and saw no reason why his sisters could not do the same.
The responsibility devolved upon Stephen.

As he came more and more to question his identification with
the crucified, martyred Christ, he began to find through his relationship with me an identification of himself with the beloved
Son, the dearly beloved Son, who is also our Lord. I loved him,
and Rebecca loved him, and I approved of his loving Rebecca.
In spite of a certain amount of midwestern propriety, Rebecca
was a wonderful person, and she was willing to wait forever for
Stephen. She was a very attractive, very marriageable young
woman, and I advised Stephen's bishop that I approved of his
marriage. I did what was necessary so that the bishop could rest
comfortable in the fact that this was a good and proper marriage
insofar as human prognosis could indicate. At the same time,
Stephen decided that he would spend one more year at the seminary to get a graduate degree. He would also continue treatment
so that he and Rebecca would "have the benefit of whatever
advice and counseling" in analysis I could give them.

At that time Stephen told his mother and sisters that he intended to marry Rebecca. Surprisingly, his sisters and mother
came through. His mother decided that she would turn her
martyrdom to good account. She went and got a job where she
was needed and had something to do, with the result that this
poor, sickly, fragile woman began to bloom. She had suffered
more and more as the children had grown up and, now in meno-
pause, she was a widow who did not feel needed. But here was
an opportunity to sacrifice for her dearly beloved son.

His sisters said, "Look, you put us through school. We'll put
you through school. How much does it cost?"

Rebecca's mother said, "Well now, just exactly what's the best
date for the wedding and what do you want?"

Rebecca's boss said, "My dear, I can't see how we'll do without
you, but if you insist on getting married—certainly at twenty-
seven you have a perfect right to think about getting married,

and I've always liked that young man of yours. I'll see about getting you a job in our New York office."

Suddenly everything that seemed so impossible now became completely possible, all because of the change in attitude, and not at all because of a change in circumstances. The attitude, the fact that Stephen decided this was what he wanted and was right for him to want—only this was needed. He found that he did not need to lie down under endless suffering, but to scrutinize life in all its aspects and take it and turn it to good use. After that, one thing after another fell into line.

The final problem was one I have with clergymen quite often, that is, preparing them for their wedding night. I have done a lot of marriage counseling, but the problem of preparing two virgins to get married always seems almost an insuperable and an unnecessary one. But, both Stephen and Rebecca felt that it should be this way even though at first Stephen bitterly resented my talking about sex. He felt there would be plenty of time to talk about it after the marriage. I said, "Well, we'll talk about it now. That much I will insist upon. You are planning to get married, and it is my duty as your analyst and your doctor and your counselor to see that you are prepared for the marriage bed."

He said, "You far exceed the proper marriage instructions."

I replied, "After you have been properly prepared for your marriage and after you have been enjoying a good marriage, I think you'll know much more about the province of marriage instruction."

We struggled. His vocabulary and mine were quite dissimilar. I refused to discuss sex in "churchy" language. It is all right when one is discussing theology to speak about the relationship with God as foretold in the happiness and unity of a good marriage, but when you are trying to help people achieve a good marriage, it does not help to talk about theology, because they do not understand what you are talking about. Besides, the best and quickest way to get attitudes of sin and guilt about sex out in the open is talk about it in the plain ordinary words of the ancient Anglo-Saxon language. We struggled with talking about the marriage bed in four-letter words. But we were able to accomplish a great deal, and their honeymoon was a reasonably satisfactory one. The marriage is now of some years' duration, and it has become more and more satisfactory as the years have gone by.

After they got back from their honeymoon, Stephen discovered that, when he attended the Eucharist early in the morning, he was apt to be irritable, annoyed, and angry. It was seldom the happiness of the communion with God that he felt it should be. One day he was particularly annoyed and decided not to go at all. He and Rebecca sat down for breakfast. Usually Rebecca ate by herself, since she was working at this time and could not allow herself the added hour of religious observance in the morning. As he sat and drank his coffee and chatted over breakfast, he found his annoyance vanishing. He was enjoying life. He was happy. Suddenly he felt very much at peace with God, with Rebecca and with himself. Everything was good. He looked at his watch and realized it was time for Rebecca to leave and that he might only be a few minutes late at chapel. He walked quickly and briskly, in contrast to his usual dragging steps at this hour of the morning, and found himself getting there in quite good time. For the first time, he felt happy, relaxed, enjoying the service, enjoying his participation. Suddenly this was a good experience. He came up with the observation that the only difference between that day and other days was the fact that he had had breakfast with Rebecca—a few minutes of happy, leisurely relationship with another human being, but especially a very special human being whom he loved and who loved him. And after all, this was what Holy Communion is about. Somehow, when he had enjoyed the warmth and the fulfillment in those few minutes of a mutually responsive human relationship, he could find this same warmth with God in the chapel. He mulled over the various problems—the fact that, according to tradition, one must be fasting when going to our Lord's table. Yet, there was nothing he could find in the Scripture that indicated that it was of necessity. Indeed, our Lord had broken his fast on several occasions when he needed to. Stephen decided that perhaps it was necessary for him to have both the human and the divine— that to be able to enjoy coffee with Rebecca made it possible for him to welcome the Sacrament of Communion at our Lord's table. This is, after all, the meaning of much theology, in which we have to decide many matters according to the better of two goods, or the lesser of two evils.

This was some years ago. Stephen is successfully married, has been reinstated, and has become a beloved parish priest. In every way he has become what he once wrote to me on a Christmas card, "a real person."

❧ JAMES ❧

James [1] came into therapy voluntarily. He was becoming depressed, anxious, and scarcely able to keep up the pretense of appearing poised and interested in his work as a seminarian. At twenty-two, he was personable, attractive, and to all appearances a comfortably masculine man. Coming from what is called a good family, he had all the earmarks of good breeding. He had the ease of manner, the charm, the sophistication to appear as a welcome guest at any tea or cocktail party. On occasion he could be a delightful raconteur. All in all, James had all the personality assets to make a successful minister. He alone knew this to be a consciously and carefully built-up façade.

James was the child of devout and "good" people. His father was a hardworking man and his mother was sickly. James was a healthy, good baby. The doctor proclaimed his destiny: He was so healthy, so strong, that he could be put out to pasture—and that was his childhood. He was put out to pasture. He was given only the care that a child needs physically. He was a lonely baby, but he did not cry; he was good. He slept and he played by himself. Later, he learned that he must always keep quiet because mother either had one of her sick headaches or would have a sick headache if he made any noise. They lived in a beautiful big house in a beautiful suburb. The house was surrounded by beautiful shrubbery and a garden. There was even a tennis court. But James could not invite any of his friends over, when he tried to make friends, because the sound of boys running through the shrubbery playing hide-and-seek or, later, playing cowboys-and-

---

[1] A short summary of James is given in "Therapeutic Implications of Analytic Group Psychotherapy of Religious Personnel," by Margaretta K. Bowers, M.D., Bernard Berkowitz, M.S., and Sylvia Brecher, Ph.D., in the *International Journal of Group Psychotherapy*, vol. VIII, No. 3, July, 1958, pp. 249–250.

Indians would surely start a headache for mother. So, he would try to go off to play in other little boys' yards. But that worried his mother, and he must not worry his mother, either. If she did not know where he was and what he was doing, she worried about him, and that might bring on a headache. He read voraciously, became overweight, and had fewer and fewer friends.

In his thirteenth year he was a young hellion. He was getting A's in everything except deportment, and usually a B in that, for seldom did his teacher catch him misbehaving. She always knew that he was the guilty one, but she could never prove it. After his thirteenth year, however, his grades began slowly to go downhill and his deportment became good, better and better. In fact, there was an increasing correlation. His deportment got better and his grades got worse, slowly but definitely.

In college and in seminary he continued to make barely creditable grades. Socially, he had gone through the proper pretense. He belonged to the proper fraternity, double-dated, escorted the proper girls to the proper dances, and developed an excellent pretense of having fun. Even though he was unhappy, miserable, lonely, and uncomfortable, his social graces got him through tough situations. Nobody suspected that under his placid, calm, easy-going exterior, he was a mass of anxieties and fears. His feelings of insecurity had mounted to the point that if, on a Sunday afternoon, he had made no plans and no one asked him to go along on some adventure, he would become more and more anxious. He would develop a panic unless someone dropped by his room, or somehow he was able to drop in casually on someone. His feelings of depression—the source of which he could not quite trace—were deepening. He could remember a time when he was occasionally depressed and later moderately depressed, but now he was always depressed; and yet, he had trained himself not to show it. He had trained himself always to appear calm and placid.

He couldn't think quickly; living and working in a group that relied almost entirely on brilliance of intellect, he found himself more and more at a loss. Consequently, he withdrew more and more into the background. As a result, at the end of his first year in seminary, many people told him that his professors were somewhat concerned. They felt that he was indifferent. The dean was concerned about him. His grades were all right, average, but nothing special, nothing to be proud of. The dean spoke about his apparent disinterest; some of the professors even felt that he was sleeping in class. It was hoped that he would meditate on this and show more interest and enthusiasm in his work the following year.

He talked these things over with his rector when he went home on vacation. This man had been like a father to him for many years and James would talk to him about his problems. The rector asked a few questions about how his social life had been, and then he asked him about his religious life in seminary. James had always felt quite at home at church. During the past year, though, he told his rector, he was acutely uncomfortable in the seminary chapel. He found himself sleeping late, not waking up with the alarm clock. He had to make it a matter of discipline to get to Communion in the morning. In view of the fact that this was a new development, the rector felt that this was a matter for concern, and a decision was reached for James to enter into psychotherapy. His rector had considerable experience in counseling, but he felt that this was something that needed more than counseling. James's bishop was informed only to the extent that was required, and every effort was made to keep everybody calm, cool, and collected, as was proper. Father and mother and bishop knew only enough to give permission and to write the necessary checks.

A few weeks after the beginning of therapy, James entered a therapy group. He was slowly able to make friends in the group. He seldom said anything. Everyone liked him but no one knew him very well. Later, he would tell me of his intense fear when there was too much anger in the group. And as he learned to trust me a little, he told me about intense feelings of pain, as if his nails and teeth were being pulled out. Slowly we learned that he was terribly afraid that something would happen to his body. He was very much afraid that some illness would develop, or that something would happen to him if he did anything wrong. This sense of fear that someone would find out that he was bad was what was causing the trouble in the chapel. He was sure that every one of the serious, sedate, and proper professors was judging him, and somehow judging him to be sinful and bad.

We learned that undoubtedly he would have been judged sinful and bad had his professors been aware of his recurrent daydreams during lectures. For this shy, retiring young man felt possessed by the desire to undress and to sit on the lecturer's desk completely nude, and confound his classmates with a learned but obscene diatribe. He often drooled over the reactions of consternation he could provoke. There were many times when the fear that he might actually act this out almost paralyzed him. Then he would retreat into a deeper withdrawal, and his fingers and teeth would begin to pain him again. A few times in puberty he had indulged in mutual nudity and masturbation with another little boy in the dim security of a barn loft. His psychosexual development seemed to have stopped about that time.

We worked on the usual fears of castration as punishment, as one does in any proper analysis, and finally he was more relaxed, making more friends, and also beginning to get into trouble. For a few months I had a hard time trying to keep James from getting into real difficulty. His mischievous deeds, things that were schoolboyish pranks, we could cope with in a group. But James was more than mischievous; he was rebelling. Suddenly all the need to rebel that he had suppressed during the years he was a good boy began to break out, and he was taking a lot of unnecessary chances. After all, seminaries have strict rules. We got through these times, thanks mainly to the group, because in the group we then had a number of people who had gotten into trouble, real trouble; people who had learned a great deal and had had long years of analysis. When they realized that James was trying to get himself into trouble in his rebellion, they began to be concerned about it. There is so much that an analytic group can do in helping a would-be delinquent that no analyst can ever hope to do alone.

Shortly after this, James developed a real human relationship for the first time in years. It developed in the group, with all the intensities and the unhappinesses of group relationships. But it was good to see James coming alive and feeling, even though there was so much hurt in all that he was feeling. One day he called me up for an emergency hour and came over. Everything had broken up between the two of them. He felt that the end of the world had come. I kept forcing him to go back: When had he ever felt like this before? Whom had he lost that hurt this deeply before? Suddenly he was telling me about Grandfather.

I had never heard about Grandfather before. I had asked routine questions one time about grandparents and uncles and aunts, maids, and so forth and so on, and now it turned out that he had loved this grandfather and who he knew had loved him. He told me about how he had always felt that Grandfather loved little boys who played and who were mischievous. Even when Grandfather was getting sick, he still enjoyed seeing "Jimmy." So, for the first time, we had a nickname for our sober, sedate James. Jimmy would play, and even after Grandfather couldn't play with him any more, he would sit and watch him play, and Jimmy still felt that Grandfather loved him. Then there came a time when Grandfather was too sick to see Jimmy; Jimmy would go over and Grandmother would not let him go up to see Grandfather. But he somehow knew that Grandfather wanted to see him. Then there came the day when Grandfather died, and at this part of the story our Jimmy burst into tears, and sobbed and sobbed and sobbed. He was so terribly alone in his grief. Finally he was sobbing on my shoulder, and all of the hurt little boy was between us and with us.

Now and again there would come depressions. There were times when the anxiety would be severe and the confusion painful. All his fears came through; things were being taken away from him, things were being done to him, he would end up without any toenails or teeth, having all kinds of things happen to him—all kinds of things would go wrong with his body. As we delved into this terrible feeling of helplessness, of having things taken away from him, his depressions deepened and deepened. A transcript of one of our sessions will illustrate his feelings during this period.

JAMES: I feel like . . . like I'd like to kill a few people . . . wish I knew what was going on now. I don't understand. . . .

Somehow I think we've gotten to so much that's so important that it's on a physical level. It's like a ball or a knot. Hard to talk about. I've felt this off and on for years. Part of the constant depression, then I'd feel this way for a day. Recently I'm much more conscious of it. The iron core. The other thing is I just want to cry for the last few weeks now. I don't know why. If I somehow could just cry, cry, cry, cry. If I could, I'd somehow be free.

BOWERS: Of the core?

JAMES: Uh-huh.

BOWERS: The core would melt and become a part of you? If you could cry, and let yourself be loved until you could love? The core you've had since your grandfather's funeral?

JAMES: Yeah, I think it is, I really do.

BOWERS: The only thing to do is to go back to that funeral, find out how you felt then; your life stopped that day.

JAMES: I really think that's true. I really do.

BOWERS: Every time we've had an hour when you and I had a real feeling of relatedness, it's been in relation to your grandfather and in relation to his death. The first time we had that feeling was when you first wept over him. Our last hour we spoke of him and what he has meant to you. The tightness is the feeling that no one can replace the loss.

JAMES: No. Can't replace it. Can't do anything. . . . This is the business I've said so often . . . I'll explode. Somehow the explosion has got to come from inside that core.

BOWERS: Why don't you let the tears soften it so it won't be so frightening? What do you remember of what you felt inside that church?

JAMES: Like now. Just the tightness.

BOWERS: But you knew then what the tightness was controlling. Go back. Remember vividly. Let yourself feel again all the feelings you felt then. Remember all the thoughts. Weep all the tears that you didn't then.

JAMES: I want to destroy the whole place . . . everybody there.

BOWERS: Let go. How do you want to?

JAMES: Push the whole thing in. Run around and cut everybody's head off or shoot them. Blow it up.

BOWERS: What happened to your grandfather?

JAMES: He died.

BOWERS: How?

JAMES: Got old and died. They took him away from me.

BOWERS: Who?

JAMES: Everybody, and my mother, and God . . . the priest there in front.

BOWERS: And whom did you most want to destroy?

JAMES: My father or the priest . . . or both of them. My father said, "Be good while the church takes Grandfather away." Ain't got no more grandfather.

BOWERS: Who was the most powerful person there?

JAMES: I was. 'Cause I could defy all of them and cry and cry and cry. Then I'd have upset all their nice plans.

BOWERS: Who had upset all your plans?

JAMES: My grandfather, by dying, by dying too soon. . . . My father said, "Be good, don't cry." I wanted somebody to understand why I cried. After he said that, there was nothing I could do.

BOWERS: How would you get back at them?

JAMES: By doing to them what they did to me. I would do what they wanted and hate them for it the rest of my life.

BOWERS: You would do what they wanted. You would be the good boy.

JAMES: Um um.

BOWERS: And you would hate them for having made you the good boy.

JAMES: Um um . . . *forever*. That's right.

BOWERS: That's what you'd do. But what was the special twist in your hate? The power?

JAMES: It would *look like love. I would become the priest.*

BOWERS: The priest, the separator of little boys from their grandfathers. You would become the scourge of God, the Death Angel?

JAMES: That's right. So that it would look just the opposite. . . . (Answers a lot of questions.) I never could have admitted this to myself, that I could have been like the ones I hated and despised most. I guess I never could become them now.

BOWERS: You couldn't come to this until you came to the time that someone would understand and would love you.

JAMES: You could love me *in spite of this?*

BOWERS: What you wanted that day is what you have now. You didn't want to be the scourge of God.

JAMES: No.

BOWERS: You wanted to be loved. You wanted to be understood. You wanted someone you could cry on.

JAMES: Yeah.

BOWERS: Now you have that. Now you can realize the frustration of a little boy who had lost everything in the world, who was all alone in the world. There was no one to love you that day. There was no one to console you. No one understood you. So you decided to become the good boy and hate them for making you into the good boy. But you would also become the priest. The *good priest.*

JAMES: That's right.

BOWERS: The man who had the power of the death-dealing, condemning God who sent people to heaven or to hell.

JAMES: Grandfather went to heaven, the others would go to hell.

James would feel wonderful for a little while and then the depression would set in again. He began having trouble with me. He felt I was more and more critical and demanding, and constantly we were finding that he was more and more overwhelmed by memories of attitudes toward his mother, who sat on my lap, as it were. He asked to have some hours with my male associate, and they helped a great deal. I felt he needed a father as well as a mother. He also needed to test me out and learn that a woman could be loving without being possessive as his mother was and still tried to be. His relationship with his own mother had not improved, but he has discovered that his father was a delightful person, even though he was a little too conscientious, a little too hardworking, and not very skillful at starting a conversation. But now that James has learned more about the art of knowing people and getting them to talk to him, he could get his father to talk to him, too. And since the two of them were now having wonderful hours together, I encouraged the

furtherance of this through my male associate, because there were
many things he could work out with a man more easily than
with a woman.

At this time in his analysis, there began to be many things he
learned he could do, and he began to talk more and more of the
things that he enjoyed doing. We encouraged him. We encouraged him to have more of a feeling of doing, more of a
feeling of his own worth and his own value. Although there was
more happiness in his life, there were many of the old miserable
stretches. Upon one occasion after a week or so of depression,
he decided he was not going to be shaken loose of it. This was a
time when he agreed to see me if I would promise not to do anything to disturb his depression. I said, "You mean you know
this depression is so shallow that a good hour's work would free
you of it?" He said, "I know, but I'm not ready. I will spend
the hour with you because it's our scheduled hour, if you promise
you won't disturb my depression." And I said, "O.K., you'll talk
to me?" He said, "Sure, I like talking to you." I said, "Well, fine."
So, I asked him to tell me how he was feeling. He described his
feelings of depression. He felt alone, all alone. There was no one
who loved him. He was alone in the world. He had no friends and
nobody really cared. He told me about how for years now in his
depressions he had a feeling of being in hell, where the aloneness
and the isolation has always been, is now, and forever will be,
world without end. He talked about how neither theologically
nor philosophically could he support his conviction that there
was no hope of being loved by God. But somehow he felt that
he was so far from the love of God and always had been so far,
that sometimes he felt that he was being excluded by an angry
God, an unforgiving, relentless, vengeful God. Then there were
times like today when he knew he could find his way back to
God and that there was a loving God; but he was still too angry
with God to go back so soon.

He was aware that his depression was something he still
wanted, he still needed. He was aware that he had isolated himself from everyone who loved him. He was isolating himself from
God's love. He was separating himself from love, companionship,
happiness. God had taken his grandfather away from him and

there were times like this when he was very angry with God, and he would rather stay in the kind of quiet, unhappy solitude of the isolation. Sometimes the isolation deepened, becoming more and more painful until finally the darkness overcame all, as if the storm clouds had darkened the face of the sun. And then there was no longer any choice. Then there was nothing he could do. He was doomed.

James's God was a changing concept. As long as his grandfather was alive, he had a concept of God who was an extension of this grandfather, a very wonderful Grandfather, a Grandfather who never got sick, who never got tired, who never lost His temper. Of course, like James's grandfather, He was a bit severe in His discipline, but after all, you never had to worry about Grandfather staying angry too long. But then there was the terrible anger at God when Grandfather died, and the definite decision that James would become the omnipotent, magical priest of God, that he would do what he wanted to with God and God's will in relation to people. Those like Grandfather whom he wanted to save would go to heaven, only he would see to it that they lived as long as he wanted them to before they died. There would be none of this dying before your time like Grandfather. On the other hand, the ones he hated he would doom to hell. And he wasn't going to have any of this nice concept of purgatory. He was going to have hell the way he heard about it at a Baptist revival meeting. Yes, indeed.

For a while after this session James was able to fantasy himself as the cruel but good priest. He could see himself as stern and as sorrowful as the holy inquisitors in George Bernard Shaw's *Joan of Arc,* those unhappy men who condemned Joan to the stake because there was no way by which they could save her soul other than by the torture of her body. In order that her soul might be saved, they, in sorrow, yes, but in righteous knowledge that they were doing the best that could be done under the circumstances, condemned her body to the stake so that her soul would be saved from everlasting torment in hell. James drew a picture of himself in which he was meting out just punishment, in which he was being the self-righteous, judging priest who preached stormy sermons so that everyone would repent and try to be good, because he would know that they were going to hell otherwise. He would make them feel the closeness and the nearness of hell.

It was during this time that he was preparing such a sermon for a homiletics class. Suddenly he realized he did not want to give this sermon because there would be someone present whom he hated, and who, he felt very certain, was damned. Now if he gave this sermon as brilliantly and with as much feeling as he wanted to, this person might be caught by it. This person might be brought to contrition and then to absolution, and then he might be saved, and James did not wish to save any except those whom he wanted to save. It took me quite a while to convince him that if the man were truly damned, he needn't worry, for the man would let no one convince him of the love of God. I reminded him that he should consider that in the past he thought he had the power to condemn, and now he was afraid of the power to save. I said, "You're still believing in magic. There's not much danger of your being so powerful to save. You heard a great many sermons when you were damned. They didn't touch you. Let go. Preach your sermon and see what happens. Believe me, you'll have much more satisfaction in your hate if the man refuses the love of God after having heard your sermon than if you had denied him the opportunity of salvation." He and I both felt that he was still a little afraid that he might save, so that he didn't really let go.

One of the many times we were able to help James release some of his aggression occurred in the group. There is a perversion of power which disguises itself in passivity. This has happened with a surprising number of our clerical patients in the group. The picture was always the same as James presented it. He was depressed, he was helpless, he was completely passive, he could do nothing to help us understand what was going on. He just sat there, miserable. He didn't want anyone to pay attention to him. He wanted to be left alone. But, somehow, he projected his misery, his helpless, passive misery, in such a way that no one could do anything, or feel anything, or think about anything but his misery. The more he protested that he wanted to be left alone, the more the group felt coerced to help him, to do something for him, to give him everything he wanted if only they could relieve in some measure this pervading misery which was dragging us all down into the same depth of blackness. It hurt James beyond measure when I pointed out to him that his behavior was exactly the same as he had seen in his fellow group members. He did not want to feel that his misery was like the others. His was real misery; this was no power operation. He remained angry with me.

At the next session of the group he held the group in the palm of his hand. He didn't talk, save for a word only now and then. He presented a picture almost the same as before, but there was a subtle difference. I knew that he wasn't suffering. I knew that he was consciously enjoying the situation. He frustrated everyone by not permitting them to help him or reach him or do anything else in the session. Somehow or other, he was able, without appearing sullen or negativistic, to baffle completely everyone except those whom he tricked into believing that he was suffering. He was not at all surprised when I congratulated him on his power operation in his next hour. He knew it was a power operation and he knew I knew it was a power operation. He knew it was successful and he knew I knew it was successful. Therefore, congratulations were in order. And having done, on a conscious level, a much superior job of paralyzing the group than he had done previously in his passive, unconscious, suffering way, he began to look at the "slough of Despond," as Bunyan called it. In the group he never slipped again, but he watched and studied everyone who did slip into this passive misery that was so aggressive in its helplessness. He was never going to get caught in this again, and he didn't. He learned a great deal about himself and about the whole mechanism of power through passivity and misery. He also became more and more aware of why he had been so anxious when the group was angry in his early group experience. But during those anxious months, he had feared that he might let go, and that would be sinful.

James's therapy was ended much too soon because of his bishop's insistence on his return to a geographical locality where further therapy was unavailable. This might have been over-ridden had he been in positive transference at the time; unfortunately his leaving was an acting out of a phase of negative transference. However, what was done in therapy was basically sufficient so that he has been able to overcome the regression that followed his leaving treatment. He made a good marriage and moved to a location where further therapy was available. He is now a growing, beloved parish priest. As a seminary student he had wanted to lecture nude to the class. Now, privileged to wear full vestments, he is satisfied and fulfilled. Celebrating a sung Eucharist in sumptuous vestments and preaching an inspiring sermon are for him socially approved sublimations. His marriage too has not only survived but continues to be a more and more fulfilled relationship.

✤ PETER ✤

Peter [1] entered into treatment at the instruction of his bishop. He had been engaged to an exceedingly promiscuous young woman whose frantic sexuality he hoped to change through the constancy of his love and affection. However, the matter became the subject of intraparish gossip and scandal, and finally a report of the situation was made to the bishop by a man who had known this girl and worked with her for many years. The bishop sent for Peter and told him that, if he wished to continue as a postulant for Holy Orders, he would have to break the engagement as gently and quietly as could be done, and he would have to go into treatment in order to work out the problem that had caused him to involve himself and the church in such a situation.

When Peter came into treatment, he was obsequiously pleasant and agreeable. He did everything to be liked and loved. He very quickly agreed that the bishop was right in counseling against their marriage plans. I felt in spite of his protests that he was much too afraid of women to go into treatment with me, and therefore I asked my male associate to work with him in private hours, but I put him in my own therapy group.

Peter was delightful in his childish sincerity and enthusiasm. It was impossible to keep from liking him. It was very difficult to keep in mind that he was really much too sweet, that he was much too agreeable, that he was much too quick to understand and accept any interpretation that was made. He revealed many fears and phobias, and in the first few months of his therapy he was coddled, protected, and supported by my associate. In the group he was liked, but no one enjoyed the occasional times

[1] A short summary of Peter is given in "Therapeutic Implications of Analytic Group Psychotherapy of Religious Personnel," by Margaretta K. Bowers, M.D., Bernard Berkowitz, M.S., and Sylvia Brecher, Ph.D., in the *International Journal of Group Psychotherapy*, vol. VIII, No. 3, July, 1958, pp. 249 and 251.

when he gave us long-winded stories of his social activities or his problems with his girl friends and his roommate, because in these long-winded excursions he always seemed to get nowhere and to say nothing.

As time went on he found another girl friend, and we lived through all his fretting, fuming, and worrying, all of his fears about hurting this girl, all of his excessive sexual morality and her sexual morality. When she decided it was time to become engaged no one in the group, nor my associate nor I felt that this was the girl for Peter. We thought she was much too immature for the life he had set for himself, so in many ways we added to her problems. She reacted to the frustrations of her situation by a physical illness of psychogenic nature, one which is most malignant and in time results in years of bedridden existence. Peter could then look forward to devoting his life to this patient, a sick, unhappy woman.

It was hard to get Peter to go back into his past, but relentlessly I made him go back. Apparently, Peter had been a brat, quite a bad little boy. He had broken windows; he had climbed trees; he was always getting into trouble. Of course his mother gave him more attention when he got into trouble, but on the whole she had behaved in quite a healthy way. Perhaps she had not given him quite enough love, but as far as she went she had done remarkably well. Peter had repressed very deeply the memories of the babies who had died. They had made his mother sick. They had threatened his kingship in the household. He completely forgot that he had been very glad when they disappeared, and he couldn't understand his mother's grief or his father's sorrow. He was quite amazed to realize that he had wanted them to die, and he began to wonder if they perhaps had died because he wanted them to die. His whole world had gone to pieces when his mother became ill and was taken to the hospital. There were long anxious days when he could not understand what had happened. He was not taken to the hospital; he could not see his mother. He was told that his mother was very ill. Then there was one night when his father took him in his arms and cried and said that his mother would very soon go upstairs to heaven. The little boy of seven didn't understand what it was all about, but he decided that he just had to get into that hospital, and he did. He got into the hall, and then finally into the room and saw his mother under the oxygen tent. He had never seen an oxygen tent before. He did not understand what was going on. His mother did not see him. Apparently she was asleep or perhaps by this time she was no longer conscious. The nurse, however, turned around and picked the child up and dashed out of the room with him. He was turned over to relatives who scolded him and carried him away. If he had only reached his mother before she died, before she lost consciousness, if somehow she could have spoken to him, if there had been someone who could have explained a little bit better to him why his mother was dying, what it meant! But no one explained to him why they felt it was such a terrible thing that he had invaded the hospital in trying to reach his mother.

He was then taken away to stay with some distant and well-meaning relatives who told him that his mother had gone upstairs to heaven. He was played with, he was pampered, he was cajoled. Whenever he tried to talk about his mother, the subject was changed, and they talked about happy things. When his father came for him, he tried to talk with his father about the whole matter, but his father broke into tears and dashed out of the room and didn't come back until he had got himself under control. He didn't talk about mother with Peter. Nobody did. Nobody understood this little boy's need to understand what had happened. As he looked back on it, a picture emerged of a need to prove himself good in rescuing his mother, and in this he had failed. There followed a succession of people whom he had tried to rescue, among whom the girl friends and I were most outstanding. He had come into treatment because he had tried to rescue a girl from her social waywardness. Then he had tried to rescue a girl from physical illness. When I was a bit sick, to him I was terribly sick, and I must be rescued. About this time he was able to speak of the sense of damnation which he had felt so deeply and so strongly in himself. Ever since he could remember, there had been times when he felt so far away from God that only in saving someone else from this same damnation would he be permitted to be saved himself. And unless I permitted him to save me, he himself would never be saved.

We were back in a dark little room where the child had hidden himself in the days following his mother's death. He was bewildered and terribly unhappy. He didn't want his mother to go upstairs to heaven. If she went upstairs to heaven, that meant she would go away from him. But he wanted her to stay with him, and he tried terribly hard to will her to be with him. Somehow as we relived the hours he spent alone at this time we came to realize that for Peter his mother had never really died. She was alive and with him in this unhappy dark little room where he had closed the door on everybody. He remembered how angry he was with the grown-ups who wanted her to go upstairs to heaven. He was very angry also with this God they talked about who wanted her to come and stay with Him. Any God worth his salt would know that a little boy needed his mother, and so he shut God out, and he lived for a time in the fantasy of his mother's being with him in that lonely dark little room. Now I was with him in the same little room, in the room of some dark, lonely, bewildered, despondent, black anger that he had known at seven.

We looked back together. He remembered that things had gone quite smoothly until his father remarried.

I said, "By the way, Peter, how are they doing?"

He said, "You know, they're very happy together now."

"Really? How long have they been happy together?"

"Oh," he said, "for several years now."

I said, "Do you have any idea why they're happy now?"

"I think so. I leave them alone now. I don't try to come in between them. I don't stir up trouble any more. You see," he said, "when I was a kid, I did everything I could do to make her life miserable. I wanted to get rid of her. I tried in every way to get her to leave Dad or to get Dad to leave her. One of the ways I could take Dad away from her was by being a devout Episcopalian. Dad would go to Mass with her in the morning early, and then he would come home and go to Sunday school and church with me. Now if I'd become a Roman Catholic, I couldn't have taken him away from her all day long. And I kept him at church as much as I could, because that was keeping him away from her. I remember how I used to visit my stepmother's aunts who were feuding with her. They helped me. They encouraged me to do everything that would annoy Mary, my stepmother."

"You mean to say that those two old maids encouraged you to become an Episcopalian even though they were Roman Catholic?"

"Yes," he said. "They would have encouraged me to become anything if it annoyed her."

"I see, and how do they feel about your being a priest now?"

"I don't know; I don't see them any more."

"Why, are they dead?"

"Hell, no. The only reason I ever went to see them was because it annoyed my stepmother. Now that I'm not interested in annoying her, I don't go to see them any more. Why should I? They meant nothing to me."

I said, "Tell me more about how you became a priest."

"Well," he said, "somehow or other all I know about it is after we moved to Centerville when my father remarried, I had a need to get closer and closer to that altar. I sang in the choir. That was closer. As soon as I could, I guess after I was confirmed, I don't remember, I became an altar boy. And that was much better. Besides, it was more fun being dressed up as an altar boy than being dressed up as a choir boy."

"And how did you feel when you were confirmed?"

"Oh," he said, "that was wonderful! I was elated for days, just simply walking on air for days and days and days after I was confirmed."

"And how did you feel after you were ordained?"

"No different from ordinary," he said. "It was exciting the day of ordination. Everybody was making a big thing of it, and I was the center of attention. The family was all excited, everybody was congratulating me. It was wonderful, but there was none of that glow that I had when I was confirmed."

I said, "And exactly how does the ceremony of confirmation differ from that of ordination?"

Suddenly things began to make sense to both of us because there is practically no difference except in the words that the bishop says as he puts his hands on the young man's head. And I think that our Peter was quite conscious of the fantasy that he was being ordained when he was being confirmed.

Peter had been very disturbed because I would not attend his ordination, but I had no wish to go. I had approved of it in the sense that I had not felt it proper or just for me to withhold my approval as far as ecclesiastical authority went. But I could not in any way lend the weight of any symbolic meaning which my presence might have for Peter, and which he might interpret as full and complete approval of the ordination. I have felt the same way about attending weddings of my patients. I feel that the presence of the analyst at such occasions lends a very deep symbolic meaning which should be given only on those rare occasions where it seems completely "meet and right so to do." I did not feel that we had gotten far enough in therapy with Peter to have the feeling that this would be for him an emotionally valid Sacrament. He had a temper tantrum in the group. He wept in the group. He begged me. The month prior to his ordination was spent in a relentless effort to make me go to the ceremony. And of course, the more I felt that his insistence was out of all proportion to reality, the more I balked. I had been invited to many ordinations. I had never gone to one, and nobody had ever put up a fuss before. At the group meeting after ordination Peter was all happiness again. He told me that I was completely right in not going to the ordination, for he was able to share it much more with his family than he could have if I had been there. His sister and he had had the most wonderful reconciliation and she had given him the feeling that he had a mother in his sister as he had never had before. And if I had gone, he would have been torn between his love for his sister and his love for me, his "foster mother."

He began to get in trouble early in his curacy. His first rector and he became involved in a long series of arguments about liturgy and ritual. Peter insisted on changing or trying to change a great many of the customs of a parish that was long established and comfortable, but was not doing things exactly the way he felt they should be done. And he showed a rigidity about problems of ritual and liturgy that one does not expect to find in a young person. It is quite another matter in a priest who has been rector of a parish for twenty years and is in his seventies, but not in a man of thirty, and a curate at that. There were constant quarrels with his secretary, with all of the staff, because of Peter's need to have everything run according to the way he thought it should be run, instead of accepting the accustomed way of doing things in a setting where, after all, he was only a second lieutenant and would be there only a limited period of time. Finally the rector could not take it, and he got rid of him so cleverly that Peter never knew what had happened, because Peter went rejoicing to help an emergency situation in an adjoining parish where a curate had recently left because of illness. There was nothing Peter loved to do more than rescue, and so his rector took advantage of this and persuaded him that it was his Christian duty to go and rescue this other parish. Peter got on his white horse and galloped off.

His new rector was a man who had had considerable training and experience in counseling and when he began having difficulty with Peter, he got in touch with me and told me that if Peter wanted to finish out his curacy, he would have to get down to work in treatment, that he was not going to tolerate so many problems in a curate. I relayed this message to Peter in the group, and for a time there seemed to be a change of pace and an increased seriousness with which he worked. We began to learn of many strange occurrences such as the time that Peter went to visit a family which had been recently bereaved. The rector had had to leave right after the funeral and Peter walked in and dissolved into tears. And to the consternation of the mourning family, he wept and wept and wept. For two hours this impasse continued, and the family was completely at a loss. Here was a man who had been sent to comfort and help them and he was weeping and helpless. They were angry because they had to comfort the man who was to comfort them. The rector got an earful from the family the next morning, and I got one within an hour. Peter could not explain it. He could recognize intellectually that his behavior was not the anticipated, expected behavior of a minister in calling upon a bereaved family, but he couldn't understand why he had done it. He couldn't understand why he had wept, or what he had wept about.

By that time we had learned that Peter had many, many expressions of emotion in his weeping. When he told us that everything was now all right because he talked it all over with the rector and had burst into tears and wept and wept, and the rector had patted him on the shoulder and said, "There, there, son, we'll work it all out," we knew that Peter had pulled a fast one, and we told him so and he admitted it. But he said at the time he was absolutely sincere. And he still has not told this man what really happened. But after that, he had the rector in the palm of his hand, and the rector did everything in the world to make him happy. He counseled him wisely and he put in a great deal of effort and a very real amount of love trying to help Peter.

It was about this time that death came into our own experience. One of the members of the group, after years of threatening suicide, carried out her threat suddenly in a moment of anger. All of us were hit badly, and Peter wept. This time, however, we were able to get deeper into his weeping and we were able to uncover the grief that had never been expressed at the time his mother died, and he began to be human and real and valid in his reawakened grief over his mother. In the end, he was a part of our grief, for his grief was for his mother, and each one's grief was double—for Lotte and for his own lost loved one.

For the first time, he was beginning to feel that he was really remembering something real about his mother and his grief was in reaction to her loss. Early in his group experience, his talk of his mother was so shallow and sugary in its sweetness that one of the older women told him that she could see no evidence that he had ever loved his mother or that his mother had ever loved him. He became very panicky and frightened in reaction to this, and I reassured him that we did not know who it was who had loved him, but that I was very sure that we would find out that someone must have loved him when he was young.

The time finally came that Peter's period of apprenticeship was over, and he found a parish of his own. He had become more and more the difficult almost obnoxiously rigid person. We were not at all happy with him. He was smug and complacent to an exasperating extent. He let his bills go, so that during this time in which, for the first time in his life, he had been earning a small income enabling him to pay for treatment, he failed to do so, and for some reason he was no longer able to permit his father to do as he had done in the past. So after many months of putting up with dull, stupid hours, my associate and Peter parted company with mutual satisfaction. In the group, his complacency and lolling about and his increasing obesity were all causing more and more annoyance, his unhappiness about his girl friend's illness notwithstanding. So it was not unexpected that as a result of a number of angry quarrels with another minister in the group, he later saw me in a personal hour and, with stiffness and smugness, he announced that he had had all the treatment he needed and that, while he was most appreciative of our efforts, he felt that there was no sense in continuing the relationship. I agreed with him and there the matter rested.

Many months later Peter called me and asked for an hour. When he arrived he told me that he was having trouble with the women in his parish. Being in such terrible need of winning everyone's affection, he realized that he did not know how to conduct himself with the younger women in the parish. He felt an intense need to be very friendly. He spoke with great envy of an older priest whom he knew, who had the gentle art of being just seductive enough to the women in his congregation so every woman was in love with him, and yet there was never any gossip about him. But Peter knew that if he let himself go and was seductive with young women, and they responded, he would feel compelled to go to bed with them. He had enough reality-testing to know that his need to be so compulsively responsive to a seductive woman was not quite healthy, and he knew that such a response was not a way to establish a good reputation for himself in his first parish. At the same time he realized that he was, in attempting to be prudent, much too cold and distant with the young women. With the middle-aged women he felt more comfortable. I asked him how he felt about me, and he told me he had always been disturbed by my seductiveness. When we searched into what this meant, it became apparent that the mildest, friendly gestures were interpreted as sexual propositions. And as he worked through these transference reactions to me, he began to talk more of the other difficulties in which he found himself.

I was amazed to see the amount of trouble that Peter got himself into. He told me how he had had to go over the parish records in order to draw up the list of the members of the parish who were qualified to vote in the annual parish meeting which would elect the vestry for the coming year. He had been horrified to find that more than half the members of his parish were not qualified canonically to vote in the election. He had gone over the canon very carefully, and the canon made it very clear just exactly what a "member in good standing" was. One rule was punctilious attendance at church, so that one was at services more often than not. This he broadly and graciously interpreted to mean that probably three-fourths of the time one should be in church and one-fourth of the time one was permitted to be absent from formal services. This interpretation did not take into account those people whose professional work made it difficult for them to attend services. He felt they should change their schedules. There was one very devoted woman who had been for years one of the most dedicated women in the work of the parish. But often in good weather she would visit her family who lived nearby and would attend services with them. He was horrified to find that she too was disqualified from voting. She never skipped church, but more often than not she went to some other parish, still Episcopalian, but another parish; therefore she could not vote, although as far as I was able to find out from Peter, she put an average of one full day's work a week into the church, and had been doing this for many years. Peter had gone to all these people in sorrow and told them about the situation, of not being able to find them qualified to vote. He had prayed with them; he had wept with them; now he was full of the most wonderful feeling that in this mutual sorrow of theirs, they had come closer to a relationship. He felt that this had done much to bring many people into the fullness of understanding their relationship to the church, their duty to God.

I said, "Peter, if I were a member of your parish, what would have happened and how would you feel? I neither go to my own parish church in Maryland nor the church around the corner from me in New York very often. I certainly don't come anywhere near to the fulfillment of my so-called Christian duty as you've elaborated in your canon. You would have to tell me regretfully that I could not vote."

This was very disturbing to Peter. He did not like facing the reality of telling me that I would be disfranchised were I a member of his parish. He began to weep and I told him he should weep. I told him very frankly that if I were a member of his parish and had been so disfranchised that under no circumstances would I ever go again to his parish. I would without question remove myself from his parish.

"You mean to say that you would leave me?" he asked.

"I certainly would."

He looked at me rather quizzically, the tears still on his cheeks, and said, "Is that the reason that you have never accepted me as your priest?"

"Among many others, it is. As my patient," I said, "I love you. If in any way, I accepted your authority as a priest, I could not have the same feeling of love for you because then you would deprive me as you have deprived your parish in such sweet, sorrowful cruelty. And furthermore, Peter, why is it so disturbing to you to have to disfranchise your analyst when it makes you so happy to disfranchise your parish? Why am I so much more important to you than your parish, so that you can be cruel to them without any awareness that you're being cruel, but it disturbs you to be cruel to me?"

Thus was the beginning of a long period of many such questions. I had become all important to Peter, far more important than I felt was good for him. The overwhelming weight of his transferent affection for me was pointed out in his reaction to a very mild inconsequential illness I had. I felt washed out; I looked washed out; and when he remarked about it, I said I had not felt well for a few days. I said I was very sorry that it had disturbed him. It really had, and I began to realize that here was valuable material, so we went into it. How was he disturbed?

Why was he so disturbed? What did this little illness of mine mean to him? He began to talk of his fear that it might be a real illness; I might die. And he talked about his feeling that there was no one but himself who could do anything about my illness. He wanted to pray for me. I could not see any reason why because I had a mild illness we should have all this fuss and bother about it.

The following week he came in *furious*. Why hadn't I called him? I said, "What do you mean, why didn't I call you? Why should I have called you?"

"Well," he said, "I couldn't sleep."

"Why?"

"You were ill and I didn't know what had happened."

"Well, I told you there was nothing to worry about. I continued to work. I got well and I was feeling very much better. I don't usually call up patients to say that I'm better or worse unless it has to do with a cancellation of an hour or so, and it never occurred to me to call you."

"Why?"

"Is that the reason that you are still in this terribly unhappy relationship with this girl? Do you have to save her too? How do you have to save her? How do you have to save me?"

He must save, he must take care of, he must protect. His mother had died, but the girl friend and I must live. He alone could see to it that we would live. No one he cared for was permitted to die.

In spite of Peter's desperate need to rescue his girl friend, she had gotten sicker and sicker. Each time they quarreled she reacted with more illness. He found out that she had had many attacks of this illness years before he had met her. He was merely one of many people who had been unable to give her what she wanted and to whom she reacted with the same intensity of physical illness. After several months, as Peter was better able to look clearly at the illness of his girl friend, he was able to break off with her entirely; much to his amazement, her health was better in the month following than it had been for several years.

Although Peter's return to therapy was voluntary, I felt that sending him back to his group would again result in failure. Peter's sense of his self was much too fleeting and evanescent as yet for him to be able to try to be good in a group where he had succeeded in damning himself, and that it might be very much wiser for Peter to try to start over again in a new group.

When I spoke to Peter about my associate's group, his eyes lit up. He had always been very much attracted to one young woman who had been with him in his old group and was now in this group. I was quite unprepared, as was he, to find that my associate did not want him in his group. He never wanted to see Peter again. His patience had been completely exhausted, and Peter's efforts at rapprochement, so charming and so gracious, met with complete rejection. Peter could not understand it. He asked for a private hour with the man and when he got there he wept. My associate would have none of it. Peter still did not understand people who could see the anger underneath his tears. He just couldn't understand anyone who didn't give him what he wanted when he wept.

Since my associate wouldn't accept him, I suggested that he talk to some of the people he knew in the group; this might start a movement from within on behalf of Peter. After a number of weeks, he tried this tactic. He spoke to a number of them, charmingly, ingratiatingly, the way a ward heeler enlists the patronage of the stupid fools who had better get in line and vote for him or else. When my associate found out about it, he invited Peter to come in and present his case to the group, and then in good democratic process, he was asked to leave and was told that the group would talk it over and that he could telephone in the next few days for an answer. However, neither my associate nor the group remembered that Peter had been an expert eavesdropper as a child. There was no peephole that was too difficult for Peter to look through. There was no door too thick for Peter to listen through. And why, because he was thirty years old, should he suddenly change? Peter stayed and listened through the door while the group rehashed their reaction to Peter. What he heard was most unpleasant. Nobody really wanted him. A most serious objection was his wearing his clerical collar and black suit. Some of the group resented this clothing of authority. They also were aware that my associate did not want Peter in the group. Some of them reacted to this in rebellion, and wanted Peter merely because their therapist did not seem to want him.

In the end Peter did not enter this group, but when I saw him the following week, he was in civilian clothes. Peter said that my associate had called him to his office and very spontaneously told him how glad he was to see him in civilian clothes. This pleased Peter, but at the same time baffled him. He knew that no one had ever wanted him to wear clericals in the old group, nor had I ever wanted him to wear them. It was hard for Peter to realize that for my associate, for the group, and for me, his round collar was a symbol of our despair that our efforts had so completely failed to be of any help in undoing the past and helping him to be a worthwhile person. Everything that we did not like about Peter seemed to congeal in the sanctimonious sweetness and smugness with which he wore his clericals. But he had wanted to wear clericals, so he turned a deaf ear on all of us. It was only when something he wanted very much came up, it was only when he realized that he very much wanted something that was not being given to him, that it mattered whether anyone liked him in clericals or not.

Suddenly Peter turned to me and said, "What good is the Sacrament of ordination?"

I asked him what he meant.

"Well," he said, "you tell me that ever since I've been ordained, I've run away from myself, and I've run away from everyone who was a party to my ordination. I have somehow the feeling that the reason that I let you question my ordination is because you did not come to it. You never seemed to accept the fact that I was ordained, never in all these years."

"No, I never have. You know very well that I was brought up a Presbyterian and these things never bother me very much one way or the other. A Sacrament is the outward manifestation of inward grace, and that I've never seen as far as your ordination is concerned. I'm still looking for the inward grace and I'm still helping you to find it. As for the outward manifestation, it was a ceremony in which you were publicly given the privilege of performing certain professional duties reserved for those who are ordained. It's to me very much the same as getting married, or having the right to practice medicine."

"You don't think there's anything special about ordination?"

"No more than any other Sacrament. No more than baptism, or getting married, or getting buried, or whatever."

"You know," he said, "you're talking just like my bishop. I never did like his sermon about the Sacraments. Did you ever hear it?"

I told him I never had.

"Well, the bishop says that the grace of God is the grace of God. And it's all the same no matter which Sacrament it is, that it is the way in which we use the grace of God that makes the difference, but the Sacraments are only ways in which we are shown that the grace of God is available at all times to us. I've never believed this. I've always felt there was something very special about ordination, a very special grace, a different kind of grace; but now I'm beginning to wonder."

We returned to the unexplained and obviously important elation which Peter had felt for a few days following his confirmation, and when I asked Peter to tell me more about this, to try to explain what this ritual had meant to him, and what the glow had meant, he began to blush. I have never seen Peter quite so disconcerted. Finally he spoke in a rather bashful tone of voice: "You see, my birthday is June 29th."

This meant nothing to me but it was obvious that it was an extremely important memory, an extremely important date for Peter. I asked him what it meant.

"Well," he said, "you see, it is a feast day."

"Yes?" I said.

And finally with great effort, he said, "It is the feast of St. Peter the Apostle."

I asked him what this meant to him.

"Well," he said, "you see, when I was little, the stories about Peter Rabbit were my favorite stories. And later when I heard the stories of Brer Rabbit, I always thought of them as Brer Peter Rabbit. I always fantasied as a child that I was Brer Peter Rabbit and then I could do all the clever mischief without ever getting caught the way Brer Rabbit did, but I did get caught and I still kept hoping for the time when I would get clever enough so I wouldn't get caught any more. And then there was this wonderful Sunday when I was all happy about its being my birthday and everybody had tried to be very, very good to me. There were wonderful birthdays gifts on the table when I woke up, and that morning when I was singing in the choir, I was suddenly amazed to find that it was the feast day of St. Peter the Apostle, and then I knew, in some way I never understood, that I had inherited the gifts which St. Peter received from Christ. And I knew some day they would be given to me."

"What were these gifts?" I asked.

"Well," he said, "if you look up in the Prayer Book you'll find it on page 246. I used to read it over and over to myself and I kept hoping and praying that I would be confirmed on June 29th and that would be a sign from God that I was really Peter and I was given the gifts which St. Peter had been given."

And I said, "And were you confirmed on June 29th?"

He said, "No, but during the confirmation service, when the Collect, Epistle, and Gospel for that day were read, I repeated in my mind the words of the Collect, the Epistle, and the Gospel, for the feast of St. Peter the Apostle, for I was sure that if I concentrated hard enough, it would make it so."

"And did it?"

He said, "For a little while I thought it did. And then I don't know what happened. And finally I forgot about it."

I said, "And what are these precious gifts?"

And finally Peter shared them with me, those gifts from Matthew 16.18, 19: "And I tell you, you are Peter, and on this rock I will build my church, and the powers of death shall not prevail against it. I will give you the keys of the kingdom of heaven, and whatever you bind on earth shall be bound in heaven, and whatever you loose on earth shall be loosed in heaven."

I knew and Peter knew why his magical power had been so very strong, had seemed so very real to him, and why he had been so sure of liturgy and procedure as a curate and why he had been so angry, so frustrated when people died against his wishes, why he had been so righteous in his cruelty in disfranchising his people. I asked him on what day he was ordained.

He said, "Again, it was June but not the 29th."

And so I said, "Peter, when did you first begin to doubt your terrible gifts?"

He said, "When I was in seminary. It bothered me terribly when I learned that the Greek word for Peter, which means a rock, is a neuter noun. I could never quite understand how this could be neuter, because I wasn't neuter, I was a man."

I said, "Yes, Peter, you are a man. And this is the first time in all these years that you have acknowledged your humanity. It's good to hear. Try to remember that in being human, we are our best selves and we can become our best selves in no other way."

I looked into the rest of the Gospel as quoted in the Prayer Book and I noted a number of things. When Jesus was questioning His apostles as to the understanding of His true identity, it was only St. Peter who could sense out and give Jesus the wanted and expected answer: "You are the Christ, the Son of the living God."

I became even more curious and remembered vaguely something that went "And Peter wept." With the help of a concordance I found the story of how, as Jesus had foretold, Peter denied Christ three times, and then the cock crowed and Peter remembered, "And he went out and wept bitterly."

There are also references to the time when Peter tried to walk where Jesus was walking so easily; but Peter could not. Peter had to swim, and be rescued by Jesus. There are other times when this overwhelming irrational self-confidence of St. Peter's is spoken of. And St. Peter too came to a time when he was imprisoned, just as our little-boy Peter was imprisoned inside the façade of the empty shell that was the seminarian who came into treatment.

Peter began to realize that he could have confessed his magic, his dreams of being the sorcerer's apprentice, to a woman and only to a woman who—because she refused to go to his ordination, he had always believed—had seen through him, just as he had always felt his mother could tell when he was lying about who had broken the window, or who had brought the little garter snake into the parlor. Yet he couldn't understand why I had so consistently refused to help him out of his trouble with my male associate. I asked him, "And how did your mother handle your problems in relation to your father?" And he remembered that his mother had never betrayed him to his father, but neither had she mediated between him and his father, when through his naughtiness he had brought down his father's wrath. He had always had to deal directly with his father in his mother's lifetime. Later, with his stepmother, he could play the one against the other. And he had done so to their terrible unhappiness. I pointed out to him that his problem seemed to be one in relation to men rather than to women and I suggested that he come into my almost all-male group since my associate's group was closed to him.

I said, "After all, Peter, your problem as a rector with your vestry is a problem that so many rectors have. You don't know how to deal with men, man to man; so in order to effect your wishes, you connive with the women in the parish who will then manipulate your male vestry. This causes an endless amount of difficulty. It's so much easier to be straightforward and open in your manipulations, so come on into this group."

Peter, for once in his life, took his courage in both hands, and walked into what he felt was a den of lions. It was a strong, hardworking, cohesive group, a group that would not tolerate the sham of weeping and long-drawn-out stories that had no point. Peter tried to stay in the background, but inadvertently he would get caught.

Shortly after this I went away on a rather lengthy summer vacation. I suggested to the group that I would ask my associate to carry on if they so desired. They were delighted. Many of them were in private hours with him, and this would give them another dimension in which to understand their relationship to him. When I came back, the group was on a delightful honeymoon. They might be much too angry if this new-found father was taken away from them, so we decided to try the experiment of giving them both a mother and a father in the group.

In my absence Peter had worked out a very real relationship

with my associate. It was a little harder for him when we were both in the group together, but finally even this became comfortable. Peter grew in those succeeding months, when for the first time since he was a tiny boy, he had a mother and a father. He was called to a new perish about the time that my associate and I discontinued the experiment, but Peter had had the time that he needed, and now in this new parish some six and a half years after he began treatment, he found a woman whom he felt was finally the right one. He guarded this relationship very jealously, which was easy to do because his new parish was two hours' driving distance from my office. But Peter could seldom come to the group more than once a month. After six months he discontinued the group and was married. Several of the group went to his wedding and reported that they had never seen Peter so very much a man, so happy, and that they were most pleased with his wife.

Now, several years later, this progress continues. The marriage seems in every way a happy and fulfilling relationship for both of them. Peter's work with children is beginning to attract favorable comment. He has a knack of interpreting religion to youngsters which is unusual and delightful. Several of our clergy have reported that they have never seen a children's Eucharist so beautifully done, with such happy participation, as when Peter celebrates it. Peter says that somehow this is the Eucharist in which he personally feels his greatest devotion. The abandoned little boy has succeeded in converting his grief and guilt into a source of comfort and spiritual warmth. His compulsion to save found not only a channel of proper theological expression, but one that led him to a state of psychological equilibrium as well.

❧ MARTIN ❧

Martin, for a big, rather handsome, well-put-together man, was unbelievably awkward, both physically and verbally. It was hard to believe that he had had the intelligence to have graduated with honors from one of the finest seminaries. He was born and brought up in the Episcopal Church. His parents had been good, salt-of-the-earth kind of parishioners, supporting the church in its functions, and going to church more often than not. They had in no way revealed to Martin their personal devotion or lack of it, for when I asked him about it he said he really had no way of answering the question; whether their religion was a matter of perfunctory ritualistic observance or whether it was a matter of personal devotion he did not know. His life had been a chaotic mess of many false starts. He apparently had followed many rabbit tracks but had never learned to follow the scent of the fox, and he still had no feeling that he knew where he wanted to go in life. He had suddenly realized during his last year in college that he had to make up his mind and decide on some career; it was one of those things that is expected of men in our culture.

Since he had no idea of what he wanted to do, he made a list of all the various professions, and considered carefully each one from the standpoint of the courses he had in college, the people he knew, what he knew about that type of life, and whether he would like it or not. When he came to the ministry there were suddenly more things on the positive side of the ledger. The course he was taking at that time in Old Testament literature was one of the most interesting courses he'd ever had in more than three years of college. The instructor was an able and fascinating lecturer. He was moreover a very charming, warm, friendly, and interesting person. Martin realized immediately that of all the older men in his acquaintance throughout the years, he liked this man the best. And it suddenly occurred to him that

this man was an ordained minister. Never before had this fact
been a matter of any consequence. He began to feel that he
wanted to be a minister just as this man was a minister. He
was sure his family would approve of it; they were church-going
people; there would be no problem there. There would be no
problem in getting the bishop to okay it. He had been a dinner
guest several times in his parents' home, and his parents had
always been heavy contributors to one of the wealthiest churches
in the bishop's diocese; the old boy would naturally have to go
along.

Having figured all this out, Martin looked over his calendar.
There were no important classes the next day and so he set his
alarm and arose early. He put in a long-distance telephone call,
and informed the bishop's secretary that he would be there and
that he wanted to see the bishop. Somehow his arrogance worked,
and the bishop's secretary made the appointment. When he
arrived, he found that the bishop was busier than the secretary
had thought. They did manage to have lunch together, however.
The bishop accepted Martin as a postulant for Holy Orders and
set the proper wheels in motion for him to be screened by a
psychologist and psychiatrist. Later, when I talked to the bishop,
he revealed to me the fact that he expected the young man to
ask permission to make some sort of marriage against his parents'
wishes, or something like that. It never occurred to him that the
young man would say he wanted to enter the ministry. He had
known the boy all of his life and had never dreamed that he
would ever want to become a priest. In spite of his surprise, however, there was no reason to turn the man down, except a nagging
feeling that something was wrong. The bishop sensed very
strongly that the boy had no vocation, that his desire to go into
the ministry was founded in superficial motivations. The bishop
did not feel that Martin was called by God and later the bishop
was found to be correct. But since the only basis for this feeling
was the bishop's intuitive concern, he had decided to let the
man have a try at his vocation. In seminary Martin would have
time to find out whether or not he had a religious vocation; if
he had a real vocation and were told to test it by waiting until
he was sure he knew what he wanted to do, he might be dis-

couraged. Now the bishop felt even more unhappy when the psychological screening report came in, for the psychologist and the psychiatrist were both extremely hesitant about this man's fitness for the ministry. The reports stated that here was an unhappy, sullen, restless man who gave no evidence of knowing what he really wanted to do. The only thing that was clear was that he was rebellious of authority. The report concluded that there was no specific evidence indicating that he should be excluded from the ministry, but psychotherapy was definitely advised. This was what the bishop had feared.

Shortly before Martin began his theological training the bishop had told him that at the seminary to which he was going there was a great interest in therapy. He explained carefully that this was a way of understanding oneself and one's problems and that the screening psychiatrist and the psychologist felt that such a project during seminary would be very helpful to Martin. Martin said he would think it over.

Upon his arrival at the seminary he had a conference with his faculty advisor. The advisor welcomed Martin to the seminary, congratulated him on the grades he had made in college, and then brought up the question of therapy. They spent an hour discussing the various therapists in the area, which was all very well until a couple of months later when the faculty advisor saw Martin at his next scheduled conference and realized not only that Martin had done nothing about beginning therapy but that he had no intention of doing so. The faculty advisor and the dean had a conference with Martin after this; they told him that for the good of his soul he ought to go into therapy. Martin replied that he did not want to. They informed the bishop, who also had a conference with him. But no one felt right about telling him to put up or shut up, and so he went on through seminary, pressure being put on him constantly to go into therapy, and he refusing to yield an inch. His clinical training was delayed because it was felt that students for whom therapy was advised should have begun it before they went into clinical training. Nevertheless, he managed to have his clinical training without his therapy. He graduated with honors, and everybody was just a little puzzled, wondering if those psychiatrists and psychologists knew anything about the business of religious vocation. After all, Martin had done a beautiful job; he was one of the top half dozen in his class, well-liked by all of the students.

Amid due pomp and ceremony Martin was ordained. He began his ministry in a curacy and for a year he served his internship under an excellent parish priest. After this he was most successful as rector of a small but worthwhile parish for a year. Then he decided to go into hospital chaplaincy, and to prepare for this he took a full year of clinical training. This is where he was caught. A very intelligent, well-trained clinical supervisor was able in a discussion-group situation to learn enough about Martin to make him so uncomfortable that he realized he had to go into treatment. He made Martin admit that he had done a skillful job of trying to mold himself into the pattern, picture, and role of the good clergyman, only with a view of pleasing people. Unfortunately, the supervisor had used pretty rough methods to break through very well-laid defenses, and he had uncovered only the first layer. The result of all this was that Martin had abandoned clinical training and had gone to the bishop to resign from the ministry. He did not really belong in the ministry, he said, and had only been trying to make himself look, talk, and think like a minister. It was now clear that this was no more than role playing. He was through. "I'll be goddamned if I'm going to make myself into an actor, no matter how good an actor I am. Just because I can do a good act, there's no reason why I should want to be an actor. I want to be myself."

The bishop asked him who he was and what he wanted to do. "Bishop, I don't know what in the hell I want to do. I don't know where I've been." There was a long pause. Then he said, "Bishop, you've been trying for years to get me to go into therapy. Do you know an analyst that might be halfway decent? I don't want any blundering idiots like that clinical training supervisor. You know, somebody that's got some sense about things." Martin did not like the idea of a female therapist. Women were stupid. But the bishop had insisted that he try it, and Martin had come.

He was a patient who came in every hour sullen, depressed,

unhappy, incredibly clumsy, and yet so skillfully clumsy that his clumsiness could not be questioned, until gradually we began to know him after he had been in group therapy for several sessions. He was still sullen and silent, and yet you had a feeling he was really a good-natured man.

We learned more about Martin's childhood. We found out that he had always lived this same sullen, unhappy existence, only in childhood the pattern showed a more understandable goal. Being the eldest child, he never seemed to get as much attention from his parents as did his younger brothers and sisters. There was, for instance, the year that he had made straight A's in everything, including an A-plus in mathematics, which happened to be his father's hobby. So what? There was no fuss about it. He got no attention. Nobody seemed to realize that this was a wonderful job for a nine-year-old. His brothers and sisters were brilliant and capable youngsters too, and in this family, where everybody was doing unusually good work, such accomplishments were taken for granted. So the next year he decided he would get some attention. He flunked. He made F's in everything. He was sent to the family physician to be checked over; his parents thought there might be something wrong with him physically. When the doctor said that he was all right, they asked the school psychologist. This man informed them that the school authorities were baffled by Martin; he did not seem to pay any attention to anything, and he had not been interested in his classes that year. At this point his parents shrugged their shoulders and hoped he would straighten out the next year.

The next year Martin settled down to making good grades when he was interested and poor grades when he wasn't. Finally he was making exceptionally good grades when he was interested and mediocre grades when he wasn't interested. Then he decided he would try sports. After all, one of the younger brothers was doing well at figure skating, and one of the little sisters was beginning to be a dancer. That summer the family had a house in the country, and there was quite a bit of interest in tennis. Martin went to work, and he became the champion tennis player of the summer colony. So what? The family expected this of him. Of course he was the champion tennis player. Nothing happened. No love. Martin stopped being a tennis player. The family accepted that, too. This was the pattern of Martin's life throughout high school and college. He became the outstanding freshman football player in college, but everybody took it for granted. Of course Martin was the outstanding football player on the freshman team. So he dropped out. The same reaction from his family: if Martin doesn't want to play football, he does not have to. Nobody got upset about it. Martin brought home different girls. Everybody was very happy. Martin wanted a girl, fine. He decided he wanted to marry one of the girls. This girl had terrible table manners; she was gauche and unattractive. The family did not understand what he saw in this girl, but felt that, if she loved him and if he loved her and wanted to marry her, it was all right. Anything Martin wanted to do was all right by them. This was not what Martin wanted. He wanted them to say, "Martin, we love you, don't do this; this girl isn't for you." Martin wanted to know that they cared. All through life they had been so understanding, so permissive. They had never imposed their own standards on Martin. They had done a fine job of being intelligent parents and letting Martin do just exactly what he wanted to do. But they never understood that Martin never wanted simply to do what he wanted to do. He wanted to know that he was loved. He wanted to know that they thought he was wonderful, and this he never heard from them. They never showed him this.

When he was in seminary, one day he heard a lecture on Martin Luther. He heard how Luther had struggled through twenty or thirty years to be good. He had done good works; he had become a priest and a monk. He had worked very hard, and never had there been a single moment of feeling that he was saved, that God loved him. But suddenly one day Luther was saved. He felt the complete acceptance of himself by God. He knew the answer then. Man is justified by faith and not by good works. You were saved not by anything you yourself had done, but only because God loved you; and if you had faith that God would love you and if you accepted yourself as totally worthless of being loved, then the time would come that God would take pity on you, and the awareness of His love, of His grace, and of His forgiveness would be yours.

As Martin was telling me this, there was a change in his whole being. He was suddenly sitting very gracefully for the first time since I had known him. His big clumsy body was suddenly beautifully composed. He was alert. He was exciting to listen to. He told me a great deal about Luther, and I could well understand that he had been a tremendously fascinating person for Martin. He told me the story of the Protestant Reformation and became really eloquent as he described that whole period of history. Finally I asked him to give me briefly and concisely the theological conceptualization of what we had been talking about—the doctrine of justification by faith. At this his whole being seemed to change. He spoke in a very ordinary tone of voice from which all the emotional intensity and excitement were drained. An intelligent, cultured, quiet voice gave me briefly and succinctly the theological definition he had been taught.

Justification, he said, is "our being accounted righteous by God because of the merits of Christ and by reason of our living faith in him. Faith is steadfast loyalty to Christ as Savior. Thus justification by faith is our appropriation of the atoning work of Christ."

Now when Martin finished this statement of the doctrine, I asked him to compare it with what he had been telling me about Luther. He did not understand me. He could not see that on the one hand he had stated that God, because of the atoning work of Christ, accepts us as the persons we are in our essential integrity as human beings and not in spite of our wrongdoing or because of our rightdoing, and on the other hand that because of the atoning work of Christ, God accepts us as the persons of integrity that we really are, and since this is done neither because of our good actions nor in spite of our bad ones, we await the event of our salvation. The catch, as far as Martin was concerned, was "await the event." This meant that there had to be a sign that God had bestowed his favor before Martin could know that he was saved. I could find no way in which to get the two compartments of his mind to communicate with each other. Each was completely airtight and his personal religion never came into contact with his intellectual, seminary religion.

The conflict between Martin's seminary training and his personal religion had to be made manifest before he could see it. Some of the symptoms of this conflict had come to me in the report of his bishop's screening psychologist and psychiatrist. When I questioned him more about the doctrine of good works, I got more of the history of the Protestant Reformation and also an unmitigated anti-Semitism of the worst and most ignorant variety. He was thoroughly convinced that the theology of the Jews was completely COD. It was his feeling that the Jews believed in an accounting system whereby you had a certain number of merits or demerits for everything you did. If you committed adultery, that was so many demerits; if you contributed $500 to the synagogue, that was so many merits. On this type of a merit and demerit system, good works are certainly a matter of anyone's contempt. He could not believe in the idea of good works in identification with a God of mitzvot or of a Jesus whose mission in His human existence included such good works as healing, comforting, and helping. There was no way this could penetrate Martin's one-track mind.

It was not until much later that I was able to tie this problem to Martin's anger with his father, whose profession it was to judge people's actions. He had displaced onto the Jews the accumulated hatred of his father, who had been an unusually intelligent and careful judge, always most scrupulous in examining the evidence before pronouncing judgment on the prisoner at the rail. And of course, this man had leaned over backward all of his life in trying to avoid judging his children. As a result, he had failed also to praise them. And so Martin could love his father and hate the Jews. It was a happy solution, unless one were concerned for the welfare of the Jewish community in Martin's jurisdiction. Martin had failed to get his father to love him in the ways in which he needed to know that he was loved. His father had refused either to judge him or to reward him. He had not been given love in a way which he felt proved that his father loved him. He had tried very hard to get his father to love him by being very, very good, and had never received any approval for his trouble. He had tried very hard to get his father to be angry with him by being very, very bad, but his father had been very understanding and had never become angry, and had never punished him. Therefore he could not possibly have loved him. Consequently the concept of a father in heaven who could be relied upon to love one if one remained in a totally depressed attitude concerning one's self, was most appealing. As long as you were depressed and unhappy, and considered yourself worthless and useless, and honestly felt that nothing you had ever done was any good, and that nothing you could do would be of any value in helping yourself get love from God, could God ever in your fondest hopes reach out his hand toward you?

Once I asked Martin if he felt he had ever done anything well. I was wondering if he had ever had a feeling of triumph, and of personal excitement and pleasure in what he had done. In response, he told me of a time in college when he had overspent his allowance and was finding himself very proud about not asking for any extra money. He decided instead that he would earn what money he needed the way some of the other students did. One of his friends told him he could get him a baby-sitting job. As a matter of fact, the friend was supposed to baby-sit that night, but he was feeling tired, and wanted to skip it and get a date. So he called up his erstwhile employer and said that there was an important examination for which he needed to study. Could he send over an excellent person to take his place? The baby would be well cared for; he would vouch for that. And so they went over and he gave Martin a quick briefing as to how to look after babies. Thus, this clumsy young ox of a boy, age 18, who had never bothered to find out about babies because he never wanted his little brothers or sisters when they came along, suddenly was alone in a great big house with a year-old baby. The baby was sound asleep when he arrived and Martin sat himself down with some books and was studying away. Everything was fine; he was beginning to say to himself, "My God, this is a snap; all you do is come over and study in a comfortable room; hell, I'll do this more often," when the baby started to cry. Martin tried to remember what he had been told to do. The baby's screaming and yelling and kicking indicated that he most definitely did not need much of his bottle. Martin felt the baby; he was wet. He therefore took the diaper off, and he was amazed at the mess! Hence he took all the clothes off the baby and got a towel, water, and soap, and washed the baby; and then he got talcum powder and put that on the baby. He was not sure of the proper way to pin a diaper on a child, but he "got them on" as he told me proudly, and then he changed the baby's crib sheet. By that time he and the baby were great friends. He held the baby in his arms for a while and was beginning to like the little mite, when all of a sudden the baby was sound asleep. So he put the baby back in the crib, turned the light down, and went back to his book. In about an hour the parents came back. The woman was furious. She couldn't imagine how anyone could be so stupid; the diapers were on completely wrong. Martin could not understand then and Martin still could not understand. "After all," he said, "I cleaned the baby up, and I fed the baby; the baby and I had a wonderful time, and the baby went to sleep. What if I didn't pin the diapers on right? They were on."

This was the only time that Martin had done anything that he was really proud of, really satisfied with. Here he had enjoyed doing something and had pleased himself in doing it in spite of the mother's disapproval. He had retained a feeling of pride in his job.

Martin began to review his life and found that he had always enjoyed his work with young people in the congregation. He looked into secular work with adolescents and found a job working with street gangs. He slowly but surely began to find himself. He was given promotion after promotion as he proved himself capable and responsible. As this work became more fulfilling, he found himself less and less inclined to continue in the priesthood. He was unable to find any deep motivation for his continuing, and nearly four years after he had entered therapy, he resigned and was deposed with honor. Martin had never had a vocation to be a minister as his bishop had so surely sensed in the beginning. He had not gone into the ministry for the professional and unconscious desire to express his being through the functions of that ministry. He had gone in only for the purpose of finding God's love. Once he found that he was happier in the pews than at the altar. His devotion during the same time continued to grow so that slowly he began to have periods of feeling he was loved and saved, and the moments of doubt troubled him less often. He came to see that his doubts were concomitant with times when he was troubled and depressed. He realized more and more that it was only as he reached out to God that God's grace was evident, and his hopeless waiting for sudden conversion ceased.

✤ SAMSON ✤

Samson was brought up in a female-dominated milieu. His mother had married late and the marriage had not gone too well. She and her husband lived in the tenant house of his grandmother's big plantation. Samson quickly learned that all of the important decisions were made by Grandmother Hecate in the big house on the hill, and his father obeyed them just as did the other tenant farmers on the plantation, black or white. Grandmother Hecate's real name was not Hecate, of course, but this was his private name for her because she represented to him the implacable fates, as had the Greek goddess Hecate. The little boy grew up not really belonging in the big house on the hill, although he was a frequent visitor there, and not being permitted to belong to the social group of the tenants either. He was lonely, without playmates, and he never learned the give and take of games. As a result, he turned to his mother, who spoiled him completely. His father, suffering from a passive inability to cope with dominant females, tried "to make a man" out of his son by letting him win at everything. When they played checkers, the little boy always won; when they wrestled, the little boy always won; when they ran, the little boy always won. In everything the father did with him he connived for the child to do better than he did. So the little boy began to feel contempt for his father. This plus the pampering of his mother gave him a feeling of magical superiority which was completely unrealistic.

Occasionally there were family reunions in the big house on the hill, and once in a while he would meet the one male member of the family whom he respected—his uncle who was able to preserve a few shreds of his masculinity by being away from home a great deal. He was a traveling salesman and was frequently away for months at a time. When he was at home, he was never there for more than a few weeks, sometimes only a few days.

Samson was permitted to have the extraordinary right to choose his own religion, and in defiance of his grandmother's wishes, he went to the Presbyterian Church with his father. He knew that when he went to the Episcopal Church with his mother and his grandmother and the rest of the family, there was always a special reward for him. But he refused it because this was the one area in which he could rebel against Grandmother, and often the need to rebel in order to preserve some shred of independence was greater than the temptation of the goodies at the big house. Besides, there were always strings attached to the largesse of his grandmother.

Samson's father, rather incapable as a farmer, became increasingly less successful, and finally when Samson was in college, Grandmother Hecate put her foot down. The situation was becoming economically impossible and she was losing too much money every year on this "trifling, no 'count husband" of her daughter. Therefore orders came out of the great house on the hill, and Mama told Papa that things had now come to an end. Shortly thereafter Samson received a letter in which he was told that Mama and Papa had been unhappy for many years now, and since he was in college, they felt they no longer had to make the sacrifice of trying to live together for his sake. Hence she was going back to live with Grandmother Hecate, and Papa was going to get a job in town. Papa found a position working for a wealthy and somewhat elderly widow, and soon strange bits of gossip circulated about his exact position in her household. As far as Samson was concerned, his father died the day his mother's letter came. He felt frightened and insecure; there seemed no longer to be any possibility of coping with Grandmother. Since his uncle's death several years earlier, Samson's only possible ally had been his weak father, and now this, his last ally, his only ally, was gone.

In the weeks that followed he began to review his decision to be a Presbyterian. After all, was there any other reason for being a Presbyterian besides the fact that it was fun to go to church with Father because Grandmother was always so annoyed about it? He had even wanted to be a Presbyterian minister because this infuriated Grandmother and made Father so proud and so happy. But no longer had he any desire to make happy the father who had betrayed him through weakness. He thought more and more about the value of changing his religious allegiance. Although he was not very interested in becoming an Episcopalian, this was the only other religious group he had any acquaintance with, and he decided he would talk to the rector at college about it. The rector encouraged him to become an Episcopalian, and explained that it was important for him to enter the present confirmation class at once, because in a few months the bishop would come to the parish to confirm the group. Samson suddenly remembered the occasion many years before when his grandmother's bishop had graced her mansion with his presence. He recalled his astonishment at her almost frightened respect for this great man. He began to realize that there would be advantages to being an Episcopalian. Such a bishop would be a wonderful man to protect him against Grandmother, and he would have the social prestige she always felt so important. Not long after this he spoke to the rector about the fact that he had always planned to be a minister, and now that he was becoming an Episcopalian he felt that he wanted to become a postulant for Holy Orders. The truth of the matter was, as a priest he would have not only equal social prestige with his grandmother, but beyond that he would at least share in that spiritual power which she had so envied in the bishop. In this respect he could be superior to her, and therefore quite secure against her hateful control of so many of the forces that influenced his life. As soon as he was confirmed, he was accepted as a postulant by the bishop, and in due time he was off to seminary.

Samson had never learned to play with people his own age and the situation was no better in seminary. He was as lonely as ever there, and lived an almost isolated existence. Consequently it was to be expected that his loneliness would sooner or later influence his conception of his coming ministry. He decided that he would become a celibate priest and as soon as possible after that he would become a contemplative monk. This would be a life in which he would not have to talk to people;

he would simply live in dignified, devout isolation and meditation. He did not realize that this was how he perceived the nature of his grandmother's life, because he had never seen her save on rare and important "state" occasions.

During the course of his seminary years he had become a very High Churchman, to his grandmother's consternation, and after his ordination his southern bishop was happy to transfer him to another diocese. In the new diocese he found the ideal strong and impressive bishop as well as a situation where Anglo-Catholic practices were most completely observed. It became much more important to him to follow the latest liturgical decrees than anything else. He was horrified lest anyone should know that he had once been a Presbyterian. He became the assistant in a parish where the liturgical practices were executed in accordance with his own principles, and he became associated with one of the monastic orders in the Episcopal Church, taking yearly vows of celibacy. His preaching was outstanding and his charm began to be more apparent. He used his free time to earn a graduate degree in theology. As a result, when there was an opening on the staff of the cathedral within his diocese, he was immediately asked to fill the vacancy. Although here too he filled only the position of an assistant, his usefulness to the aging bishop, both theologically and administratively, gave him unusual opportunities to be seen in the right places, so that he soon had the social prestige of those who were by many years his ecclesiastical seniors.

Acquiring at so early an age such an enviable position by his brilliance and scholarship, his charm and wit, was, to say the least, an unfortunate thing for this young man. Such a phenomenal success in social climbing was in marked contrast to the years he had spent in loneliness, and he had not the sense of reality testing to avoid being swept off his feet by such success. This lack of a sense of reality testing, which would become such a severe problem later, became obvious when he joined with a group of clergy and seminarians, signing a statement criticizing the bishop on a recently issued statement of policy. He vividly recalled how the bishop summoned all the signers to his office, and standing them in one long row, paced up and down before them, roaring in his wrath, and told them that he would not tolerate such rebellion. From that point on Samson knew where he stood at all times with his bishop. He had found the strong, good father he had always sought.

Everything went very well for a few years, until the old bishop died. Samson betrayed none of his real feelings during the bishop's funeral service but he was secretly indignant that his father-in-God had betrayed him in dying, that no one had realized that only he should have been the celebrant of the Requiem, and that only he should have delivered the funeral sermon.

A few months after this the dean of the cathedral called him in to discuss with him very seriously the problem of his relationship with a young acolyte. Samson thought he lied his way out of it, but apparently the dean never believed him, and the new bishop transferred him to another parish. The dean continued to watch him closely and one day suggested to him that perhaps he was not really cut out for the celibate life. He mentioned to Samson that the problems young celibate priests had with acolytes often disappeared when they got married, and asked him if he knew any nice, eligible young ladies. Samson took the hint. He looked around and chose a very fine, very quiet young lady, a woman who had been brought up to be the most respectful of the clergy. She had been reared in such sexual prudery that she had come to have the deep-seated notion that only in marrying a priest of the Episcopal Church would she be sure that she would do nothing wrong in sex and marriage.

The problems with acolytes gradually disappeared, as the dean had predicted, and nothing of that nature ever came to the notice of the authorities again. Samson was finally able to get a small parish of his own and, much as he resented its size, still he enjoyed the prospect of freedom from the strict surveillance of the past few months. He and his wife settled down there, with nice neighbors and a lovely house. There was almost nothing in the way of money, but fortunately his wife respected her position and accepted their poverty. When Samson finally yielded to gentle persuasions and she was permitted to have babies, she became even happier. Everybody delighted in this radiant young woman, everybody except her husband. For a while he had en-

joyed a marriage in which he was the only child as he had been
at home with his mother, but now he felt excluded and unwanted. Of course this was only his reaction, and in no way the
reality of the situation. He had always had his way about everything; he had always lived in such a world of omnipotence that
now he could not tolerate the competing omnipotence of his
infant children. Naturally his attentions began to wander, and
the inevitable happened: there appeared a damsel in distress
disguised as a pathetic young parishioner with a very severe
marriage problem. Her husband had deserted her, and she was
desolate.

Samson comforted her. After a while, however, he found it
inhibiting to execute his pastoral ministrations in the austere
premises of his study, so he began to drop by her home when
he would be making a parish call in the neighborhood. Gradually
he found more and more occasions to drop in to solace the lonely
young woman. He paid no attention to the matter of discretion;
he came and went as he wished, in daylight or moonlight or
dark of night. In the course of a few months the village was
disturbed to learn that things had been going on of which it did
not approve. The matter came to the attention of the vestry,
who were still recovering from the misbehavior of the previous
rector, who, over a period of years, had also been quite indiscreet
from time to time, both within and without the parish. This man
had been very much loved by his people, and Samson had tried
to be like him in order to win the approval he needed. Unfortunately he lacked the reality testing necessary to discriminate
between the qualities for which his predecessor had been loved
and those in spite of which he had been loved. The gossip about
his predecessor had been a real factor in Samson's lack of discretion. The vestry brought the matter to the attention of the
bishop, who was quite angry, as well he might have been. As a
result Samson and his bride were uprooted very suddenly, and
he was put in a situation where he would supposedly have more
supervision.

This was not a clever move on the part of the bishop. Demoting
Samson from a rector back to a curate upset him no end, and
placing Samson in the charge of a very severe, moralistic, Low

Churchman was even more annoying, because Samson loved to walk gracefully in his vestments. He loved the rustle of silk and lace. He delighted in the number of yards of material that went into his surplices. He fancied himself as being graceful and very beautiful. But his new rector frowned on all this. He felt that vestments should be more simple and plain. Indulging in richness and extravagance was unseemly in a devout atmosphere. He therefore thwarted Samson at every turn. He did not approve of Samson's delight in the use of confession, especially with indiscreet young ladies. He told Samson he intended to announce that confessions would be heard by appointment only, and that the rector himself would do this work, as it should be done by someone with experience, sobriety, prudence, and so forth. He felt that Samson was really getting much too big for his britches, and he was absolutely right. Samson had been enjoying his sacramental functions because of the magical omnipotence they seemed to give him. He enjoyed remembering that part of the ordination service which declares to the ordinand, "Whose sins thou shalt forgive they are forgiven; and whose sins thou dost retain they are retained." He unconsciously interpreted these words to mean quite literally that he had received the keys to heaven and hell to do with them as he wished. This young man was at heart and in his own personal religion a staunch Calvinist, and he knew unconsciously that if he could determine who was saved and who was damned, he was in effect not only the instrument of God's grace, but God Himself.

Samson continued to be angry about this, and about many other things. The rector insisted that he should visit the old, the infirm, the sick, and the poor. He had serious ideas about the duties of a parish priest to the widow, the orphan, and the bereaved. Samson felt, on the other hand, that the only people who should receive his visits were damsels in distress who needed to be comforted, or people who made him happy, so that he would feel almost as if he were having tea with his grandmother when she was in a rare mood.

Eventually, Samson again found a young lady to comfort. This time he was more discreet, but his wife had learned to read the signs. Fearing to go to the rector or the bishop, she went to the priest who had been Samson's first rector. This man called him in and reasoned with him, and prayed over him; but Samson continued to see his Delilah. His wife then went to the dean, and he too saw Samson, and told him that his marriage was sacred, that he must give up this illicit relationship, that his unhappiness was his cross to bear. The dean also sent him to a priest-counselor, explaining to this man the situation and some of the background. For some months they spent several hours a week together. Unfortunately Samson never mentioned his problem directly, and because the counselor had been trained exclusively in the classical, indirect approach in psychoanalysis, neither did he. Finally, realizing he was getting nowhere, he referred the case to a psychiatrist he knew to be trusted by the church, who put the matter to Samson very plainly, whereupon Samson cancelled the next appointment and never saw him again.

So matters went for nearly two years with everyone trying and praying but being most ineffective, while Samson became more and more careless, until finally the gossip reached the ears of the rector. So the conscientious, respectable, hardworking rector had to go to the new bishop and confess that he had been a complete failure in putting Samson on the straight and narrow path. The bishop responded quickly and with great authority, removing Samson from the parish, suspending him from the exercise of his priestly functions, and giving him permission to work in a civil capacity. He also put him into psychotherapy with me. Samson was so surprised by the swiftness with which these things happened that he accepted treatment with little ado. The psychological study done at this point reveals clearly the clinical picture before therapy was begun. The report compares the study done nearly a year earlier at the request of the psychiatrist mentioned above.

> Mr. ———, on the surface, was pleasant and willing to please and readily verbalized his previous experience with the Rorschach test. He probably can be very charming and ingratiating in his superficial contacts with others, when he so desires, and in fact, attempted to handle the session as if it were a social rather than a test situation.

His approach to the Rorschach plates however, revealed that his eagerness to prove how cooperative he was, was a façade, for in actuality, delaying tactics as he attempted to control and suppress his spontaneous ideas, were very obvious. There was much talk (which at times was rather pedantic) and intellectualizing which reflected not only obsessive character traits and deeply embedded feelings of insecurity and insufficiency, but his feelings about the task-like character of the situation.

At present the man's interests are rather restricted to himself and the predicament he is in and he is depressed and disappointed in himself. His inability to cope with his difficulties in a masterful way seems to have revealed to him just how weak and inadequate he actually is as a man; feelings which he has probably always tried to escape from and which he compensated for through his drive for prestige and recognition and through his manipulation of others. He probably does not quite believe or accept the self-derogatory statements he makes about himself at present, for they are too unacceptable to the self-image he has always striven to maintain.

The patient verbalized some of his feelings in a comment to plate X: "this way it looks like a series of lines . . . pointing to a non-existent point on the plate or table—the whole thing brings your eyes down. . . . I can see two things; I feel very much in this case I'm involved in that so much depends on one man and his reactions and this pinpoints to a day, when Dr. B. will see the Bishop.(?) I was going to say before, not so much the pinpointing . . . the pointing down, a feeling I get about myself— feelings that I have not taken advantage, have not gone up as I should but have drawn people down in the sense of making them sad and unhappy; pointing to something, pointing down, losing status that I've had . . . all the objects and colors have no other connection except being pulled down by my own folly . . . stupidity . . . stubbornness." His response suggests too that he feels that life is rather somber and the outlook for the future bleak. It is likely that he does not know how to plan for the future and that there is a longing to return to the past; to a childhood which he probably fantasies as a pleasant retreat from the threatening present.

On the whole his behavior can probably best be described as indicating a reluctant conformance with regard to environmental and social pressures. Though the man is intellectually well aware

of social conventions, he displays a strong desire to flout conventions—to see what and how much he can get away with
secretly under the guise of conformity. He probably can be extremely negativistic and stubborn in his attempts to cling to his
own standards and decisions or in his attempts to manipulate
others so that they appear less of a competitive threat. His
obstinacy and argumentativeness are probably usually most obvious when others (and especially authority figures) try to sway
him from his chosen path, so to speak.

The patient has probably always needed to offer to others a
picture of strength and individuality and this can be related to
his basic feminine identification and resultant feelings of weakness and inadequacy. His basic conception of role in life appears
to be a rather passive and submissive one and it can be speculated that the maternal figure (or surrogate) played a much
stronger role in his early childhood environment, than did the
paternal figure.

In view of the feminine identification and confusion about
sexual role, underlying homosexual leanings are quite likely. It
is also probable, however, that the man may try to protect himself from and deny his homosexual desires through flight into
heterosexuality. A true love relationship is doubtful since he is
very hostile towards women and seems to regard them as ex-
ploitable objects rather than as people with feelings and needs
of their own.

His orality and underlying castration fears are apparent in
both records, though now he is not as preoccupied with pregnancy and his irritable feelings towards his wife as he was a
few months ago.

On the whole, a comparison of his present Rorschach with his
previous one reveals a general personality constellation that is
basically the same though at present there is less emotional irri-
tability and he displays a better control over his stronger and
more labile feelings and impulses. That is, acutely overwhelmed
by his intense feelings and fears (though he still seems to expect
punishment from the paternal figure or surrogate) and thus is
less inclined to hysterical outbursts. He still longs for freedom
and escape from his responsibilities and his difficulties, but he is
well aware that this is not attainable.

To Summarize: The man's personality difficulties appear to
be deeply ingrained in the character structure though they have

been intensified by his present predicament. He probably can best be classified as a neurotic character with obsessive and hysterical components. Therapy is recommended though undoubtedly it will be a prolonged procedure. Not only is he very negativistic but probably it would be very difficult for him to accept his basic dependency. It is likely that he will attempt to intellectualize and prove his superiority under the guise of cooperation.

A fantastic story began to unfold before me. It was the story of the sorcerer's apprentice. In his tiny, angry, little-boy self Samson wanted to get back at the rector and the bishop. He wanted to make the whole church pay for daring to make him leave his comfortable little rectory where he was having so much fun doing just exactly what he wanted to do. He wanted to get even with the old bishop for dying, and with his father for being so weak. He wanted to get even with his wife for having other babies beside himself. He wanted to get even with everyone who had let him down. He saw no anger in himself toward God, nor did he see himself fearful of the wrath of God. He had known he was saved ever since he was a small child playing in the backyard. But what was back of this memory and why he came to this conclusion he didn't know then, nor has he yet remembered.

For several months he played with various fantasies of leaving the church in a blaze of scandal, and in telling me of this even likened it to Samson's pulling the temple down about his head. During this time he showed real initiative in finding for himself a civilian job, and for his family a place to live. He moved them into the new apartment and helped them get settled; then he packed his bags and left. After all, if he had to go into treatment, which he began to realize was nothing he wanted, why should he stay with this foolish little woman who loved her children so. He did this against my advice and in spite of my efforts to show him that this action would seriously jeopardize the ever-diminishing possibilities of his avoiding deposition.

For a few months Samson made the pretense of living at a hotel, although he was really living with Delilah, which made it possible for the bishop to keep him on suspension, and also gave his therapy an opportunity to be effective. But at length his anger became too much to be endured, and he gave up his hotel room and let everyone know he was "living in sin." He demanded that his wife give him a divorce on grounds of adultery. This, he hoped, would make the headlines, so that the church would suffer. In the end he caused just enough scandal so that the bishop was forced to act decisively. Samson was deposed.

When I saw him a few hours after this he looked ashen. His world had collapsed. He was like a small child who did not know what had hit him. The source of his magic was now taken from him. Suddenly he understood what I had meant when I spoke of his magical thinking, his omnipotence, and omniscience and realized that in reality he had none of these.

At this point he tried to go back to his wife. During the time of her abandonment she had grieved desperately, but when he returned seeking her love she could remember only that she had once loved him. She knew she had been in love with her fantasy of a Sir Galahad on a white charger. She had forgiven him but she could find no present love. She could find no basis for their renewing a marriage, and for the first time in her life she had the courage to say no and to start life over again.

Samson was furious with me for letting all this happen. Every session was a battleground. He used every possible way of coercing me into coercing his wife into taking him back. He began to realize that he had had a real marriage, a wonderful wife whom he loved, children he cared for. He became angry with Delilah for "leading him astray," and with me for treating him as a conventional person. He left Delilah and went to live alone. But even when his wife believed he really wanted what he had lost, she still could not take him back.

This was a time when Samson began to grow up in the grief and remorse over what he had destroyed. He now began to realize that he had a real vocation in the priesthood. His grief was deep and real, but there was still too much anger with himself for him to feel the compassion of his analyst and his bishop. I agreed that he should find a job away where he could start life over. This he did.

He began to realize that our work in therapy was sadly incomplete, and all on his own found a male therapist with whom he could discuss his religious conflicts and find his devotion. He began going to church, then finally to confession and Communion. When the very quiet divorce was arranged I received from him a storm of angry letters. Then there was a long silence of about two years, during which time he was out of therapy completely. This silence was broken by a telephone call. Of course I could see him. We had two wonderful hours as only old and combat-tested friends can have. The little boy had become a grown man. The charm he had formerly was replaced by depth, warmth, and sincerity. He told me of his approaching marriage and it sounded like a good one. He had gone forward wonderfully in his new career, which was in the field of advertising. In this field he found an identification with his uncle, and the dignity and prestige he had lost by deposition. He could no longer preach, but he could sell and he could do creative planning. He no longer felt any sense of deprivation in this work.

I spoke of his ministry. Had he considered asking for reinstatement? He answered that for many months he had struggled over the question. He could not now accept the reality of taking celibate vows, and he knew it could be difficult for the bishop to reinstate a divorced and remarried priest. I reminded him that nothing in canon law forbade this, but we both knew it was very difficult socially. Then I asked him if he had forgiven the church and all the well-meaning but ineffectual people who had tried to help him. He was startled at this. He had thought only of needing forgiveness for his own acts. I went on to express my feeling that as long as he was deposed the church suffered as one with a wound that never heals. I also asked him if he had considered going back to the Presbyterian Church. His answer was that he would rather remain a communicant of the Episcopal Church than be an ordained minister of any other religious body. Only in the Episcopal Church does he feel the emotional validity of the Sacraments. Intellectually he agreed that in other churches the ritual and intention could make a valid Sacrament, but even there he would not find a complete emotional fulfillment because the ethos of their worship was too foreign to him. This does not appear to be an instance of the use of his old magic in ritual. He expresses his satisfaction in quite simple and ordinary language without having to make it certain by officiating. And he is now accepting a very wide range of practice and opinion within his church. He knows he is saved, and now his salvation is real. He no longer has to prove it. His conversion of convenience has become a conversion of depth of conviction and of devotion.

❧ JACOB ❧

Jacob came into treatment at the suggestion of his internist who felt that his patient was much too young to have a gastric ulcer which responded poorly to treatment. Jacob was in his early thirties; he was teaching Semitic languages at a local university. He had gone through seminary, but had refused ordination. He felt a keen lack of devotion, which caused him untold suffering. He feared constantly that this lack might be discovered, especially by a congregation of devout, sensitive people, and that he would thus be considered "phony."

Being a conscientious Jew, Jacob was aware of the doctrine of Kavanah. Theologically, the significance of Kavanah involves the necessity of achieving a state of correct intention in prayer. Thus, for instance, if the devotion of the High Priest while making the sacrifice in the second temple at Jerusalem faltered or was lacking, the sacrifice was of no avail. This is in contradistinction to the Roman Catholic dogma that the Sacrament is of grace itself, regardless of the intention or the state of grace in which the properly qualified person might be. In Jewish theology the hope of efficacy in ritual or in prayer is wholly dependent on the individual's achieving a proper state of concentration and devotion, which is Kavanah. Bachya Ibn Pakuda denied all value to outward acts of religion devoid of Kavanah, and Maimonides declared that a prayer without Kavanah is no prayer at all. Under this discipline it is an act of deliberate impiety for a rabbi to lead his congregation if he is without personal devotion. Knowing this, Jacob could not approach ordination.

Since Jacob felt more self-esteem as a scholar, he went on in a teaching situation, extremely conscientious, poorly paid, working much too hard for what his job required. He had translated some minor works which he had not been able to push through to

149

publication. He had had one year of previous psychotherapy with an excellent woman analyst, who was also Jewish.

Jacob was a middle child. There was a brother three years older, and one three years younger. The father was angry and rebellious against everything his rigid Orthodox father stood for. He was rabidly atheistic, his political views were intense and radical, his business dealings, though unscrupulous, were always unsuccessful. During the depression years the father's inability to do more than eke out the barest essentials added severely to Jacob's life of insecurity, for in the quarrels between father and mother the martyred mother could always justify her complaints.

Jacob's only refuge was the synagogue and its Hebrew school. Here he found the only approval and sense of belonging he ever knew. Here too he learned to have a contempt for his mother's religious ignorance and superstition. Yet at the same time he could not find an acceptance for or by his severe grandfather. This man was "Calvinistic" in the cold Mitnagdic rabbinic tradition.

He fell in love with a girl whose home was equally troubled, and they rebelled together against orthodoxy. Unfortunately her rebellion extended beyond giving up a kosher kitchen; she wanted no longer to be Jewish. They were married, and as time went on there were more and more times when she saw in her husband her abusingly angry father. With each child she felt more and more insecure, and by the time Jacob came into treatment they were considering divorce.

The psychologist's report at this time so very clearly describes Jacob that we will quote from it at length:

> The patient was overproductive, offering a total of 105 responses to the Rorschach test, yet was very disappointed in himself because he felt he was not being productive enough. In many instances he seemed to be "forcing" percepts in a seeming attempt to "impress" (both himself and others) with his ability and in this way compensate to some extent for his underlying feelings of personal inadequacy. His percepts thus not only tended to be repetitive, but many (32%) were projected in small detail (and space) areas.
>
> Outstanding, too, were the man's "gentle" manner and at-

tempts to ingratiate himself. There seems to be a very strong need to make himself acceptable to others (and thus gain love), even at the expense of yielding part of his personality so as not to jeopardize the respect and affection which the environment can give.

It would seem that the man's desire to act in an expansive and spontaneous manner has been thwarted. Not only is there a self-imposed inhibition of action, but he seems to repress and deny his basic problems and feelings of weakness and inadequacy in spite of his habit of self-analysis or self-observation.

Feelings of inner unrest and anxiety would be quite likely since not only does he seem to experience his promptings from within as hostile and uncontrollable forces working upon him and which have to be inhibited (to prevent anticipated punishment) but he feels impotent and concerned over controlling outside forces as well.

There is little in the content of his Rorschach responses to indicate truly deep religious convictions or beliefs or needs. In fact, he is not overly interested in other people as individuals and seems primarily concerned with gratifying his deeply ingrained dependent (and oral) needs. He thus would appear to be a basically immature individual, whose self-concept is a very weak one, and who is given to mulling over conceptions of role in life which he considers desirable though unattainable because of external difficulties and/or personal incapacity.

Sexual concerns are also reflected and the quality of his sexual percepts suggest that the man not only has a strong need to constantly affirm his virility but that he is unwilling to come to grips with his basic sexual problems. While the female figure or feminine role is conceived of as being essentially a nurturent one, he at the same time sees the female as frigid, rejecting, castrating and ungiving (especially in terms of satisfying his oral dependent needs). He probably entertains fantasies of a hostile, sadistic nature against the wife (or mother) and in general there seems to be a sensing of unstable equilibrium and tension associated with his relationships with her.

Diagnostically the findings suggest deeply ingrained conflicts and the patient can probably best be described as a neurotic character. Obsessive-compulsive features are most outstanding, and in view, too, of the strong emphasis on repression and denial as mechanisms of defense, hysterical features are also likely.

Jacob was ambivalent about coming into analysis with a Christian, and he was honest about this reservation. I encouraged him to speak freely about his concerns and to ask any questions he cared to ask me. Soon he asked me the expected one: How could I as an intelligent scientist have such an unintelligent religion? My answer was that it is possible to find a mature adult religion in Christianity. Then he wanted to know more, particularly about whether I believed in the Sacraments and whether I received Communion. When I told him that I did, he wanted to know what I really felt about this pagan ritual. I spoke of how I had learned to think about religion in symbolic language and of the symbolic mystical meaning of the Eucharist as a very beautiful way in which we were shown the physical symbols of God's love in the bread and wine. He was quite relieved that I could put it into such language, and he began to tell me more about himself.

I asked him to tell me about his prayer life. How did he feel when he prayed? He told me that he never prayed, that he could not remember when he had last prayed. When he attended services, which he did regularly, it was a disciplined, empty, and meaningless task. I asked him to feel what this meant. I asked him to try to pray and describe to me his feelings. He began to talk about how hungry he was. No one was listening to him. No one paid any attention to him. He was hungry and empty, and he began to have a yearning, whining, crying note in his voice. After a while he sat up. "I can't take this, my stomach is beginning to act up," he complained. "I'll have to take some medicine."

So he went and took some of his stomach medicine and, when he came back, he sat up and we talked about the fact that there was something very, very deep within him, a crying, hungry little baby who never felt heard, either by God now or by mother long ago. Jacob began to tell more about his feelings of being abandoned by his mother, especially after the birth of his younger brother when he was three or four years old, and how hungry he used to get as he watched the little baby nurse. But there was seemingly no way he could make himself understood to either his father or his mother. However, when he started going to Hebrew school, he was able to get some attention from his teachers and soon he began to be an excellent Hebrew student. When he be-came a bar mitzvah, he was the rabbi's joy and pride, but his father did not come to the ceremony. Somehow his terrible yearn-ing that his mother should feed him and his father should under-stand him and love him had never been satisfied. The only person from whom he ever got the encouragement he needed was the rabbi and so he continued with Hebrew school. He began to teach Hebrew in the synagogue and later, when he went to seminary, he found that the one field he really enjoyed was Semitic languages. After he had finished seminary, he went on and got his doctorate. Yet there had always been a feeling that something warm and secure within him was missing. I asked him if he had ever discussed this with his first analyst. He had not. It would have been too humiliating for her to know that he was not devout. With a devout Jewish analyst he would have been embarrassed and humiliated; with an agnostic one, his whole defensive structure would have been reinforced. Only with a devout Christian analyst could he have opened the subject. He added that his doing it would have been extremely unlikely had I not been so honest in admitting to him my own religious de-votion. He had to know about me before he could dare tell me about himself.

I found that owing to his excellent defenses it was almost im-possible to get through to him in private hours. Still, he would provide me with a great deal of material about what was going on in his life, and in the group I would often find ways to make him talk about incidents which I thought important and provoca-tive of group interaction. It was on one such night that with my help the group got him cornered. He became terribly angry with me. He felt I had ridiculed and humiliated him and that the whole group had aided and abetted me. He stormed out of the group telling us that he would never come back. He remained in a rage, angry with everybody. His wife was afraid of him for the first time in their marriage. His students were given the most terrible examinations they had ever received. One day he was in the synagogue, and suddenly he was praying as he had never prayed before.

"Goddammit, God, do something. I've worked, and worked,

and worked, and it's time for you to do something now." For half an hour this man, in his mighty wrath, wrestled with God. The next time I saw him he announced with pride: "By heck, it's up to you and God now. You can do it. God can do it. I'll not do another goddammed thing to help you." This very softspoken man had become abusively angry in a vehement, decisive way. For about two weeks he continued in this very angry vein. Soon after he was asked to read a paper on some theological problem at a meeting of rabbis. He became passionately absorbed in this project and read what he felt was the best paper he had ever written in his life. He was caught up in it and suddenly he felt that here was a message that he had to give these people. Here was something about God they needed to know that he had learned by scholarly research. At the close of the meeting a rabbi whose person, character, and devotion he had always admired gave the benediction. For the first time in his life, Jacob had the feeling of being blessed by a benediction. God was pleased with him, and he had done well. For the first time he had a feeling of fulfillment in his devotion.

There have been many times since when he was profoundly angry with me. Each time he has followed the same pattern. He gets angry with me, then gets angry with God, and in the working through he is able to get rid of some of the attitudes of his father and his mother that have marred and defiled for him the face of God.

Once Jacob came in very, very upset. Before coming into treatment, he had worked out an intellectual, philosophic, naturalistic religion of law and order, but God was so castrated by being bound to the natural order that it could hardly be called a religion.

Now that he was finding a warm, personal religion, he was having trouble harmonizing it with the God of outside reality. There had been an earthquake in the Near East. A thousand people had been injured, and many hundreds killed. Jacob began to rant and rave. "Why did God let this happen to these people? Some of these people were good people, why did it have to happen to them?"

I asked him who it was that was always letting things happen, so that little boys got hurt, and little boys didn't have their supper, and little boys didn't have a clean shirt to wear to synagogue.

"Oh," he said. "Mother?"

I said, "Yes."

He began to see that mother and father had always been very careless about taking care of the reality situation. His father had not done well in business. His mother had not done well as a housekeeper, and so Jacob had the feeling that God wasn't much good as a manager of the universe. When he got the divine reality cleared of all the messiness of the human reality in his childhood, he began to develop an awareness and, in the end, a deep fulfillment.

Jacob had difficulty in understanding the concept of a present state of being in hell. He could not accept a Jewish Gehenna as anything but superstition. He argued that he felt deprived of a sense of devotion; he felt depressed, but he couldn't understand the Christian concept of hell. I asked him when had he ever felt completely abandoned, helpless, and hopeless. When had he felt himself to be judged to be incurably bad and unforgivable? He remembered once when he was eight or nine, he had disobeyed his father on one of his father's worst days. And his father had locked him in the smelly little toilet of his shop and had made a pretense of calling the reformatory. For hours Jacob didn't know it was a pretense. For hours it was real. His father wouldn't listen, wouldn't relent, and any moment he would be taken away. This was his hell. Great is the mechanism of denial!

One of the things that caused strains between us was my observance in group therapy of some of the religious holidays, both Christian and Jewish, as they come along through the year. I do this because it is helpful in forcing patients to work through religious conflicts associated with the particular holidays. Jacob had steadily refused to light the candles and say the blessing on Jewish holidays, though he was frequently the only Jew who knew how. One night during Chanukah I had as usual a menorah and a Christmas tree on the mantel. About half way through the evening I said rather wistfully that I hoped someone would light the menorah. Jacob said he had lit his at home and said his blessings before he came to the group. His duties were completed.

Several of the others spoke about doing it. One of the peripheral Jews said he would light them, except that he would be embarrassed because he did not know which end to start with, nor how many candles to light. One of the Christians said she would like to light them, but she did not know how. Jacob sat there, angelically innocent of the fact that he was not only refusing to light the candles, but making it difficult for anyone else to light them.

I found that I remained annoyed about this, and it is my custom to work through any annoyance which I have with my patients. At the next group meeting I said that I had been annoyed with Jacob and thought it was time to discuss a number of problems hitherto restricted to his private hours, among them religion. He became very angry and said very curtly that he had made quite clear to me the fact that he could not discuss such things in the group.

The group picked up their ears.

I explained to them Jacob's feeling that out of courtesy he ought not speak of his feelings about Christianity in this group because there were devout Christians among them, including clergymen. It would be very inconsiderate if he said anything that would ruin their faith.

This presented the challenge I expected. He was vigorously reassured that there was nothing he could possibly say that would interfere with anyone's devotion.

Then Ben, a devout but nonpracticing Jew, asked Jacob how he felt about my interest in things Jewish. This was the right question. Jacob burst forth with a flood of anger toward me. I was always sticking my nose into things that I had no business being concerned with, and I should stay out. I should stay with my silly Christian God where I belonged, and not poke into things where I wasn't wanted and didn't belong. The extent of his violent, irrational, anti-Christian feelings shocked even him as he heard himself shouting. There was a moment of silence which seemed like hours. Then he turned to Ben and said: "I can't sit here and endure the contempt in which you hold me."

We were able to show Jacob that he was sitting in judgment of himself, and that he had projected this terrible self-hatred onto Ben. He sank deeper and deeper into his suffering, helpless state, until someone remarked, as happens often in groups, that Jacob was the most Christian in the room, being nailed more securely to a Cross. When was he coming off it?

That evening Jacob began to realize we were all concerned for him, that we cared for him and were trying to understand him. Though I had been angry with him at the beginning of the session, my anger had long since dissipated. Jacob slowly emerged from his mood of depression, but there was soberness in the succeeding ten days and the emergence of much greater depth in his personality as a result of our having penetrated so deeply.

Toward the end of that evening Ben spoke again: "What is it that you hate in me?"

Jacob answered: "You saw so deeply into me and, when I don't like what I see in myself, I don't want to have anyone else see so deeply."

This was the turning point for Jacob, and the crux of the whole problem. Those who are truly devout and truly fulfilled in their devotion do not fear having someone see deeply into their souls and minds. But the professional religious person, be he Jew or Christian, is intensely afraid of having anyone skilled in the art of seeing deeply into the human soul realize what he himself knows too unhappily, namely, that he is empty.

When Jacob first found his inner devotion, he kept it as a precious secret between himself and God, giving me occasional glimpses of what was going on. Finally I challenged him. When was he going to begin to share this with his family? He felt it was too new, that he would never be able to share it. Soon, however, he became interested in taking part in services at the synagogue. He was delighted that now he felt real and that he was real and his devotion was real when he read a service. He suddenly knew he wanted to be a rabbi and had always wanted to be a rabbi. His wife and children were overwhelmed. In their attempt to understand, he was forced into talking about his new feelings. The traditional Friday night blessings were brought back. The children, at first confused, became interested and then delighted. His wife confessed that she had always resented that the whole burden of the children's religious life had fallen on her shoulders, but now it had become a shared happiness. Strangely she could never confess her devotion because she knew he suffered because he had none. She was frightened, however, at his being a rabbi. How could she be a rebbetzin, a rabbi's wife? She could give up some of the rebelliousness such as shopping on the Sabbath, but as a Jew she felt so unwanted, unaccepted, that she was nothing. So he had to begin to share his devotion with her, and as he did so he began to know for the first time his real love for her. He was no longer angry with her for not feeding his hungry inner self, and he began to cherish her for herself. He began to tell her why he had come to be proud to be a Jew, and gradually, as he shared his learning, his devotion and his love, she began to bloom in the joy of being loved and loving, and she could dare face the new life ahead.

So Jacob was ordained and called to a busy congregation. Everyone was happy except the university, but it was hoped that he would find time to go on with his teaching and his research.

In Jacob we have the case of a man who in every respect could teach a mature and good religion to his people, but who had been cut off from any inner satisfaction in that religion by the frustrations of his childhood. He was able through therapy to develop into a healthy, energetic, industrious, socially minded person.

✤ ISAAC ✤

Isaac came into treatment after about five years of previous psychotherapy with eminent and well-trained analysts. He was a man of about 54, vital, alive, very intelligent, and a person who worked well in psychotherapy.

He had for many years been unable to go into any house of worship without suffering intense anxiety. He would emerge within a few minutes with the sweat running off his face, his heart palpitating, his breath coming in short quick spasms, and he would leave as if he were escaping from some impending destruction. Any time he went into a temple, synagogue, or church, any time he tried to attend a wedding or a funeral, there would be the same terrible, overwhelming, unbearable anxiety.

When I inquired about his orientation, he gave the intelligent, philosophical, mature attitudes of a well-educated Jew. He insisted that his previous analysts had worked through all of the material well. But, fortunately, he was most cooperative and told again what he had told his previous analysts.

I found that he had come to this country at the age of four from a small village ghetto in Poland, and that, for the first ten years of his life in this country, he lived on the Lower East Side of New York City.

His father had left Poland first, leaving him with a frightened, irrational mother who, in later life, became a severe paranoid schizophrenic. The outstanding memory of his life in the old country was his devotion to his beautiful, affectionate young aunt and his feeling of being completely abandoned when she married. He remembered her wedding, her going away, and his weeping over her. His next memory was of his intense fear, when traveling on the boat with his family to join his father, that the boat would sink and he would disappear into the abyss of the ocean.

When he met his father in New York, Isaac found him a strange, angry, frightened man. Life in New York was difficult. His father had a little shoe shop on the Lower East Side, and the family lived in the back of the store. In many ways life in New York those first few years was even more terrible than life in Europe. His parents seemed even more afraid. Everything was so strange. The city was so big. However, he was able to find a gang of little boys, and these three or four little boys would meet in a cellar and, as little boys do, they would indulge in masturbation.

One afternoon when Isaac had been particularly bad, his father made him stay in the shop and work. Suddenly there was a terrible noise! Everyone rushed out on the street to see what had happened. They found that a cellar wall had caved in. Under the wall were the bodies of three little boys. This tragedy proved to Isaac what he had always been told: the punishment for sin is death, especially for sexual sin.

One summer he was sent to camp by well-meaning Christians who were trying to do good among the poor of the Lower East Side. There he was in terrible fear of the evil magic of these strange people. Before he left for camp his mother taught him how to close his eyes and whisper intently to himself Hebrew incantations against the evil eye of the Christians when they said blessings at meals. It was all very frightening for him.

As he grew older, he tried to talk to his father about the terrible things his mother was doing. She was causing constant embarrassment to him as well as all the rest of the members of the family. She would come to school, rant and rave, and make paranoid accusations against him to the teacher. He was taught that one must honor and obey one's parents. But how could this intelligent little boy honor and respect a mother whose craziness was obvious and humiliating?

His father said, "She's your mother; you must respect her; you must obey her."

The rabbi said, "She's your mother; you must obey her; you must respect her."

Everyone quoted the Ten Commandments to him.

When he was about twelve, Isaac decided to inquire more

into the Christian religion. Maybe there would be more common sense about this irrational command. For a while he found the Christian religion wonderful, and he was about to become a convert when he listened to a sermon on "Honor Thy Father and Thy Mother." He was horribly disillusioned to find that the Christians had the same Ten Commandments that he was trying to run away from. There was another occasion in his twelfth or thirteenth year when he listened to a noted evangelist speak about the horrors and the dangers of sexual sin. He had the feeling that this man was looking right at him, and that he was being accused before all of the people. He broke into a sweat and left.

From that time on he had been unable to go back into either a church or a synagogue without feeling excessive anxiety. On the High Holy Days this devout man would stand all day at the door of the synagogue. Once in a while, he would muster up enough courage to step just inside the door, and would be able to stay as long as three or four minutes before panic became too great. He subscribed large amounts of money to synagogues and to worthy Jewish charities. He was repeatedly asked to become a member of this congregation or that congregation because of these contributions, but he always wiggled out of it. There had been no change in his symptoms, and he insisted that he had told all of these things to the three previous analysts.

I asked Isaac more about the later history of his mother. He told me she had died the year before he had begun therapy with his first analyst. I then asked him what seemed to me a logical question. "And were you able to say kaddish?" [1]

I might as well have struck him across the face. This question had never been asked. And it was the key, because he knew that I knew if he had not said kaddish, then he feared his mother's spirit was still wandering the world, wailing and weeping. Apparently, neither the two Jewish analysts nor the one Christian analyst had sufficiently inquired into the superstitious beliefs of the uneducated Jew, especially the Jew of Poland or Russia. Isaac told me how he suffered during that year after his mother's

---

[1] For a year following the death of a parent the devout Jew goes each day to the synagogue to say kaddish. It is a beautiful prayer of thanksgiving for the blessings God has given us and is used as the traditional prayer of mourning.

death, how many times he went to the door of the synagogue. He did not want to say kaddish for his mother, but he knew that he had to. He was the only son left alive. His father was long since dead. The enormous amount of repressed guilt over a superstition he could no longer believe in, yet which he had devoutly believed in as a child, and which at moments after his mother's death had come to fleeting awareness, could at last be given some expression.

As he was able to realize that for six years he had been condemning his mother to an eternity of lost whirling existence, he was able to begin to reconcile the two parts of himself. The watertight compartments were at last broken down. The little-boy religion and the mature-man's religion came into communication with each other, and the superstitious religion was slowly worked through. The sexual guilt and the real Ten Commandments now became available for contact. There was no longer the emptiness of an intellectual understanding. We now had a working through of real emotional depth so that the benefits of all the previous six years of sound and good psychotherapy were realized. This interpretation was like the keystone of an arch which holds up the whole arch, but when it is removed the arch suddenly collapses.

It was gratifying when, after only a few months, he came to his hour beaming from ear to ear. The night before he had attended a board meeting of the synagogue to which he had been making heavy contributions over a long period of time. He had been invited to these meetings periodically, and this time he impulsively decided he would go. He went in and before he had time to wonder whether or not the old symptoms would come back, he was overwhelmed by the friendly welcome that met him. These people were so happy that he had come. They were so happy that he had decided to be one of them. They told him freely that, as much as they appreciated his contributions of money, they needed him as a member of the board of the congregation. They needed his services. They had always felt badly that he had remained away from them. He was immediately appointed to some post of responsibility so that there was a real reason for his returning to the next meeting. And the following Sabbath he went to the synagogue and was comfortable.

The whole course of his life began to change. He lost interest in his business and turned over more and more of his responsibilities to younger, capable men in his employ. He became engrossed in the life of the synagogue. He served as president of the board of his congregation. He became concerned about his lack of formal training in Hebrew and began to take courses. It was not enough to learn to transliterate the Hebrew so that he could join in the responses. He wanted to understand what he was saying, so he continued his studies. He went to Israel and stayed until his use of conversational Hebrew was excellent, and he felt that by this deep immersion in the life of the Jewish community, he had really become the Jew he had always wanted to be. When he returned he retired from his business and found a home among a community of retired people in a gentle climate. He found that this Jewish community was too small to have a full-time rabbi, so he began tutorial courses with a nearby rabbi and became the lay rabbi of the congregation. Here he has lived for several years enjoying the life of study, worship, and work among his people from whom he was so long exiled.

✣ PATIENCE ✣

Patience came into treatment with me after a series of clerical counselors and one medical analyst had concluded that she was so acutely and severely disturbed that skillful therapy was needed to avoid hospitalization.

I can best describe Patience as she presented herself in her first hour—a bedraggled, starved, frightened little alley kitten. Disproportionally tall and thin for her slender frame, she tried to lessen her gangly height by her stooping, caved-in posture— a picture of intense angularity. She was wearing clothes designed for somebody else. I found out that the unattractive dress she was wearing had been selected for her by her husband as a birthday gift; he too wanted her to be something she wasn't. She was about as unpromising a patient as I have ever seen.

Patience was in her early thirties and looked ten years older; she had borne and tried to care for three children in five years of bitterly unhappy marriage. Shortly before she came into treatment her husband had been critically injured in an automobile accident and had nearly died. There followed many long and difficult months of convalescence during which she began to drink secretly. As she had been brought up in a severe fundamentalist Methodist environment, her chain smoking and drinking were terrible sins to her.

She was the daughter and granddaughter of Methodist ministers and the wife of an Episcopal priest. Her marriage had been very much the reproduction of her parents' tragic one. She was the youngest of a large brood of unhappy children; she was often frightened by the cold quarrels between her parents and the more violent ones between her parents and her siblings. Her siblings were rebellious and brought much shame and humiliation upon the parents. Patience had been the "good" child, trying desperately to please, and never succeeding in meeting the impossible standards her parents and grandparents set for her.

She had the same problem in pleasing her concept of God; she needed the assurance of a conversion experience to know she was "saved." Throughout her childhood she tried desperately at every opportunity, especially at revival meetings. Sometimes she would momentarily "feel" what she thought she was looking for but the "feeling" never lasted more than a few hours and she was left more hopeless and despondent than before.

Patience had met her husband while they were young adolescents; they dated because they couldn't find anyone else rather than because they liked each other. After many years of failure to attract men Patience married the only man who wanted her. His reasons for marrying her were equally negative. They were virgins when they married. Their honeymoon was a nightmare in which she was raped by her equally frightened and anxious husband. Her resistance was expressed in pseudopassivity, with fists clenched as tightly as was her vagina. In consequence penetration had been effected only after repeated attempts which brought out all the latent brutality of an inadequate man. The quickly succeeding pregancies had all been of this pattern: She would delay putting in her diaphragm because she didn't want sex. He would force her and they would have intercourse without protection and she would be pregnant again.

She spoke of her secret and unrealistic fear that her husband would get into trouble and be deposed. She was sure he would divorce her then. She was unable to realize that she herself wanted a divorce although she could speak of her anger toward him. He refused to have any part in the responsibility of caring for the children. In fact, he was rarely home at all. He was busy being a charming and a much-beloved pastor.

She confessed with considerable embarrassment that for many years now she had been unable to pray. Church services were an ordeal. As though it weren't enough to suffer trying to control her brood of restless children, she had to have as her minister the husband she was so angry with. She had to listen to his preaching and take Communion at his hand.[1] This was doubly hard because she knew that she was not in the proper devotional frame of mine to take Communion at all. She was much too angry with God and man, but what would the congregation think if she didn't go regularly to the Communion rail?

After a few sessions and with much trepidation I brought Patience into a therapy group. Although she appeared quite poised I knew she was terribly frightened. The group quickly developed a sensitivity, a protectiveness toward her. Perhaps it helped that, being a fair-skinned blonde, she blushed easily and could rarely conceal her embarrassment. For this overprotected, intensely prudish woman was frequently embarrassed by the often vulgar language of the group, the like of which she had never heard before.

Fortunately, she had a keen intelligence and her need was desperate. She listened and tried to understand that a fantasy was not reality and her marriage vows would not be violated or threatened if she fantasied in her relationship with the men in the group or they with her. There was nothing immoral in enjoying a man's arm around her shoulders and finally she could accept our calling a spade a spade.

It was not difficult to show her that she had been making herself as unattractive as she could as a means of defending herself against her sexuality. It was also an unconscious way of saying "no" to her husband. The men in the group were slowly able to persuade her to say "no" in consciousness to her husband when she was angry and to say "yes" in fantasy in the group. There was never any concern on my part that any sexual acting out would take place after group parties. On these rare occasions, after a drink or two, she could let go and enjoy dancing with an abandon which proved that she was essentially lovely and graceful. The men understood only too well that she could not endure any over-burdening of guilt that would result from overt sexual acting-out.

[1] This is a problem I have found quite often in the wives of clergy. It would be such a relief to them if they could go to some other church where the minister could serve as a good symbol. But tradition insists that the wife should attend her husband's services at *all* times.

In her need to please she responded to every suggestion that the group made. She wore her hair a dozen different ways until she found a way that pleased both the group and herself. She never wore a dress a second time if the group disapproved. She began to thrive on her dawning realization that here were people whom she could not only please but who were most pleased when they knew she was pleasing herself. The group soon realized the danger of the lengths to which she would go to please and soon impressed upon her that what was most important was that she become her real self.

At first Patience's womanliness and warmth were mainly expressed in mothering qualities but after a while, as the group expressed their resentment at being mothered, she became more and more woman. She gained weight and with the new curves came a grace of physical movement. There were moments when she would suddenly become beautiful.

Slowly she began to trust us. Finally she told of her secret which she had never told anyone. In college she had met a man, and they had fallen in love. He went away and was killed in an accident. It had been so brief, so passionate. They hadn't "gone all the way" but she felt she had "gone much too far" and she felt she had been disloyal, for she was engaged to her future husband at the time. She had never dreamed that anyone could forgive her and was amazed that the group could feel only compassion for her loss.

During one session the question of Patience's deliveries came up. Her deliveries had been strangely traumatic; they were all essentially normal but each time she had suffered acutely from a panic of fear and pain. Each time she had bravely denied all that she could. She had an ideal of how a woman should give birth and she suffered greatly because she reacted so differently from the way she felt she should. The worst time was when she had an obstetrician who was applying the new technique of painless childbearing without hypnosis and who lacked the sensitivity to realize that Patience was bravely faking. An edited transcript of this session follows.

BOWERS: What happens when you first start feeling the pain?

How do you feel aware of them? Then what happens?

PATIENCE: Well, they're very low down and they're not too bad at first; but then they get worse and. . . .

BOWERS: But how do they feel?

PATIENCE: They feel as though there's something inside that's just trying to tear you apart.

BOWERS: It's a stretching pain.

PATIENCE: Yes, it's stretching. Yes.

BOWERS: And you can't do anything about it; it's there.

PATIENCE: You know darn well that it has to be, because that's the only way that the baby is going to come out. But it is horrible while it goes on.

BOWERS: It's the helplessness of it.

PATIENCE: Very much so.

BOWERS: How helpless are your feelings?

PATIENCE: Very helpless. You wish that you could press a button, and say, now if this is going to last for five minutes, if I can somehow magically make it last five minutes, then I can last. But the uncertainty of never knowing how long it's going to last; you just have no control. I know in the final stage that you do.

BOWERS: But tell about how this pain just keeps coming in wave after wave after wave. I mean it's absolutely and utterly inexorable.

PATIENCE: And it gets worse and worse; you feel that you're on a boat that's at sea. And each wave gets a little higher and higher and you hold on to the sides of the bed, and you say, how much more can I take. And the waves keep getting higher and higher, and the pain worse and worse.

BOWERS: And the pain keeps coming closer and closer together, so that you can't seem to get your breath between pains. Keep on telling about it.

PATIENCE: And you keep asking and saying, is it going to keep on getting any worse? And you grasp on to whatever hand is closest and you hold on tightly, and you feel sort of lost; won't somebody help you? Won't somebody do something to end this a little bit faster? But nobody cares, that's something you've got to keep on doing yourself.

BOWERS: But does anybody try?

PATIENCE: What can they do?

JOB: But does anybody try?

PATIENCE: They keep encouraging you and saying it won't last, but they don't know what it's like.

BOWERS: Honey, you've never had anyone with you; never. You've never had anyone hold your hand that you know really loved you?

PATIENCE: No.

JOB: You've never had a doctor whom you felt would really take care of you, and just the sound of his voice comfort you?

PATIENCE: Yes.

BOWERS: This is anxiety that you're talking about.

PATIENCE: I think that would make a big difference. I think the main trouble is the pattern that was sort of set by the first doctor's not making it to the hospital in time; and I kept asking for him and asking for him. Is he going to come? Oh, he'll come. But he never did come. And then looking up and seeing this strange man, I mean for the first time. . . .

BOWERS: But honey, it's been so many times that I've walked into a labor room or a cabin out in the woods someplace, and the woman never saw me before.

PATIENCE: Then why do I need it? Other women don't? Why am I so afraid of it, why am I such a coward to pain? I don't want to be. (With sobbing.)

BOWERS: That's what we've got to find out, Patience.

PATIENCE: I'm even scared to let them give me an anesthesia.

BOWERS: Why?

PATIENCE: Because I. . . .

BOWERS: Why, honey?

PATIENCE: I don't know why it is, but the thought of being out any place terrifies me, and it's so ridiculous.

BOWERS: How does it terrify you?

PATIENCE: I can't say exactly how it does, but it does. Going under anesthetic scares me.

BOWERS: Why does it scare you?

PATIENCE: Do all people when they go under panic the way I do? I get the feeling of panic. It's like a period in college when

I couldn't go to sleep at night in panic, for fear I'd never wake up again. And it's the same way when I go under anesthesia.

BOWERS: Well, what happens to you when you don't wake up again, Patience?

PATIENCE: I'll be dead.

BOWERS: And what would happen? What is being dead?

PATIENCE: Being dead is just a terrible fear, of not knowing what's on the other side.

BOWERS: What might be on the other side? What is the most terrible thing that could be on the other side?

PATIENCE: I suppose it's my fear of an angry God.

BOWERS: Is it?

PATIENCE: Or is it just the nothingness?

BOWERS: What is the nothingness?

PATIENCE: I don't know; I don't let myself think of it. I suppose more than the death itself, it's the transition from life to death that frightens me.

BOWERS: How?

PATIENCE: That it will be very very painful.

BOWERS: Why?

PATIENCE: That I want to live so badly, that to suddenly. . . .

BOWERS: Do you want to live so badly, or are you just afraid of dying? What will happen when you die? What will be more terrible than the nothingness?

PATIENCE: Facing an angry God? . . . I hate to go into this again, because you're all. . . .

BOWERS: Keep on, keep on, Patience; we've got to get through it. We've got to get through it; tell us again and again and again; tell us as vividly and as fully as you can.

PATIENCE: An angry Being that I've always taken too vividly the pictures in Revelation in the Bible. That I will be judged and cast into eternal fire.

BOWERS: You're not the Queen of heaven whose manchild is delivered and caught up safe into heaven?

PATIENCE: No.

BOWERS: Tell us; put the cigarette down, honey. Don't . . . let's get into this really; suffer a little more now and you won't suffer so much the rest of your life. Talk about what is the angry God going to do, how is he going to judge you. Why is he angry because you've been angry?

PATIENCE: Because I've been so angry that I just ignored Him, that I haven't wanted even lately to work through my anger, that I haven't wanted to get down and pray.

PHILIP: He's angrier with you since you came to therapy than before?

PATIENCE: Before I could at least go through the motions, Philip, but now I can't even go through the motions.

JOB: Does he like the motions?

PATIENCE: Maybe not, but at least you're sort of trying. Now I just won't even try.

BOWERS: Now you've got your mouth shut and you're staying far away, is that it?

PATIENCE: Yes.

BOWERS: Because He's bad? But how would He torture you, honey?

PATIENCE: No, He's not really bad; He's really good.

BOWERS: How is He good?

PATIENCE: He just is. God is good.

BOWERS: What has He ever done for you that was good?

PATIENCE: Gave me three beautiful children.

BOWERS: How?

PATIENCE: I might have been barren, might have not been able to have children. But I have three beautiful children.

BOWERS: Well, why did He make you suffer so when you had to deliver them?

PATIENCE: Because there's some quirk in me that is so afraid of pain.

JOB: And if there were no pain?

PATIENCE: Then I wouldn't have suffered.

JOB: What made you suffer?

PATIENCE: Nobody, just me. Just me.

ANDREW: Who made you, Patience?

PATIENCE: I can't go that far. I can't. I can only go so far in my anger and being angry at God, but I can't say that He is responsible for these things.

BOWERS: Who is?

PATIENCE: Me.

BOWERS: How did you become responsible?

PATIENCE: I don't know, but I did.

BOWERS: How?

PATIENCE: I'm an individual. I mean, surely He can't be that capricious. You undoubtedly, I'm sure you didn't suffer fear of the pain as much as I do, and yet He made us both.

BOWERS: How capricious is He?

PATIENCE: I can't damn God.

JOB: Ever hear say He's capricious?

ANDREW: Can you damn yourself?

PATIENCE: Yes, I've got to.

ANDREW: Is that what God wants you to do?

PHILIP: Would you like to be angry?

PATIENCE: I suppose I would, Philip. I would like to get angry, but I can't, I'm too afraid of what. . . .

PHILIP: What would happen if you did?

PATIENCE: But that would just be more, more sins upon my head.

PHILIP: What would happen?

PATIENCE: That I'd be damned even more.

PHILIP: And what would He do to you?

PATIENCE: Then there would be no out whatsoever.

PHILIP: An out from what?

PATIENCE: From eternal damnation.

PHILIP: And what is eternal damnation?

PATIENCE: Of being separated from all that I love, of being . . . I think it really comes down to fear of being all by myself.

PHILIP: Bottomless pit?

PATIENCE: Bottomless pit.

PHILIP: What have you been fearing most of your life?

PATIENCE: Being alone.

PHILIP: So what have you been in?

PATIENCE: Bottomless pit. I can reach out and touch. I might not feel close, but I know that somebody's there. But not after death.

BOWERS: But does it do you any good in labor to reach out and touch?

PATIENCE: No.

BOWERS: Why not?

PATIENCE: It would be better than being by myself. I'd go wild if I were by myself. And yet I wonder if maybe I couldn't let go and scream maybe once in a while. I've never been able to do that.

BOWERS: Why not?

PATIENCE: Fear of what people would think of me.

BOWERS: Scream.

PATIENCE: I don't want to scream now.

BOWERS: Scream.

JOB: Go ahead, Patience.

PHILIP: Let yourself go.

PATIENCE: No.

JOB: Yes, you can.

PATIENCE: But I don't want to. (Almost a scream.)

BOWERS: Scream.

PATIENCE: I don't want to.

BOWERS: Scream.

PATIENCE: Don't! (Cries)

BOWERS: Scream.

PATIENCE: Stop! (Crying) Oh! Oh!

JOB: Scream.

BOWERS: What are you thinking about? Tell us what you're thinking.

PATIENCE: I was thinking I was in the labor room.

BOWERS: Tell us about it. How do you feel now?

PATIENCE: Oh, so scared. So scared. I wanted to scream, but I couldn't.

JOB: Would it be easier to scream if somebody held your hand?

PATIENCE: No, I'd have to be all by myself to scream.

BOWERS: Scream.

PATIENCE: I can't.

BOWERS: Yes you can.

PATIENCE: I pushed it down.

BOWERS: No, let it go, scream. If Philip puts his arm around you, can you scream?

PATIENCE: No—

BOWERS: Try.

PATIENCE: What good would it do?

BOWERS: Try it though, try it, Patience. Scream.

PATIENCE: (Weeping loudly) I can't.

BOWERS: Scream.

PATIENCE: (Cries) I can't.

BOWERS: Let go—scream. Let go and scream.

ALL: Scream.

PATIENCE: No, I feel better now.

BOWERS: Just relax. When did you feel like that before?

PATIENCE: Many times. The worst was in the labor room those three times. I used to have it continually those months before I came into treatment. I'd go up to my room and I'd want to scream and scream and scream. And then the children would come up and say, "What's the matter, Mommie? and I'd say, "I'm just tired," and have to push it all down again. I guess I've never been able to get to the point where I could really let it go.

BOWERS: Nobody is going to die if you scream. And God isn't going to thunderbolt all to hell if you scream.

PATIENCE: Is that what's holding me back from screaming? Well, you know, I think I could now if the moment arose, but it's past; I really feel it's much more peaceful.

BOWERS: You see, honey, God doesn't want you as a sacrificial victim who must be so good, so patient on the altar while the knife is plunged in.

PATIENCE: But this is what is so distressing. Why does it take so long for one to really feel something like this? We went through this the other night when you helped me so beautifully. Why haven't I been able to work through it yet? Why does it take so long?

ANDREW: How long did it take me? You have to keep going over and over it until you get it.

BOWERS: How long did it take to develop, Patience? How old are you?

PATIENCE: Thirty-one.

BOWERS: It's been thirty-one or-two years making, you know.

PATIENCE: That's reassuring.

ANDREW: Think how much you got rid of of that thirty-one years in such a short time.

PATIENCE: Because after I . . . oh, when I hit low again, I think . . . what's wrong with me? After all that work and love that I should not be sure that I am loved. And that I needn't be afraid.

BOWERS: Did it feel better when Philip held you?

PATIENCE: Uh-huh, it felt very good.

BOWERS: Did you know that he loved you before he put his arm around you?

PATIENCE: Yes, but that made it even more sure.

BOWERS: Did you know that Andrew loved you?

PATIENCE: Yes.

BOWERS: Did you know that Job loved you?

PATIENCE: Yes.

BOWERS: Did you know that Mark loved you?

PATIENCE: Job frightened me. I know that Job loves me, but he frightened me too much. But I know he does.

BOWERS: Job just doesn't want you to push him away.

PATIENCE: And I don't want to.

JOB: I was the one who wanted to scream really.

PATIENCE: I wish you had. Maybe I could scream with you. I do feel much better though; something sort of broke inside.

BOWERS: Some of the iron core went out. How about you, Job?

JOB: This threw me way, way back. I was just screaming like a little baby, absolutely hopeless, perfectly furious. I—I was Patience's baby.

PATIENCE: I had that feeling.

BOWERS: Yes.

JOB: I was terribly angry. Terribly hopeless and alone. As if you were not giving me something.

PATIENCE: I was.

JOB: Not giving me something. You were pushing away.

PATIENCE: That I was so concentrated upon. . . .

JOB: If you had screamed, I think it would have been all right.

PATIENCE: Why? Why?

JOB: You could only cry, and somehow or other that was violating. If you had screamed it wouldn't have been.

PATIENCE: I don't follow that.

JOB: Neither do I.

PHILIP: Because if you had screamed, you wouldn't have been alone and neither would Job. Job would have been with you. You see?

PATIENCE: Yes, I do.

ANDREW: The scream would have included us rather than. . . .

PATIENCE: Yes—pushed away.

ANDREW: But not doing it meant something was still set back. You weren't free to give.

PATIENCE: Yes.

BOWERS: That's why I said maybe you could scream if Philip held you, because you were sitting there so alone.

JOB: But you were rejecting me. I don't mean about the torture fantasy, but you were rejecting me.

PATIENCE: As the baby, I was.

JOB: As if I were a baby you had inside of you.

PATIENCE: I was.

HIRAM: Patience, you treat the whole world as though they're your children and you mustn't distress them.

PATIENCE: What you said last week was very meaningful to me, about what you said to your mother, your vow, because I think that's very true. I'm somehow afraid I will lose love if I do distress, and yet you don't gain it if you don't. If you do keep that down.

BOWERS: You push it all away.

PATIENCE: You do push it away, yes.

ANDREW: So hard to see.

PATIENCE: It is.

ANDREW: Isn't everyone in here involved with this somehow?

BOWERS: Yes, but when we let you see our pain, then we let you in. Do you see what I mean? You see, Andrew, you let the whole of us in during the prayer of consecration.

ANDREW: It's so hard to trust, though.

JOB: Well, Patience has me inside of her and she. . . .

ANDREW: Boy, I was feeling right along with Patience like mad.

BOWERS: But she really loves you, Job.

JOB: I know, but she won't show me.

PATIENCE: I do, but I'm just afraid of the pain that you will cause. I know that it's only momentary.

HIRAM: In other words, Job was describing childbirth to you.

BOWERS: That's why I wouldn't let you stop. You see what I mean, I knew what was going on.

PATIENCE: Yes, exactly.

JOB: Do you know all the pain I suffered?

PATIENCE: While it was going on?

JOB: And after.

PATIENCE: I'm beginning to see it.

BOWERS: Do you see the pain he suffers when these fantasies are underneath his disintegration? And do you remember how disintegrated you were when you came into treatment?

PATIENCE: Yes. I feel it now.

JOB: And how I tried to kill myself when I was a little baby? Not once, but fifteen times.

PATIENCE: At a time when a child should feel the most love. And you wanted to kill yourself. But he didn't feel loved, and that's what I mean, he didn't. That's the tragic part.

BOWERS: Can you love Job now?

PATIENCE: Very much so.

HIRAM: How do you solve the problem of loving the newly born child after all the pain?

JOB: I don't see how that's really a problem.

HIRAM: It's a serious one.

JOB: Well, the more you do for somebody, the more you love, and if you suffer a great deal, then you're going to love them much more, all the more.

HIRAM: I don't agree with that.

BOWERS: No. It doesn't—

PATIENCE: No, I think that would make you angry, Job.

BOWERS: It makes you angrier. You cannot love someone who had caused you intense pain such as Patience describes; you cannot love a child whose birth is a memory of pain; that's it exactly. The thing is that there is something in the miracle of normal birth, so it's as if the pain had never happened.

HIRAM: The attempt to handle this has given rise to the self-sacrifice story.

BOWERS: But you see, you see it's in her aloneness that she has suffered. You see, what she has described is the suffering of anxiety and not of physical pain. This is the aloneness where no one would help you, no one would really reach out to you; there was no one there that you felt loved by and cared for by. I suspect that a good 90 per cent of your pain has been the anxiety of isolation and abandonment.

PATIENCE: It must be, because I don't have long labors.

HIRAM: You used to boast of your efficiency of delivery.

PATIENCE: Yes, I am very efficient as far as that goes.

BEULAH: I was thinking of my mother. She was a small woman. If she was five feet tall that was all. I think they said she had her babies like kittens. They came so easily to her. She must have had five babies in seven years; and I kept on thinking of these waves, and sort of thinking of a pleasurable sensation, and I also kept on thinking of, I wonder how it would have been with me if I had had children; and again it's probably fantasy. I've never thought of that as terrifically painful; just very naturally, just coming through.

Patience began to respond to therapy on a much deeper level and brought to the group a dream of kicking a baby sister down the stairs. This dream had been of such vivid nightmare quality that she had gone to her parents and asked them questions, and told us that she found out that when she was two years old she had had a baby brother. She had reacted to this sibling's birth very severely and when her jealousy was punished she had competed by becoming ill and for several months seemed much sicker than her sibling. Then the baby had died and she "forgot all about it." But with the dream and its historical verification vague memories came back. She felt like a murderer as she remembered how she had been punished for hitting the baby. She realized that she was accusing herself of her successful death wishes and she began to understand her overanxious, overprotective concern for her own children, her fears of being a bad mother.

Now we could begin to understand her breaking down when her husband had nearly died. Now she could tell us about the

accident, of how, while she was driving and they were quarrel-
ing, she had stopped at a red light and the car behind them had
run into them. Her husband had been seriously injured. She
had had a few ribs broken. She insisted it was all her own fault
even though everyone, including the police, assured her that it
was not. We told her, when she stopped crying long enough to
listen, that she felt it was her fault because she wished him dead
in her anger. Then she told us that the lover whom she had lost
had left her angry because of her denial of him sexually and had
died before they could forgive each other, or have each other.

Patience's most difficult times in the group occurred when she
sensed the least anger in me or projected onto me the expected
disapproval of the transference. Then she would withdraw into
herself and be very quiet. After my annoyance or my anger was
expressed and dissipated or shown to be unreal, she would relax
and tell us I had become her angry, stern, suffering father. Her
father had never punished her when she confessed to a misdeed.
He would pray with her for God's forgiveness and be very
quiet and sorrowful for a few days. He taught her that we hurt
God when we are bad and that God suffers because of our sins
and that is why Christ suffered crucifixion for our redemption.
As she worked through all this incorporation of her father's
distorted projections onto his God-idea, she became freer in her
anger toward me. Finally she could challenge me as soon as she
sensed the least trace of annoyance in me, or projected onto me
and tell me to stop being her father and examine her transference
attitudes toward me as well as toward God.

Many months later while we were trying to get her to express
some more of her anger, the group got into fantasies of cruelty.
This time they were sexual fantasies. There was a teasing, gentle
quality about them. Suddenly Patience went flying out of the
room. Job caught her and held her while she trembled and
sobbed. Finally she could tell us that only if she suffered would
anyone love her. Only if she let people mistreat her would they
love her. This time she needed very little help to understand her
self-imposed martyrdom. She had learned better ways to find
love. She wanted no more of this.

Some time later she told us that she had been to a retreat with her husband. They had quarreled and she was quite angry. The sermon that morning was on how one should not go to Communion in anger. By this time her prayer life was usually good and fulfilled, and she knew that as the preacher had just instructed her that it was her duty to pray that God would help her forgive her husband. But she found herself telling God very plainly that she was right to be angry and she didn't want and didn't intend to forgive her husband so soon. She wanted to hold onto her anger a while yet. Then she went up to the altar rail because what would people think if she didn't, and received Communion. Suddenly she felt a wonderful sense of peace and love such as she had never felt before. This was the "grace of sudden conversion" she had tried for so desperately as a child. As she told us her face was illumined and beautiful. This was real.

Patience now had the inner security to face her marriage. She was as unwilling as ever to have a divorce but now she could face her wish to have one. She and her husband began to have serious talks and he decided to go into treatment. She could begin to look into the ways that she mothered him and assisted him in his own self-destructive needs. As mutually destructive patterns were discarded they were each finding self-integrity and mutual respect. Slowly they seem to be developing the maturity to love each other.

As her unconscious wishes to castrate and kill her husband have been freed and have come to consciousness, she is slowly developing vaginal sensation. She is remembering her childhood fascination in descriptions of torture. As her husband becomes more of a man, so that he too will not need to prove how she has ruined him, their mutual anger will lessen. She will in time undoubtedly achieve sexual maturity.[2]

[2] Two years later Patience has a happy and fulfilled marriage and is experiencing regular orgasm.

✤ JOHN ✤

John came into therapy voluntarily. He was a vital, exciting, intelligent young man in his late twenties, doing excellent work as a parish minister, already getting a name as a preacher. Neither he nor his bishop quite understood why he needed psychotherapy, but his internist helped him masquerade it as an interest in gaining more training in counseling. John was having too many serious psychosomatic illnesses. Just a few weeks before he had been in the hospital for ten days recovering from severe abdominal pain with several days of vomiting, yet very careful medical studies had revealed no explanation. The winter before he had been taken with pneumonia twice. This, said his internist, was too much.

It soon became apparent that John's cheerfulness had a forced frenetic quality about it. He was really more unhappy and anxious than he realized. He could not relax and was always on the go. He worked long hours in his parish, was painfully conscientious about his counseling, suffered during his preparation of sermons, and finished each Sunday completely exhausted, often with prostrating headaches.

The oldest child in a large family, his mother had become pregnant within the first few weeks of her marriage. She was just beginning to respond to the experience of motherhood when she became pregnant again. This proved to be too much for her. She took to her bed and stayed there, vomiting, unhappy, and suffering.

John grew up lonely and feeling unwanted, shut out by all his family. He hated his brother who seemed to occupy all his mother's attention. He hated the other siblings who followed. He could never talk to his mother, who developed a pattern of going to her room and shutting the door whenever she was upset and angry. He felt ridiculed and humiliated by his father.

181

In his terrible need for acceptance John became a "good boy," his mother's helper. He learned to take care of his siblings and helped with the housework and the cooking. In school he was teased for being a sissy and could never join in games with the other boys. As an unhappy adolescent he found an equally lonely girl friend whom he married when he was still in college. Their parents said they were much too young but didn't seem to care otherwise.

He had some difficulty in making up his mind about his vocation. His interest in the natural sciences, his curiosity and pleasure in using his mind, tempted him at first to go into astronomy. Then he began to realize that there was something else that he wanted, and wanted desperately. At last, following in the footsteps of other members of his family who had made names for themselves in the Church, he entered the seminary and became an outstanding and brilliant student. Although he was exceptionally qualified in every respect, he remained restless and unhappy. Not that anyone ever knew this, because he was compulsively happy, compulsively cheerful, and compulsively satisfied. Still the pressures eventually became so severe that he began searching. At first he did not know even remotely what was driving him. He would take his wife to bars and nightclubs with the rationalization that he wanted to see "how the other half of humanity lived." He felt he wanted to be able to carry his ministry to sophisticated groups of people. He tried to "understand human nature." He took courses in counseling and spent more and more time listening, trying to counsel his parishioners. Because he was an extremely good-looking man, a large proportion of his counselees were, of course, unhappy, frustrated women.

In the meantime, poverty became a factor because his wife was having so many babies. Moreover, the more babies she had, the less he felt that she really understood him, and the more hours he put in counseling the unhappy, frustrated women of his parish.

As John continued to talk of the deep frustrations of his life, a period of slowly developing depression began coming over him for the first time he could remember. He seemed to be reliving the loss of his infancy. One morning he awoke from a dream he could not remember with the persistently repetitious thought, "I've lost my mother, I've lost my mother, I've lost my mother." Then he began talking historically of how he had "lost his mother" when he was six months old at the time she conceived her second child. He began to realize that the pattern of his grief reaction was that of a very young baby, which he was reliving.

Further cues began to present themselves. Although he was unable to find any happiness in his first child, with the birth of a second child he began identifying with the first one. To John, here was another poor displaced baby who had lost his mother. Each time they had a child he felt more unhappy, more restless, and yet, on looking into the case, we found that every single one of his wife's pregnancies had been due to his wish and decision. Once a baby was about four months old, he would begin to persuade his wife that they should have another baby. He was driven to recapitulate the experience of his childhood so that every one of his children had to endure the trauma of a mother whose succeeding pregnancy came much too soon. At the moment she conceived her first baby, his wife ceased to be the mother, the beloved virgin mother, and became the betraying mother, the mother who left him or banished him when he was such a tiny baby.

This symptom was also displayed in the therapy group. In his transference, the group was his hated family, rejecting and ridiculing him as his father had done. Like his mother, I had betrayed him by having other children (the group) before he had a long enough time with me to become secure in his relationship with me.

One night in the therapy group a fellow member had confessed a peccadillo which he considered a terrible sin and humiliation. The group was pleased and gratified at my handling of the material and at the response of the penitent. John could not see why it was so wonderful. His wife, he said, was as understanding as I was every day; besides, I was understanding only once in a long while and never for him. An older group member picked this up, skillfully and gently showing him that while it was part of my work at times to be an understanding mother, what husband would want to make his wife into such a full-time mother? John got the point but went on a month's "vacation" from therapy.

Progress was necessarily slow in the face of resistance. John was adept at maneuvering the group away from his problems, yet once in a while such psychosomatic illnesses as severe back-aches and gastro-intestinal disturbances would force him into working on them. At other times he would complain of a general-ized feeling of severe and unexplainable anxiety.

The first time John felt anxiety during the religious services was when his parents visited him. For the first time in his life he was able to talk with his mother and was discovering her to be overly sensitive but warm and lovable beneath the customary withdrawn silence. He began to realize how much she had been hurt, as he had been, by the clumsy and often cruel teasing of his father. He had become violently angry against his father but as usual could say nothing about it. It was progress, however, that at least he had become consciously aware of his anger. That Sunday morning his anxiety intensified all through the Communion serv-ice. Never before had he remembered feeling such anxiety nor had he related his anger to his anxiety for he had never felt this anger during the service. Why? It wasn't Christian to have anger in one's heart at such a time. "But," I asked, "if you had felt the anger what would have happened?" "My father would have died," was the answer. I asked why. The answer came, "If I wished it, or prayed for it during the Communion it might have happened." I said, "Really?" He answered that he knew it wasn't logical but magically he felt it might happen. So I said "try it." He regarded it as a childish game, but reluctantly decided to try out his "magical powers." The next Sunday he did and his father's brother dropped dead the following day. He lectured me severely, telling me that if he hadn't been capable of reasonable logical thinking he would have believed he had accidentally killed an innocent bystander. A week later the wife of a vestrymen died and he went into an inexplicable anxiety attack when told of the news. He felt too upset to conduct the funeral service. After analyzing the death in the light of his recent analysis he suddenly remembered what a difficult and demanding person she had always been and also remembered how on one occasion she had been so unusually provoking that he had wished her dead. He had been shocked at his wish at the time and had promptly dismissed it from his mind. Now he could realize that the cause of his anxiety came from a fear that his magic might have been effective. Reasoning with himself that he really did not have omnipotent control over life and death his anxiety left him.

It became evident that sharing a "mother," in the person of myself, with all of his group was just too much for John to endure. He transferred to a male therapist where he could feel for a time that he was the "only" one. Thus relieved of his intense anxiety, he began to experience a security with his new therapist that he had never been able to enjoy with his mother or with me. He took leave of the group and settled down to the long and hard work of growing up in the "little me" part of himself.

Thus our story ends as his real adventure into therapy was just beginning. It will be for someone else to write the story of how John "grew up" and gave up the omnipotent magical needs of the "little-me" within himself.

❧ PHILLIP ❧

Phillip came into treatment voluntarily at age twenty-three. His increasing sense of despair and loneliness had impelled him to plan to go into therapy for several years but he feared that undergoing treatment while in seminary might adversely affect his brilliant academic career. He had finished seminary with high grades and had secured one of the most prized curacies in the city.

Phillip was the eldest of three children. His father was a research pathologist who had become outstanding professionally. He was fond of his first-born son, loved playing with him, and he naturally wanted to share his absorbing life work with him. He used to take the small boy to the autopsy room when he had an autopsy to do. It seemed perfectly natural for him and the mother made no protest. It often saved spending money on a baby-sitter when she wanted to be out shopping or playing bridge.

No one realized the fascinated horror the autopsy room had for little Phillip. No one knew that he was much too young to understand that the naked corpse on the marble slab was already dead when his father started to cut with his terrible sharp knives. Phillip thought his father had killed these helpless people. Phillip's mother reinforced this idea by calling his father a butcher in their angry quarrels.

When his mother went away to the hospital to have a baby, Phillip felt lonely and lost. He was afraid his mother would die and never come back. Life alone with his father was somehow happy and frightening at the same time. After his mother and the new baby returned, Phillip began to feel actually lonely and unwanted.

He hated his baby brother and began to have temper tantrums. Once his mother became so enraged by his outburst that she

186

held him under a shower until he almost drowned. That stopped the tantrums! He became more docile and tried to please his mother. She had come of a family of musicians and it was her ambition that Phillip should be the musician she had failed to become. Music lessons were started before he began to go to school. He practiced long hours on the piano to please his mother and at the same time he made good grades in school to please his father. And he was an unhappy, lonely little boy.

As the years went on the conflict between the parents and their attempts to express themselves vicariously in their oldest child grew more pronounced. The father felt that all the mother's emphasis on culture and classical music was making a sissy out of Phillip. He had no musical appreciation, except for popular jazz which the mother abhorred. So Phillip hated jazz too, and spent hours listening to good music or practicing while the other children were out playing football or baseball.

The quarrels between the parents became more frequent as Phillip learned to be most adept at maneuvering them. He encouraged his mother to divorce his father, and when he was fourteen he succeeded. For a long time he remembered his triumph. Only later did he remember his strange unspoken pleas to his father not to leave.

When his mother sought counseling from the unmarried and attractive Episcopal rector (her Presbyterian pastor was so unsympathetic, she felt) Phillip also became interested in him, but he had a harder time gaining access to him than had his beautiful mother. He had to take music lessons from the organist, join the choir, and then the confirmation class. The day he was confirmed he and his mother had their first bitter quarrel and he left the house angrily, took her new car and almost consciously drove into a telephone pole. He smashed the car and escaped with a few bruises. Soon after that he announced his intention of going into the Episcopal ministry which created countless opportunities for long hours of talk with the rector. Then, one day the rector put his arm around his shoulder. From that time on it was easy. The rector explained that their relationship was in no way homosexual—"they loved each other."

Now he had succeeded in the second competition for his

mother. He had gotten rid of his father, and he had taken a potential lover away from her. But while he was away at college his mother married again. He felt bewildered and betrayed. How could she do this to him?

In seminary he realized that his rector's rationalization of their relationship was unacceptable to the church. He broke off the relationship slowly, never being unfaithful to this jealous and powerful father-in-God.

He had little reason to come home. His mother was happy with her new husband, whom Phillip cordially despised, and his father was happy with his new wife. His brother was going to medical school. They had never had anything in common. He had given up his music while in seminary, which made him even lonelier. It had been years now since he had touched the piano. He was disciplined, celibate, and lonely. He occasionally dated girls in a romantic, adolescent fashion but had never had any real relationships with anyone.

In his first therapy hour, Phillip keenly resented my probing into his personal religious life. He had been brought up a Presbyterian and had always known he was "saved." As an Episcopalian convert he was above such things. He expressed a contempt for people who worried about life after death. There was none. When you were dead that was it. There was, he bravely contended, no heaven and no hell. He had no personal prayer life. He believed in a religion of natural order as a foundation for an ethical code of morality, beauty, and the brotherhood of man.

In his next hour he said that he had never understood why his mother had remarried. They were each so independent, so self-sufficient; he could never understand why she needed to marry another man.

I suggested that inasmuch as he had never had a satisfactory relationship with his father and had shown such a need of a man to identify with he should have an hour with my male associate. I was concerned because he seemed to have such a need to please me and in trying to ingratiate himself with me he became more feminine and childlike. He came back a week later and reported that he had seen my associate for two hours. The first hour he had been very enthusiastic about my suggestion. He felt a pleasure in being dominated by a man. In the second hour he had turned tables on my associate and had very skillfully outmaneuvered him. He realized that this would be an untherapeutic situation. He said that he realized that he would not be able to outmaneuver me, at least not all the time. There were times, however, that he did. One time he caught me off guard and kissed me lightly on the cheek as a shy little boy might have done. Always when he loved me as his mother he was fragile-seeming and very young. When he was angry with me he would then become strong and masculine.

About four months after treatment began, his long-expressed bitter anger began to break through to the surface. In individual hours he began drawing pictures of his newly uncovered angry God. His certainty about salvation was a thin façade which had to crack.

The first picture was mostly covered with a dense black smudge, with a small figure at the bottom of the page. Phillip described his feelings about it. "Strong, angry. Throwing shit on God and the Heavenly Host. He's never done anything for me. My mother said He was so wonderful. If I'd be a good boy, I'd be happy. I've always been good and He's never done a thing for me."

The next day Phillip drew a picture of a figure tied to a rock with the sun glaring down. He said of this one: "Prometheus—God—when the sun goes down and the moon comes up. Then the sun will come up and they'll eat it again and *I'm glad*." The next picture was of a cruel Oriental God with a crown and long, pointed beard, sitting crosslegged, breaking people in his hands and dropping them into hell (at the bottom of the page). He wrote on this: "They want bread? Give them cake!! Ha! Ha! Ha!" In the next picture he drew himself in red vestments lined with green. His hands were stretched out in a welcoming gesture. On his left was a sign pointing upward reading "Heaven" and there was a long stream of people going up to the Pearly Gates. As they went through they were shown falling through into the flames of hell (also in red) above his head. Phillip explained: "I'll really enjoy camping when I'm celebrating Holy Communion with the gestures of my hand and wrist so that the sleeve folds beautifully, the profound bow, the beautiful singing. I'm sending them all to Heaven, they walk through the Pearly Gates and fall into hell and I follow them." When I studied this picture I found that although he had drawn himself in Communion vestments he had not drawn a stole. Since the stole is the symbol of the priestly authority this omission indicated that he really didn't want to act this out in life.

I realized that he needed more scope in which to act out all this angry, exhibitionistic aggression. He was doing well in his all-male therapy group where he was finding a much-needed brotherhood. He needed some place other than his parish where he could let go and shock people if he was to get through therapy without getting into trouble. So I transferred him into a mixed group where he proceeded to shock the daylights out of people. In the group we had a dedicated, hardworking, self-righteous Episcopalian vestryman who had refrained from going into the ministry because he felt he wasn't good enough. Gideon, as we shall call him, was Phillip's cup of tea. Never has anyone had a more responsive, more gullible audience. Gideon took every fantasy of Phillip's on his angry God, and on himself as the partner-in-crime as well as the tortured sacrifice as an accomplished fact, literally and unequivocally.

When it was time for Phillip to be ordained as priest he knew he wasn't ready and we had some serious hours both privately and in the group. The clergy in both groups agreed with me that in time Phillip would find his vocation and his devotion because, through it all, he had shown a well-disciplined theological grasp of what was healthy and what was distorted religious thinking and feeling. It was socially difficult to delay the ordination. The situation was much like the night before a grand wedding when the guests have arrived and wedding gifts are all over the place. Both bride and groom agonize over their doubts. Although I regretted that he had not come into treatment when he first entered seminary, we felt confident that in time he would work through it all and be a good minister.

Gideon alone couldn't accept our assurances. He felt he had a conscience, "if no one else did." He insisted that he would have to do his duty as a Christian lay person and when the question was asked in the ceremony if anyone knew of any impediment, he, Gideon, would have to stand up and denounce Phillip.

We realized that Gideon was really serious and we all tried hard to show him that, while it was too soon, it was right. Phillip took Gideon's doubts seriously, and for the first time revealed to himself and to us the depth of his sincere convictions about his vocation. At last Gideon seemed satisfied and at two o'clock in the morning we ended the session.

A few days later Phillip was ordained a priest and we felt the crisis was past. Gideon and Phillip became warm friends and Phillip felt that, for the first time in his life, he had found a man who was a good father and a brother with whom he could identify.[1]

About this time Phillip had an argument with one of the men in his other group. This was a very angry man who had had quite a lot of training in boxing and was always going to the gym to keep in trim. In addition to his physical readiness, he was a good two inches taller and probably thirty pounds heavier than our slender Phillip. Just as I thought I would have to intervene, the bigger man backed down and I heard a quality of controlled anger in Phillip's voice that made me understand why he had backed down. In another age Phillip might have been dressed in

[1] Gideon left treatment a few months later and we could not understand why. He had hardly begun to uncover, let alone work through, the many layers of his self-righteousness which had brought about the severe depression that had brought him into treatment. He had made little effort in therapy after his depression had lifted and especially after Phillip was ordained.

Many years later Phillip's rector told me that Gideon had come to him and told him of his conscience doubts about Phillip. Interestingly, he told Phillip's rector only of his fears of Phillip's distorted theology. The rector had sternly told him that what he had told he had learned under the seal of confession and that Gideon should keep his lips sealed. The rector said he had confidence in me as a therapist and that he was certain that if I approved it was right and proper for Phillip to be ordained. The rector could tell me now because it was evident that he had been right to trust my judgment. We were both very pleased with Phillip and the man and priest he had become.

This is the only instance of betrayal of confidence in the ten years I have worked with clergy in the group therapy setting. I have always regretted that we never knew the burden of guilt that Gideon bore and which was probably the reason he could not go on in therapy. Like Judas he went away.

a string tie, a black suit, and in a quick draw would have killed his man with a bullet between his eyes. He was of the stuff that made successful Mississippi River steamboat gamblers. Then I realized why he was so afraid of his anger that he could kill. He knew that he would kill rather than be killed. For this reason, he had not been able to enjoy identification with his father whom he considered a killer.

Phillip had seemed happy in the actual performance of sacred services although he was bitterly lonely and unhappy in his personal and religious life. He became increasingly restless, not knowing what to do with his energy. He began to take modern dance lessons, drawing lessons, foreign language lessons, and finally I asked him about his music. He got a piano and began to practice many hours a day. He didn't know why it seemed to ease the restlessness; at least it kept him busy. He was pleased with his polished, graceful performance at the altar. He was the first one who helped me to understand the Eucharist as a Sacred Dance. He had a beautiful voice and had been trained as a singer so that he was unusually well equipped to do what he wanted to do at the altar.

In response to Andrew's months of working through his personal distortions of the meaning of Holy Communion, Phillip's defenses in relation to the Eucharist began to crumble. He expressed the wish that he could have worked through this with the group instead of in the set-apartness of the sanctuary, where he had to go through what was for him the same agony but where he had to do it alone and in the knowledge that this was for real. Phillip experienced a great feeling of loneliness and anger; he identified himself as the beloved Son who was sacrificed, and although he said the words beautifully and clearly, he learned not to hear them any longer in their literal meaning. He experienced a nonverbal, happy sense of relationship to God at the altar, a feeling that must have been previously experienced in early childhood. He had faint memories of happy times playing with both his father and his mother, and as long as he stayed in the realm of primary-process thinking, unconsciously symbolizing the time when he was loved and happy, Holy Communion was a happy, beautiful, and fulfilling devotion for him. He said that once in a while he forgot and heard the words in their literal meaning; at such times his anger at his angry God would return.

A few weeks after Phillip had helped me with his angry young strength to put Andrew through his ordeal in the prayer of consecration, he expressed the wish to celebrate the Eucharist in the group. The group was of one accord, everyone feeling that it would be good for Phillip to bring his own conflicts into the shared experience of the group. I made only one request: no one was to be denied Communion. Phillip asked me if I meant Job, an assimilated Jew. I said I did and Phillip agreed, irregular as it was. The service was a profoundly devotional one for everyone. Andrew served as acolyte. Phillip chose for the Epistle, Isaiah 63.4, "For the day of vengeance is in my heart." When it was over we broke the tension with the Kiss of Peace and asked Phillip to tell us about it. He was pleased because he felt for the first time that he had shared with, and brought in, his congregation. I was the only one he excluded, but he could not tell me why.

In spite of all we could do, the performance of the Communion service was becoming too terrible for Phillip to endure. He had to work through his distortions of the sacrifice. So when his contract as a curate ended, Phillip asked for permission from his bishop to do secular work for a year. He didn't know if he wanted to stay in the ministry or to study medicine. He practiced the piano and slowly and painfully worked through his distorted, unhappy childhood and the image of his angry Father-God who so loved his Son that He killed Him. He had many fantasies of his father and mother being fatally injured and comforting them in their dying. There were endless variations of this theme in his preoccupation with death. He drew two pictures during this period. One was of an angry man holding a small boy by the neck and swinging a hammer with the other hand. The second was of a recurrent nightmare of being in a long, dark tunnel with a slave collar around his throat, chained to the wall and the floor so that he couldn't move without choking. His first association to this was of his mother holding him under the shower till he

nearly drowned. But as we went deeper into it he began to remember his fascinated horror in the autopsy room and all his
fantasies that his father really killed people with his knife.

He fell in love with an older woman and for a few weeks he
was happy. He was thrilled with the excitement of being a man
in a sexual relationship with a woman. Too soon he realized that
she was as possessive as his mother had been. When he stayed
away from her a few days she got sick. Then he was sure he had
found his mother and it was over. He had had enough of his
mother.

Some time after that, perhaps in response to my own illness,
we got bogged down in a period of negative transference which
neither of us could understand. He couldn't remember any
dreams or give me any other clues. So I suggested to him that I
listen to him play. He was flattered at first, then quite skeptical.
He was sure I wouldn't be able to sense anything through his
playing. But it was worth a try. So I went over to his apartment,
and listened while he played for over three hours. Once in a
while he would speak to me and I would encourage him to go
on. At first the music was the beautiful classical music his mother
had taught him to love and I knew he was making love to me as
his mother. There was some sad music I later learned was a
funeral march, then suddenly he was playing jazz. He was im-
provising, he told me later, because he had never played jazz
before in his life and had no scores in the house. He asked me
if I liked it. I said I did and he seemed happier. I knew he was
playing happily with his father, that somehow he and his father
were happy together and I was his father now. Then he was off
on his own, far away and very happy. I knew he had left me far
behind. This music was for someone and with someone he would
some day find and love as a man does a woman. The phone rang
and the dream was broken. It was late and as he walked me
home he asked me what I had learned. I told him that deep inside he knew what he had told me and in the succeeding days he
would let it come to consciousness. Slowly it did and with it
came also his awareness that in the playing he had begun to find
moments of devotion that he had never experienced before.
Gradually this feeling of freedom and of devotion deepened.

One day he was asked to supply during the vacation of a curate and he was excited. It was a High Church parish and he was delighted to be able to celebrate sung Eucharist in full vestments. The music was wonderful and the congregation responsive. His major duty was to be acting chaplain in a hospital for chronically ill and dying people. The rector gave him excellent supervision and soon he was enjoying his ministry in bringing solace and comfort to those who hungered so for it. He learned to sense out their need and their response even when speech was no longer possible for them. He was living out the fantasy of ministering to his dying parents but the guilt of causing their death was long since gone. He knew now he had his vocation in the ministry and began looking around for the kind of place he wanted.

His anger-with-his-mother transference to me could now be expressed in the direct honest anger of a man. He no longer needed to regress to the little boy and seek my affection. He was secure in his relationship with me so that he could be unafraid either of hurting me or of my retaliation. It has taken a long time and a lot of consistent effort to rid himself of the need to make me into his mother and to come to the time when he could see me for myself.

He has continued in therapy, working through his problems steadily; we both feel that the worst is over.[2]

[2] Three years later our hopes have been fulfilled. Phillip is happy and fulfilled in his ministry and has recently married.

✿ ABEL ✿

Abel came into therapy diffidently. He had interviewed a number of therapists over a period of nine years and had even tried therapy for a short time with what he considered disastrous results. He came to me first to ask for consultation regarding his counseling of a parishioner, and some months later took the plunge. His main overt problems were homosexuality and drinking.

During the nine years of preparation, he had carefully drawn up his autobiography, and it was immediately obvious that I had best be patient and listen. He was very meticulous and circumstantial, and droned on in a very monotonous voice.

He began with his parents. They had been married many years before he, the first child, was born. He was apparently a happy, healthy baby until about the age of two, when his grandmother, who had always lived with them, died. After that he had night terrors for several years. He could not remember this grandmother but was told that she had been fond of him. He went on describing in detail his first day at school, his playmates, his developing interest in girls and then, suddenly, I heard: "I should tell you of an incident that occurred in my thirteenth summer. My sister died in an accident. That fall I entered high school and—" I stopped him and asked for more details about this "accident." I did not remember his telling me that he had a sister at all; I thought he was an only child.

He went back and told me that he was ten when she was born and that he hadn't paid much attention to her. The accident had occurred while he was taking care of her, and he didn't remember much about it. In response to further questioning, he told me the accident had occurred in the backyard. Something happened, he ran for a servant who was nearby, and there was some commotion. He remembered standing alone across the street that evening, watching the family gather. No one talked to him about it and he was taken to the funeral by the family doctor. Why? He didn't know, except that they were good friends. He had always planned to be a doctor, and he recalled the doctor talking about his plans on the way to the cemetery, considering the different medical schools, and which one he would decide to go to.

It was too soon to make an interpretation, but at the end of that hour, which was only the third session, I could not contain myself. I blurted out, "So that's why you became a homosexual— so that you would never run the risk of hurting or killing another woman."

Abel reacted with surprised and almost pleased alertness. He was intellectually excited to realize that his chaotic, troubled life might be open to some meaningful interpretation. In succeeding hours he reported having difficulty in sleeping for the first time in his life and feeling "shook up."

He went off on a two weeks' vacation and when he returned he entered a therapy group. He shocked the group by announcing himself on his entrance as a "murderer," but his self-dramatization subsided and he got down to work. He was somewhat difficult in the group because of his monotonous droning and his difficulty in expressing any feeling—especially his anger. One of his fellow clergymen in the group was a personal friend of Abel's who knew a great deal about Abel's life, and he felt torn between his duty to Abel as a friend and his inclination to tell me and the group what he felt was vitally important for us to know. Finally, he resolved his conflict by telling us of his concern about Abel's whirlwind courtship. Eventually, Abel himself told us that the evening of his revelation of the accident he had had his first date with the girl he had loved for many years. He had been her friend and confidant, standing by while she went through several engagements. Once in a while when very drunk he would talk about how hopeless it all was, and how much he loved her. Now that he would soon be "all cured," they were going to be married. Abel was convinced that all of his difficulties originated in one traumatic incident and that it would surely take only a few more weeks to clear it all up.

I wanted to know why Abel hadn't mentioned the girl voluntarily, but all he could say was that he had never told his parents
anything.

In his next individual session he was able to tell me more. It
was evident that he really loved her, and that she loved him.
She seemed to him in every way a girl who would make a good
minister's wife. It was all wonderful and romantic, but he was
nearly forty and a virgin. When I questioned him about his
sexual response to his fiancée, he suddenly showed real feeling.
He wanted terribly to have sex with her and she was willing, but
it was sinful. At this, I asked him which was the greater sin,
risking a disastrous marriage or indulging in a bit of fornication?
I pointed out that they intended to get married and that this
should be considered as preparation for marriage. We talked
seriously about his fears and anxieties.

Soon after this session he rather sheepishly asked me if I had
seen the papers. His engagement had been announced. Again, he
couldn't tell me until after it was in print. He was sure I would
have wanted him to wait, and after all, he hadn't told his parents.

He kept going back over the accident and, finally, in a group
session, his grief broke through in almost uncontrollable sobbing.
He recalled how angry he was when his sister was born, how
jealous he was of her. She was so cute, and everyone loved her
so. Once when he was angry with her he burned one of her dolls.
He had no doubt of his death wishes for her. He still felt sure he
had murdered her. We were uncertain, we went over the scene
in the garden minutely. He remembered more and more and
gradually a picture of what had really happened emerged: While
Abel was occupied with the plaything he was making he heard
a crash, ran over to his sister, and saw that she had been hit by
a timber some workmen had left behind. He called for help and
people came but no one asked him what had happened. He recalled again having stood across the street, watching the family
gather, and wondering what they were saying. His mother's grief
was overwhelming, yet at the funeral she was as composed as
the rest of the family—it was that kind of family. No one accused
him, no one blamed him, no one said anything. He remembered

the bleak funeral service, and that he sat apart from his family with his doctor friend.

Neither Abel nor his mother were able to go back to the Congregational Church after the funeral. His mother became an ardent Christian Scientist; his father, though he did not follow her, asked Abel not to do anything opposed to her convictions. During a summer in college Abel spent some weeks at a Trappist monastery in the mountains and acquired an interest in Christian mysticism from the monks, but couldn't feel any certainty about the vocation of a monk.

World War II began about that time and Abel served in the medical corps, but he no longer felt that he wanted to be a doctor. He became interested in the Episcopal Church, was confirmed, was accepted as a postulant for Holy Orders, and when the war was over he entered seminary. When I asked him why he preferred the Episcopal Church, he said it was because of the beautiful ritual of the Eucharist. He could never understand the lack of ritual in the Communion service in the Congregational Church. When I asked him what Holy Communion meant, he said it was a funeral service in memory of Christ's death. That was why clergymen wear black, he further told me, because they are in perpetual mourning for Christ's death.

"Or your sister's?" I asked him. It had never occurred to him that there might have been a relationship between the bleak, heart-broken despair of his sister's funeral and his choice of the ministry as a means of living and attempting to master the tragic experience. Then he volunteered that for many years he had celebrated Holy Communion with one intention (or prayer), and that is that God would make him a eunuch and relieve him of the burden of his guilt over his homosexuality. At first he meant this in quite a literal sense; later, he prayed only that God would take away his homosexual desires. After his first contact with me and during the months he was trying to decide whether to come into treatment with me, he prayed that God would grant him the fulfillment of a good marriage.

As we began to learn more about his adult life we found that Abel had much for which to forgive himself. His drinking and his homosexual behavior had begun while he was in the medical corps during the war. He had reacted very severely to the horror of sudden death, of blood, and suffering. There was so little that one could do. After the war he entered seminary. He realized that the seminary would expel him if his homosexuality were ever discovered. He was very careful to hide it on the psychological testing and tried to be very discreet. He somehow got through using his high intelligence to cover his emotional difficulties and, as a result, became more and more unable to express any real feeling, especially any anger.

When he graduated he went home, was ordained deacon, and was sent to a parish which had just suffered the traumatic experience of having had a rector who had committed bigamy. The parish fell to pieces as the papers were full of the tragedy. In the midst of their very real need for an experienced and mature person to help them through this crisis in their lives, they were confronted with a young immature deacon. Their anger knew no bounds. They took out on their deacon all of the anger, the frustration, the doubt as to the meaning of Christianity and of a God who could let such a thing happen. The once thriving parish fell away. People deserted the church and removed their children from confirmation class. Abel told, with deep bitterness, about how his bishop had come for his yearly visit and when he found that Abel had no one to present for confirmation, roundly upbraided him. Abel had done all he could do in the situation and deserved praise for his efforts instead of the blame he received. He resigned and went as a missionary to the furthermost missionary district he could find.

There among the poor, Abel began to thrive. He was in his element working with the tempestuous, unhappy people of the mission. There he could be worth while, he could do something he could be proud of. At the same time, the pressure of his unconscious drives drove him to bouts of very heavy drinking. He would begin the evening in a social situation with social drinking and then, still in his clericals, he would begin to cruise the bars getting drunker and ending the evening in a fight or picking up a man and, taking him home, violently demanding to be raped, and raped he was. Even after he found a fellow minister whom he could love and be loved by, the pattern continued. It was one of those open secrets. Everyone knew that he was living with a man. Everyone that knew him loved him too much and liked his "roommate" too much so that his bishop never suspected. As these relationships go, his was a very good one. They each really cared for the other. One night, as they were driving home, they forded a swollen creek, the car turned over and the friend was drowned. Abel was driving. He reacted violently with more severe drinking, and then in his guilt-ridden grief, he became overwhelmed by remorse. He resigned and sought refuge in a monastery. For a time he found peace. His deep mysticism came to the fore and he seemed at last to find himself.

Then the unrest began and he had to leave this haven of security and peace. There seemed no way he could find atonement. He came back home and found a little rundown parish that was still there because the church and the rectory had been there for several generations, while the congregation had drifted away. There was little to do and much time to meditate. He thought over his tempestuous life and could make no sense of it. He knew he had hidden his troubles and they had come home to roost. He decided to go into therapy and after a few more months had come to see me.

As his therapy progressed, the Eucharist became less painful for him but there was still no joy in his work. He continued, he felt, out of habit and the need to earn a living. In the meantime, concurrently with his engagement, his interest in medicine revived and he started applying to medical schools.

Less than a year after Abel entered therapy, he was married. He came back from his honeymoon happier than we had ever seen him. He came back into treatment under protest, and only because he had promised. He couldn't see any reason for continuing it. They were going to have a baby, he said, beaming, and they did, happily, nine months later. I had asked them to wait for at least a year but, in the light of his prayer for the grace of becoming a eunuch for so many years, it was understandable that he couldn't wait. He felt that the birth of a healthy girl baby was a sign of God's forgiveness.

Toward the end of Abel's third year in the group a young senior seminarian began to talk about wanting to test his vocation by reading the Communion service in the group. He had been tearing paper all evening until finally someone asked him what he was doing. He replied that he was learning how to fraction the Host properly, which should be done, his professor had taught him that day, by tearing, not breaking, the Wafer. He asked a lot of questions about our experience of the Communion in the group and there was much discussion both pro and con, which continued with considerable heat for several weeks. Finally, theological approval was sought and found; the authority said the service wouldn't be valid but under the circumstances it could be considered a practice session, a "dry run."

The boy surprised us all. He read the service beautifully and with real feeling. It was for most of us a real, "emotionally valid" Communion. For Abel it was much more. At the end he crossed the room and kissed and thanked the woman who had at first opposed the ceremony, and then came to me. He embraced me and broke into sobs. It took a long time for him to tell us what it had meant. First of all, it meant that his "family" had accepted his ministry in the Episcopal Church. On a deeper level, he felt that somehow he found approval of himself in his vocation and, with it, his first sense of being loved by God. After a few weeks we realized that it had been a conversion experience for Abel, for he told us with great happiness the pleasure he now found in the Sacrament of Holy Communion, which had always been such a sad and painful ordeal.

It was after this experience, in his third year of therapy, that Abel was at last willing to ask his family what had really happened when his sister had died. He was at his parents' home for a part of his vacation and felt himself to be a part of the family for the first time he could remember. He found that his parents were quite unaware of how traumatic his sister's death had been for him. There had been a neighbor woman taking care of his sister at the time the accident had occurred. He had been playing quite a distance away. She had run for help at the time he had heard the crash and had run over to his sister's body. Nobody had realized that he felt any responsibility. They had tried in every way to shield him from their grief not knowing that all their efforts had been interpreted as their rejection of him. So he realized that he had built his whole traumatic fantasy out of his misunderstanding of their reserve and their overprotection of him.

After this experience, it no longer mattered to Abel that he wasn't able to find a medical school that would accept a man past forty. He found fulfillment in his vocation, his marriage, and his child, and most of all in himself.

Abel is now a respectable husband, father, and priest, but has still not recovered the aggressive zeal which characterized his earlier work. He is still in treatment and we hope this too will come.

❧ JEROME ❧

Jerome came from a very mixed religious background. His father's parents were Southern Baptist, his mother's mother was Episcopalian. They all lived together with his mother's spinster sister. He felt unwanted by his father, loved by his grandmother and his aunt, and possessed by his mother. He spoke almost happily of his mother's slips of the tongue when she would introduce him as "my husband."

As a child he went to his father's church; about the age of nine or ten he experienced "sudden conversion," at a camp meeting and in the language of his father's church, "he gave his life to Christ." By this was meant a life of dedication in Christian service. His grandmother also used to take him to her Episcopal church where he sang in the choir. When he was about sixteen he was caught kissing a girl in the choir and before the fuss was over he had promised to become an Episcopal minister. In college he became a fervent atheist and when he got over that phase of his rebellion he made an intellectual decision to enter the Episcopal ministry because he wanted no more emotional upheavals and because he felt that the Episcopal Church was more liberal in its theology. He felt sorry about hurting his Baptist father but, after all, he never felt that his father really mattered.

When Jerome was twenty-nine, his father suffered a heart attack; soon after that Jerome began to suffer from vomiting fits. Before going to the hospital to see his father he wrote his bishop saying that he was ill and would need a supply priest for a few weeks to look after his parish. In referring to his father's illness he invariably thought and usually said, "when my father died," even long after his father's recovery. Also, within a matter of days after his father's heart attack, he maneuvered his wife into intercourse without protection and she promptly had another pregnancy which, although unplanned and much too soon, as all the others had been, she was healthy enough to accept and enjoy. Jerome vomited "for her" each morning, and on many days quite often, until she delivered.

A few months later Jerome entered into therapy voluntarily with an analyst who was uninterested in religious problems and seemed quite unimpressed with the fact that whenever Jerome tried to talk about his church he would begin to get nauseated and frequently vomit. He had worked terribly hard as young enthusiastic rectors are wont to do; he had driven the congregation through a fund-raising campaign and had built them a fine new church. Now he was called to a new parish where he felt they also would lie back and ask him to take care of them and build them a fine new church. He was tired of taking care of people. He was fed up. He was furiously angry with his analyst because he would not help him ventilate his anger at the congregation that was waiting for him to take care of them. He was angry because no matter how much he did for his people, they did nothing for him. He was angry at his wife, too. She was a wonderful mother to their babies but she didn't realize that he, too, was a baby. He had found some comfort in a flirtation with a pretty young secretary, so it was evident that he was headed for behavior problems as well.

As soon as he came into one of my therapy groups he began to be angry with me, too. He had a very difficult time expressing this and would frequently be nauseated and sick the next day. At other times he would develop severe headaches during the group session. Several times when we got into his religious conflicts in the group, he would react with such acute illness that he was quite honestly afraid he would be unable to carry on with his work.

We had hardly begun to try to understand why he spoke of his father's heart attack as his father's death when his grandmother died. At first he insisted that he felt no grief. She was so very old and had been so weak and frail. It was a blessing, really. He came back from the funeral very angry with his mother. She had stolen the show. It was her funeral, really. Gradually he remembered that he could always go to his grandmother when he was a little boy. She always had time to rock him in her lap and talk to him.

He said he began to understand that our working through grief experiences was worth while. He said he felt that he was unusually fortunate that no deaths had occurred in his family until now. Then much later we learned that when he had been in trouble at sixteen he had gone to his father and had been overwhelmed by his father's gentle kindness and understanding. He realized for a moment how very much he loved his father, then suddenly he was furious with him. Why all these years had he never helped him in his troubles with his mother; why had he never shown him this side of himself before? He remembered all the bitter theological arguments he had had with his father. He remembered his mother saying that his father "had had something" when he had been studying for the ministry as a young man before he had given it up in order to earn a better living for the family after Jerome was born. So now Jerome resolved he would become not just a minister but a priest. He would take that "something" for himself which his father had had so briefly. He would go to seminary and learn so much theology that he would be able to argue so well with his father that his father would have apoplexy and die. So that in fact his becoming a priest was a way of taking his father's power away from him and onto himself until finally, by virtue of his ministerial power, he was able to kill his father. So his severe overreaction at the time of his father's severe illness; his "death" becomes understandable.

At this point, Jerome began to regain his compulsive cheerfulness. He was delighted with his new baby. He felt he was really practically done with therapy and expressed his feeling that he would probably stay in treatment a few more months because he would learn skills in counseling which would be helpful in his parish work.

There is a point at which a group will not tolerate phoniness.

One night, when there was nothing pressing and his cheerful helpfulness had been more obnoxious than usual, the group challenged him. Who was he really? They drove him into a corner as he got more defensive and bewildered. All he could say was that he felt very little and lost. The next week he told us that this feeling had continued and that he had a memory of wandering about the house and no one talked to him or seemed to notice him. He began to remember more, and slowly the memory of his grandfather's funeral came back. Then he remembered that just before his grandfather's death he had slipped into the room where his grandfather lay in bed; the old man seemed to want something so the four-year-old boy went over to the little altar in the room and brought him the Crucifix. Then someone came into the room and sent him away.

He remembered that before his grandfather's death he used to kneel at the little altar with his grandfather when the old man said his prayers. After his death he continued to kneel there with his grandmother and think about him. He remembered that grandfather was Roman Catholic and religion was a sore point between grandfather and father. There were other vague uncertain memory shadows that he couldn't remember clearly enough to understand. He went to his parents and they told him that during the eighteen months before his grandfather's death there had been two other deaths in the family, one of which was that of a great-uncle who had been very fond of him and had played hide-and-seek with him. After his death, the two-and-a-half-year-old child couldn't understand where his uncle had gone and for days kept looking in closets and behind doors trying to find him. The other death had been that of his mother's sister and, although he had not known her very well, his mother's grief had been dramatic and there had been a great deal of talk in the family about it.

Jerome also remembered very vividly his reaction to the death of two pets he had loved. The first one, a dog, died as a result of his mother's carelessness when Jerome was about seven years old and he accused his mother of killing it. He still feels acutely that his mother was a murderer. A year later his father brought home a duck. The little boy fell in love with the new pet and played happily with it for weeks. Then the duck was killed and cooked and Jerome sat at the table horrified, watching his family eat his friend. He couldn't understand how they could do such a thing. He was nauseated and unable to eat anything on the table.

About this time we found that Jerome had begun services of healing. He had read a great deal about spiritual healing but had never mentioned the subject in therapy. Although it is permissible in the Episcopal Church, I felt some concern because of the dangers of such powerful mechanisms in the hands of an enthusiastic amateur. Jerome described the wonderful success of his first service—how much better everyone and especially he himself felt afterward. It was so very different from Holy Communion where he felt that he was bringing God's love to the people, but never felt loved himself. He merely felt drained and tired. After the Service of Spiritual Healing he felt happier, more loved, more himself than he had ever felt throughout his whole ministry.

Quite early during Jerome's treatment I asked him how he felt during the celebration of the Eucharist. He said, "Oh, all right, I don't have any trouble." I said, "How do you feel during the prayer of consecration?" He replied, "My voice is always very firm, well controlled, well modulated." I repeated my question, "And how do you *feel?*" He said, "I feel all right, but my hands tremble. But nobody can see my hands tremble, and my voice is always perfectly controlled." I asked, "And what comes to mind when your hands tremble?" And in a strange, somewhat small voice that came straight out of the depths, he said, "I kill my father, or I kill myself."

I had not tried to delve into this further at that time; it seemed much too soon. But now I went back to it and asked for more details. He said he always kept his eyes closed during the prayer of consecration. Once he had looked into the polished surface of the chalice and had seen his reflection and felt that it was indeed his body and blood that were upon the altar and in the chalice. After that he had kept his eyes closed. This is what he had felt it meant when as child he "had given his life to Christ." At the altar he became Christ the Sacrifice. He would die or he would kill his father. But in the service of spiritual healing he did not have to appease an angry God. He was with a *loving* God who would heal, comfort, and love him and his people. He didn't have to sacrifice himself in order to bring God's love to his people as his pet duck had been sacrificed to feed his family.

Jerome was away on vacation during the worst of a serious illness of one of the group, and when he came back the ill member was in the hospital. I asked Jerome if he would do spiritual healing on this member in the group when he returned. Jerome blew up. He had given him a book about it, he said. He could only do it in his own church in the right way. He became more and more defensive. One just didn't do such things spontaneously. It was obviously not safe. As he got deeper and deeper into his fears of his own magic if it was not properly controlled by his obsessive rituals he began to realize the extent of his omnipotent magical thinking.

That was the end of his Services of Healing.

We are slowly helping him find himself. Every time the group finds a way to help him reveal more of his distortions of religion he is sick for a few days and bitterly berates me. Yet, he has begun to develop a sense of healthy devotion to match the excellent theological training he had brought with him when he came into treatment.

It is never necessary to point out to Jerome that he has revealed childish distortions of religion. It is enough to get him to let the unconscious thoughts break through to consciousness. Once he hears himself say them his mature theologically trained mind can come to bear on the problem.

Recently I asked Jerome to describe what his life would have been without therapy, in the light of his present awareness of his uncovered personal religion. He told me that his life would have been one of suffering the burden of the road to Calvary, identifying with the One who suffers and angry with the one who causes the suffering. Every time he celebrated Holy Communion he himself died a symbolic death in identification with Christ.

But by the life of selfless devotion to the welfare of others, he would in death find salvation.[1]

[1] Some months after I had recorded Jerome's case, he reported a series of three dreams. In the first dream he was in the balcony of the church he remembered going to as a child. As the service was proceeding an old woman turned around and he was frightened by her ugly face and by her hair hanging down over it. His associations revealed that the woman was his mother and the ugly face with hair hanging down over it represented female genitals—which he has never dared look at. He felt that his interest in sex was perverting his relationship with God. That was the reason why he was in the balcony and not with the congregation.

In the second dream he saw himself as a priest celebrating Holy Communion. As he was communicating the congregation his deacon prevented him from giving communion to a woman in the congregation whose conduct had been sinful. In his associations he saw the deacon as his severe, puritanical condemnation of his wish to be a loving person, and he was preventing himself from being forgiven and loved.

In the third dream he was again a priest celebrating the Eucharist. His congregation was singing and dancing around the altar and he felt they were about to sacrifice him. He awoke in a state of severe anxiety. His associations again indicated his persistent feeling that he was the sacrificial atonement for his sins and the sins of his congregation.

To Jerome these dreams seemed to confirm his previous feelings and attitudes; he saw them as a turning point in his therapeutic progress.

✻ ANDREW ✻

Andrew sought treatment voluntarily at the age of thirty. He was handsome and well built; his physical movements were almost feline in their gracefulness. His manner was charming and his social skills were superb. He was highly intelligent and sophisticated both in the ways of the world and in his scholarship.

Andrew descended from a long line of proud American stock on his father's side—ministers, teachers, all talented but rarely capable of effectiveness in business. His mother was foreign-born and never felt quite at home in the rigid social pattern of a small East Texas town. She was already considered a "spinster" schoolteacher when she married Andrew's father—a middle-aged bachelor whose mother had recently died. Andrew was always sure that his father had married in order to have a housekeeper. He also felt that they were not happy together and that he was not wanted. As he wrote in the autobiography he prepared for the referring psychiatrist, "I am her only child—a second died at birth—as, previously, my mother and I almost did." She never let Andrew forget how terrible this delivery had been. He was brought up in the belief that he caused his mother irreparable physical damage by being born. He was also deeply impressed by the fact that he, too, had almost died at birth because everyone had been so busy saving his mother's life that his presence for a time was almost overlooked. To him this meant that he had never really been wanted at all.

His childhood was a lonely one, with few playmates. His father's younger brother, who lived nearby, would occasionally take the child with him and his family on fishing and camping trips. This uncle seems to be the only person in the family who ever really talked to him or seemed to care about him.

211

His father was a rigidly authoritarian, sternly Calvinistic Congregationalist. He was usually depressed and talked endlessly of his theological concerns. His mother was a lapsed Roman Catholic who had made a half-hearted attempt to placate the father by joining his church. As time went on she became more and more withdrawn and had many illnesses. She always worried when Andrew was out of the house, so he would stay near her and read or practice the piano whenever his father was not in. She encouraged Andrew's interest in music in the face of her husband's disapproval.

Andrew remembered little of the Congregational Church except the Sunday-school custom of giving as a reward for perfect attendance a paper goldfish which would be glued onto the picture of a goldfish bowl. He was fascinated by the fish, and as he grew older he set up an aquarium. He spent many happy hours taking care of the tropical fish that were his only pets. He was never allowed to have dogs or cats.

It was only when he went to college that he began to find a positive meaning in religion. His musical ability gave him the opportunity to become one of a group of organists and choirmasters. Through an Episcopal priest whom he admired he got a job as an organist in an Episcopal church. He found happiness and satisfaction in the beauty of liturgical music. As a result of his growing desire to belong, and of his wish to share more deeply in the emotional and devotional quality of the music, he was confirmed as an Episcopalian. This pleased his mother, who felt that her son was returning in some measure to the "true church," and angered his father, who felt that this was the beginning of his son's damnation.

Andrew had delayed going into the Army at his mother's insistence. She felt it was enough that his uncle was in service. She saw no reason why he too should be "sacrificed" for the country. Nevertheless, he was drafted and news of his beloved uncle's serious injury reached him in training camp. Up until that time he had felt no emotional involvement in the war but remembered that moment as his first conscious awareness of hate in his whole life. From then on the enemy was his enemy also.

On one occasion during his army days, he was looking at a

folio of prints of English churches. One of the pictures was of a beautiful English cathedral, and the drawing reflected the perfection of the stone work. The walls were tall and strong and high up were lovely windows. It was a magnificent church with a wide courtyard and a road leading to it. He remembered that the church in ages past was the center of all the community roundabout, and that it was there that on the holy days all the people would gather. As he studied this picture a sudden decision to enter the priesthood formed in his mind. The decision was felt very intensely and despite the impulsive quality of his decision he went at once to the chaplain and the necessary protocol was worked through. He was accepted as a postulant for Holy Orders. In his autobiography he wrote only, "My unaccountable decision to become a postulant while at Officers' School."

After he completed his seminary studies he found himself unable to go on to ordination and spent three years teaching English. When a curacy was offered him and he felt pressured to be ordained he decided to seek psychotherapeutic help. He suffered keenly from feelings of indecision and lack of willpower, and hoped that he would find "a clear path ahead."

It was at this time that Andrew prepared his autobiography, in which he made the following notes concerning his vocation.

The Ministry—reasons for.

A strange *unarticulated* [1] almost mystical *impulse* toward and attraction for it.

Feeling that I *ought* to or really should.

Sense that I have *obligation* to use certain talents.

A growing realization that *meaning* somehow is *only to be found in this area.*

Reasons against.

Dislike of my future colleagues.

Restriction on private life and eccentricities.

Great divergence *between my ideal of the priesthood* and what I feel I could do with it and would do to it.

Fear of being "found out" re: my psychosexual nature and its expression. Questioning my own moral life.

A vague uncertainty somewhere inside me of the truth of much that the church does and says.

[1] Italics mine.

Andrew also gave an account of his psychosexual history:

> Early shy circumvention or indignant reactions to sex.
>
> First contact I remember was when very young: I was taken up to the attic by boarding student at local academy who saw to it that I watch him masturbate successfully.
>
> Remember only one high school homosexual experience— although I longed for many more with a number of individuals who seemed impossibly distant. I was completely inhibited and painfully shy whenever approaching sexual matters in conversation.
>
> First experience with an adult was when I was picked up by an organist while hitchhiking back from an Organists' Guild convention when a senior in high school. This proved a most unpleasant introduction to "adult" sexual behavior.
>
> While in college I had a few experiences before going into the Army. There were a few isolated experiences in the Army. There were many tortured hours and unfulfilled desires but my inhibitions and shyness kept me from being adventurous and doing all that might have been done.
>
> The lid really blew off when I returned to college. There I found many compatible and intelligently understanding people. There was great experimentation and many sexual experiences filled those two years.
>
> The following two years abroad were warm and uninhibited. Here I had my first experience of having a lover over a period of months instead of just weeks. It was a tremendously happy and relaxed but pointed life.
>
> I had a number of casual experiences at the seminary. They were unsatisfactory and frenetic. Much time was wasted in searching and talking and much energy lost in frustration and unhappiness. There were many bright spots, of course, that made continuing possible.
>
> Last year was one of almost complete abstinence from outer contact and this year has brought last year's loneliness to a focus by experiencing much more relaxed behavior.

It was not surprising that his initial behavior in the therapy group followed the pattern of his behavior in life. He would go into a situation impulsively and then slowly retreat from it. He was moody, often quite depressed, with occasional bursts of hyperactivity. He was facile in developing an elusiveness that was maddening at times. He was surprised that others longer in therapy were angry with their mothers. He was shocked and horrified and thus had a hard time staying with the therapy group at first. His defenses were sturdy and seemingly impenetrable, yet he seemed guileless and innocent.

We tried at every opportunity, which came all too seldom, to understand why this man could not go on to ordination. His first rationalization was that, as he had stated in his autobiography, he was afraid he would be "found out." His next was more startling: If he was ordained he might be compelled to act out homosexually in such a way that he would be deposed. He could not explain why he would be "compelled" but he spoke with such depth of earnestness that we knew he could not safely approach ordination until this unknown force was understood and resolved.

As he became freer, he could finally tell us that he could not be ordained because he could not be the perfect person a priest should be. By this he meant that a priest should be celibate, and he revealed a guilt often displayed by Episcopalians over the marriage of priests. He felt that a married priest was not a completely good priest, and until he could be a completely good priest, he could not be ordained. But he could not believe that he could ever give up his wish to marry or to be able to give up his sexual life to the extent required of a celibate priest, and he could not compromise.

Slowly, we were able to get him to understand that his faithfulness to his God was truly his faithfulness to his mother; he could then begin to understand why he always spoke disparagingly of his girl friend, whom he managed to keep chasing him for five years. He had never permitted her to meet his mother although she was an attractive and socially acceptable person. He was sure his mother would say the girl was simply not good enough, beautiful enough, virtuous enough, for him. He began to understand more of his identification with his mother who was so stiff and puritanical, so "perfect." He could begin to understand that he was psychologically bound by the same corseting which stiffened his mother's body. He remembered his mother's indignation when he was drafted, and her bitter complaint that her only child should be a sacrifice for the welfare of the community. He came to understand that his mother meant that he was *her* sacrifice, and that he was to remain her sacrifice alone.

When he had been in therapy about a year and a half he developed the desire to renew his musical activity. He changed jobs, and became the organist for a choirmaster, and in many respects a curate, in a large and busy parish. He was now out of the cloistered atmosphere of the college where he had been teaching. He had an apartment of his own. He began to have a feeling that he was about to begin living a life of his own and would not need to be his mother's sacrifice. He was able to begin to tell us of some of his unhappy sexual fantasies of cruel tortures, including the torture of the Christ figure upon the Crucifix. Although Andrew's fantasies involved a sexual teasing and tormenting of the Christ figure, the profound understanding of the therapy group to whom he confided showed him that this was a part of himself, a part that was in identification with the crucified Christ. Later he would be able to see himself not only as the torturer, the sacrificer, but as the victim, the sacrifice.

Andrew had a dream about this time, a dream in which he was an observer, stationed high in the rafters of a cathedral. He knew in the dream that he should be at the organ, but an unknown, unseen organist was playing a mighty organ with such skill, with such vigor, that the whole church vibrated. As he looked down, marveling, he saw me walk into the aisle of the church followed by a group of people. We interpreted this in the group as a group dream in which he was acknowledging the group's awareness of his inner real self, the unseen musician, with the strength and beauty and devotion that made the rafters shake. This very strength, this very love, this wonderful musical ability, this devotion which was so beautifully used in the dream, was that same tortured love that had come out in the distorted fantasies of his sadistic lovemaking and his sadistic sexual teasing of the Christ figure.

Another time Andrew dreamed he was celebrating Mass at the high altar of St. Peter's in Rome. At the altar rail were the Pope and the cardinals, and as he communicated them, he spilled some of the precious contents of the chalice and saw that it was blood. The Communion service had always been an empty ceremony for him. The setting of the dream in a completely Roman Catholic situation meant that he was concerned with the possibility that the bread and wine become actually and literally the body and blood of Christ. It is interesting to note that in medieval times an accusation of ritual murder was made against anyone who accidentally broke or defiled the wafer, and it was thought that if the wafer were broken drops of blood would ooze out of it. Also, in Roman Catholic tradition the sacramental wine is partaken of by the priest alone, whereas in the Protestant tradition both the wafer and the wine are given to the communicant. In offering the chalice to those at the altar rail in his dream, Andrew was thus combining both the Roman Catholic and the Anglican concepts of Holy Communion.

The blood in the chalice had been, in his associations, the blood of the sacrificial victim on the altar. He had said at first that it was his blood. But I asked, "If it is not your blood, whose would it be?" and he said, "My mother's." His associations pointed to the ghastly amount of blood she had lost when he was born and to the belief he had held until coming into treatment that women lose a dangerous amount of blood during each menstrual period. The blood would soak through the mattress and make puddles on the floor and this is why little boys should not go under mother's bed. The blood would drip on them and get them all dirty.

A few days after this dream and the subsequent discussions about it in the group, Andrew suddenly found himself at the altar rail almost unable to go through the ritual of Communion. The taste of the wine was that of blood in his mouth. No longer was this a meaningless, empty ritual. It had become a frightening and terrible mystery. It required many sessions for him to understand the symbolism of blood *as life* and not as death. In an effort to get him to understand the unconscious meaning of his distortion, I asked him to fantasy whose body was on the altar. Was it his? Would he be the one sacrificed? Or would he be the priest wielding the sacrificial knife and would *I* be the body on the altar? This hit at the root of his sadomasochistic sexual fantasies and he began to realize how he had sexualized Holy Communion.

Andrew continued to progress in treatment. He undertook to finish his work at the seminary, including some of the canonical examinations required before ordination. I felt it best that he do these piecemeal, because at first there was danger of his acting out the old fantasy of being deposed for sexual immorality. He might be overwhelmed by getting too close to his goal too suddenly. A few months after he had taken the first of these canonicals and within a few weeks of being able to take the remainder he displayed disruptive behavior at the beginning of a group session. This was quite unusual because Andrew, as a rule, had to be brought out in a group, and here he was demanding attention and creating considerable anxiety and anger. He said that all day he had been driven; he had done a mass of detail work that had accumulated during his recent depression and had finally become so lonely that he had fallen back on his old pre-occupation with fantasies of torture. He said that the one which had come to mind a number of times during the day was a particularly unpleasant one of a man tied down in a kneeling position with an earthen flower pot strapped to his back in which a rat was placed. The rat was then driven frantic and crazy by pushing a red hot poker into the hole in the bottom of the flower pot, forcing him to eat his way into the man's body and out again in order to escape. As Andrew was telling this story he sat flourishing a knife, taking a considerable time during the telling of the fantasy to cut a piece of the cake which was in his lap, using the knife throughout to highlight the dramatic fantasy. The group responded with some anger to the fantasy as well as to the cake carving. There was a general feeling that he was both the man who was being tortured and the man who was torturing the rat with the red hot poker, and that the group was symbolized in the rat which he was trying to drive crazy in order to torture himself. He could accept this interpretation and began trying to work with it when he again picked up the cake to cut another slice. At this point, I asked him how he would feel if he were at the altar and were saying the prayer of consecration, the cake being the Host. His reaction was immediate and very severe. He fumbled and could not remember the words of the prayer as I asked him to say them. When I told him to go ahead anyway and break the cake as he would break the Host, he became ashen and was unable to force his hands into action. Using as a springboard the anger he had evoked in the previous two hours by his disruptive maneuvering of the group, I asked him whom he would like to have say the words of the prayer so that he could repeat them afterwards. He chose Phillip, a young priest, who had himself gone through repeated reactions to Holy Communion in relation to Andrew's dreams that were told in the group.

Phillip, riding as I was with the controlled anger that made our demand on Andrew impossible to be evaded, spoke the words clearly, firmly, implacably, and Andrew recited after him phrase after phrase, in a shaky, broken voice while the tears ran down his face and the sweat poured off him.

> For in the night in which he was betrayed, he took Bread; and when he had given thanks, he brake it, and gave it to his disciples, saying, Take, eat, this is my Body, which is given for you; Do this in remembrance of me. Likewise, after supper, he took the Cup; and when he had given thanks, he gave it to them, saying, Drink ye all of this; for this is my Blood of the New Testament, which is shed for you, and for many, for the remission of sins; Do this, as oft as ye shall drink it, in remembrance of me.[2]

The silence was intense. Andrew's hands were shaking; he looked as though he were in shock. I said, "Break it. Break my body." And he broke the cake that served as the wafer. There was a feeling of relief but the devotional intensity dissipated only gradually. I continued, "You have broken my body and I live. You are a man. Oedipus was blinded for this. But you have your father's love and approval. You are a man." His shirt was wet, but he radiated strength and he spoke about how meaningful it had been, how difficult it had been to break the piece of cake, and how it had actually seemed to be his body and mine. As he

[2] Book of Common Prayer, p. 80.

had broken it, it had seemed as if he would actually die; but now he felt more alive than he ever had. He said he knew that Phillip and I were his father because his father always finished things and always made him finish things. When I asked him to fantasize putting my body [3] upon the altar and take the role of the sacrificer, he showed considerable emotional response. He appeared to prefer to die as the sacrifice rather than as the priest, the sacrificer, who would have to plunge his knife into the breast of his beloved. So, both Phillip and I had been his father; and I had also been his sacrifice, as he, too, had been the sacrifice. He could not describe to us then, as he did later, his feeling of an intense and very real identification with Jesus as he was repeating the words, so that it seemed for a moment that he *was* Jesus, and his body which he broke, and mine, was the body of Jesus.

Perceiving the controlled anger of Phillip, the group, and myself as a vehicle of love and strength, Andrew was able for the first time in his whole life to experience the intense and deep emotional and religious devotional experience of being one with God and being loved by God. In explaining why it took nearly three years to come to this time, he spontaneously said, "It took so long because it could not come until I trusted you; and when I came into therapy, I had never trusted any human being." As expressed by Hiram, an artist member of the group: "At that moment he experienced total involvement, and with the total involvement came perfect freedom." In other words, he experienced the rhythm of total emotional involvement with another human being and with God, a moment of incomprehensible mutual love such as is experienced by fortunate couples in mutual orgasm, which is followed in healthy individuals by a feeling of complete freedom and integrity. He had endured his ordeal in a relationship with people whom he loved and who loved him. He had been at that moment the "perfect holy priest." He had not killed nor had he died. He had experienced an over-

---

[3] Compare "In my opinion, the eating [of the Totem sacrifice] is really the eating of the mother," in "Some Aspects of Semitic Monotheism," in *Psychoanalysis and the Social Sciences*, vol. IV, Géza Róheim, ed. (New York: International Universities Press, 1955), p. 203.

whelming flood of emotion and was more alive than he had ever been in his whole life.

We are often aware in psychotherapy that there is for the patient a conscious or unconscious timetable. In Andrew's case it was his beloved uncle's death. He, as so many other patients, needed to find a time of being able to express his love to the loved one before it is too late.

It was only a few months after the ordeal of the prayer of consecration that his beloved uncle came to the end of the long years of suffering that had begun when he was severely injured during the war. As a last resort, he was brought to a hospital in the city where Andrew and I live, and some impossible miracle was hoped for. For many weeks he was here in the city and Andrew was the only member of the family who could conveniently visit him. Much as Andrew admired his uncle's courage, he hated himself for not being able to comfort him. He hated himself for his self-centeredness, his helplessness. During an individual session I handed him the Prayer Book and said, "Your uncle is dying. For the moment we will say he is dead and you are going to read the funeral service." It took us over two hours, for often he could not go on reading while tears were streaming down his face. The deep sobs would break through. He would put the book down and after we had talked some more about his uncle and how good, brave, and kind he had always been, he would begin to read again. Sometimes he would insist he couldn't go on and I would drive him on as I had before in the prayer of consecration, not letting him skip any of the alternate prayers and psalms. The part of the service when the body is committed to the ground was the hardest. But at last it was done and he sobbed a while on my shoulder, then looked at his watch and realized how much time had gone by. He was late for his visit to his uncle in the hospital, so he dashed off.

That was the first time Andrew was able to be as he liked himself to be with his uncle. He was able to reveal his love, he was able to comfort his uncle as two courageous men can mutually strengthen their ability to face death with fortitude, with dignity, with faith. There was an almost unspoken understanding between the two that became more and more vividly real as the days went on. When the end came Andrew felt grief again but there was also peace within himself.

At the funeral Andrew's anger with his father surfaced. Over the years, their relationship consisted of nothing more than theological arguments, but now to have no more of a father than a doddering old man beset with religiosity was suddenly too much for him. His uncle had been real and Andrew himself was now too real to be content with this travesty of a man.

We then began to review Andrew's relationship with his father. It appeared that he was a depressed, beaten, middle-aged man when he was presented with a child he didn't want or know what to do with. In consequence, Andrew was really his mother's child. His father seems to have taken no responsibility for him or exhibited any awareness of him until he was twelve or thirteen years old. At that time, for some unknown reason, the boy was circumcised. He remembers that when the doctor came to take out the stitches, his father sent his mother out of the room and held his hand. He remembers the frightening pain and the comfort of his father holding his hand. Apparently, a penis was something one could have only in the presence of men. He could remember nothing about his penis before this; it's as if he had never had one until the circumcision. He began to masturbate soon after this.

Also about this time he read Stevenson's *Treasure Island* and began to have fantasies of having a wooden leg or a glass eye. This fascination and identification with mutilation continued throughout his life.

In adolescence he realized further that he must stay away from women because if he gave vent to his sexual desires he would violate them and cause them to get pregnant, and it was a sin to cause illegitimate pregnancies. So his awakening sexuality continued to be fixed in the circumcision trauma. One caused pain or experienced pain in any sexual expression. His father's love could only be secured in enduring sexual pain and his mother's in being a good boy which meant sexual abstinence, since women were fragile, so easily and irreparably damaged by a penis. For example, it developed that I was for him a man. I had just returned from a vacation rested and tanned in the face of his perception of women as pale, sickly, suffering from backaches—like his mother. Men, on the other hand, were strong, tanned, and vital. Castration fears were so deep and pervading that sexual arousal could rarely break through and then with such fear, guilt, and anger that sadomasochistic punishments or attacks of arthritis made sexual expression possible.

The group Andrew was in was all homosexual but later he entered a mixed group and began to have fantasies of sexual sadism with women. His first one with me was that he would bend me so far backward in sex that he would break my back. He could see the transference with his mother's backaches which, like her dangerous delivery, must have been caused by the brutality of sex, and his concept of normal male behavior as brutal, destructive, hated, and dangerously punished by women took a long time to work through. It was hard for him to make any of the necessary aggressive moves which are required of a man in our culture. As a homosexual he had always been passively seduced and even then was frequently impotent.

As we worked through his sexual distortions, his body began to change. He lost weight and became lean and hard. The cat-like, seductive grace of movement was replaced by angularity and with it he became more outgoing and aggressive. In this new masculinity he could realize his ego ideal: he could be the celibate "perfect holy priest," and about three and a half years after he entered therapy he was ordained as deacon. It was an occasion of great happiness for him; even his father's need to tell everyone at the reception of his theological disapproval failed to mar Andrew's triumph. He contrasted it later with the intense, wrenching unhappiness he had felt when he graduated from college. College had been his first haven of love and security and it was a cruel birth experience to have to leave and go out into a world he didn't like and in which he felt so unwanted.

Being ordained deacon was for him the beginning of a new life, the life he had glimpsed more than thirteen years before when he had had the first impulsive awareness of his wish to be a priest.

Fortunately, his rector was secure enough to enjoy seeing his growth and gave him the opportunity to expand in scope and responsibilities as curate while continuing his work with church music. An assistant organist was found so that he would be free to be in the sanctuary. He continued to enjoy playing the organ but he was also finding devotional fulfillment as a minister. His ordination as priest was thus a very natural expression of his growth, and a most fulfilling experience.

As Andrew has incorporated and integrated the extensive realignment of his personality structure and the changing concepts of his theology, he has displayed one peculiar quality of patients who make good recoveries: He tends to falsify the past. It has always been as it is now. It takes a conscious effort for him to remember how different he was five years ago. His intellectual understanding gives him help in the present and makes him an exciting and insightful group member but he has no need intellectually to concern himself with his past. He is a religionist and a musician. He has no need to be a therapist, unlike those clergymen who find a real vocational expression in training themselves to be skilled counselors.

It was only after Andrew had been celebrating Communion for several months that he could tell me that he could not fully enjoy the experience. He has trained himself not to hear the words of the bloody sacrifice. He has tried to experience it as a Communion, as a sharing of the bread and wine as symbols of God's blessing. Once in a while he would feel sad and tears would come to his eyes. Then he would sternly suppress this feeling for he knew he was headed for a reliving of his death in the sacrifice of the altar. Again I asked him, "If you do not kill yourself as the sacrifice whom will you kill?" This time he said, "My wife."

It is obvious that much is yet to be worked through. The history is unfinished. Andrew is still in treatment and still growing. Having achieved his ego ideal of the celibate "perfect holy priest" he is becoming aware of his loneliness and his body is becoming expressive again, but in a new way. When talking to or sitting near an attractive woman, an exciting quality of masculinity emerges.

Andrew knows he has the choice to remain celibate or go on

to marriage. Since he has never wanted to go into an Order and become a monk, and since he continues to work on the problem, it is indicated that he will marry.

For the present he has found direction, energy, and fulfillment in his life and his work. His depressions are a thing of the past. He has achieved the goal he had set when he entered therapy: He has a "clear path ahead."

PART THREE

Conclusion

As with all studies of an exploratory nature, many questions are raised which must remain unanswered until more work is done and reported. The very wide range of the spectrum of religious belief and practice indicates that in working with religionists of all denominations and creeds many yet unexplored distortions of the meaning of doctrine and ritual will emerge. The advantage of studying religious conflict in the clergy lies in their greater involvement in religion as they daily perform this professional function. It is harder for them to evade their conflicts than for the lay person who can more easily escape this confrontation except in times of stress or crisis.

A deeper insight into the meaning of religion and ritual is found in the depth analysis of living religionists rather than in studies based on historical or anthropological data. This depth analysis in turn validates much of the hypothetical study that has been done. Studies of the personal psychopathology of great religionists of the past have indicated that their unconscious needs determined doctrinal, ritualistic, moral, and social reforms. Some of these movements have been heretical. Some have caused holy wars and inquisitions. The living religionists I have worked with have had a similar impact on society even though of a less powerful order of intensity.

Lengthy case histories in which the unfolding of complex dynamic patterns are described present a much more difficult picture to evaluate than the use of anecdotal material confined to the limits of specific illustration. Anecdotal material is much more susceptible to the personal interpretation of the writer. In

229

a lengthy case history the reader is given much more opportunity to draw his own conclusions. Thus the case history presents the reader with much more of a challenge. It is, in fact, an open invitation to the reader to bring his own insights and experience to bear on the problem and comes very close to the give-and-take of a case seminar presentation.

Space does not permit an exhaustive report on my own conclusions because the ongoing nature of my work in the field has taught me that there is much unexplored territory ahead. My experience is still too limited to the sacramentally centered minister. What will be the experience with more extended studies of other religionists whose central preoccupations express themselves in relation to others remains to be seen. I feel, however, that many of these themes will present themselves in other forms.

In the one religious ritual that has been most studied, the Sacrament of Holy Communion, many of the healthy and pathological meanings have become evident. For example, in the case of Abel, Christ's death became a repetition of his sister's funeral which he used as a bargaining agent with God. For others it became the theater for their magical omnipotence. In such cases their infantile striving after love and their angry frustration are caught in childhood fixations brought about by the abandonment of loved ones through death or illness.

The frequency with which pathological identifications with the Christ figure occur, especially in the highly charged emotional atmosphere of the Sacrament of Holy Communion, is disturbing. One cannot help but wonder how much pathology is induced by the impact of the literal words and actions, and in what measure the Liturgy is a projective stimulus which is singularly able to express with extraordinary sensitivity the personal pathology of the priest.

The recurrent theme of placating an angry God through atonement and sacrifice has many variations. Since many clergymen begin to decompensate after ordination, one must consider how much reinforcement or feedback occurs as a result of their deep participation in the intense moment of the Consecration and the breaking of the Host. It is at this moment that personal pathology obscures the true meaning. One of my clergy patients solved this for himself by separating these two actions in time so that by breaking the Wafer just before communicating his congregation he avoids identity. Others have so completely worked through their pathological investment of the Liturgy that it has become what it is intended to be—a blessing. The words and actions have been deconditioned of their distorted meanings. The problem of how much the Church is imposing a sick religion onto its teachings and Liturgy as a result of the distorted religion of its clergy and primary-process misunderstandings of the words and action of the service is one that I cannot answer. I doubt, however, that healthy people are easily led into such distortions. But how many of our people and our clergy are healthy? Certainly a sick minister can worsen the psychopathology of a sick parishioner. Certainly the distorted religion of the parents has an even much greater effect on the developing mind of the child.

One point is worth noting. In my early cases there was no awareness of the problems centering in the Eucharist. Some of these men may have had similar problems but they had not yet included the Sacrament because they were still seminarians or, more importantly, they may not have been recognized because I had not yet come to look for them. It is essential to keep an expectant attitude—each patient is a unique and new adventure.

The frequency with which severe attitudes of religious prejudice have occurred in a population of enlightened, socially minded religionists such as Jacob and Martin is also disturbing and warrants further study.

Vocational choice, if it is to be satisfying, must, in the long run, fulfill two kinds of needs. It must meet the expectations set up by the conscious motivational dynamics that had originally led up to it, and, more importantly, it must gratify unconscious needs. Martin, for example, illustrates a case where there were no deep needs to be fulfilled in the ministry. He needed love and acceptance but his real vocational interests could only be found in work outside the ministry that did satisfy his unconscious needs. In others, such as Phillip, Abel, and Jerome, distortions of the meaning of core religious sacramental rituals made it impossible for them to enjoy the practice of their vocations. Without psychotherapeutic intervention in this area Andrew would never have been able to go on to ordination. How many of our clergy are similarly crippled by their anxieties can only dimly be realized.

It has been found that many patients have gone into the ministry in search for love; never having experienced sufficient human love, they hope to find love in God. However, as time goes on—time spent in ritual observance and in service to others —they begin to suffer acutely from a lack of *both* human and divine love and, consequently, begin to regard the ministry as failing to provide sufficient human and divine approval. Such a development—frequently observed in patients—confirms *my thesis that human experiencing of love is preliminary to and a prerequisite of the experiencing of God's love.* These patients, such as James and Jerome, feel that they are "pipelines," "agents," by whom the love of God is relayed to the congregation, but they themselves hunger and thirst. Many types of psychosomatic illness are seen in clinical practice as resulting from this frustration and anger—obesity and gastric ulcer in particular, as seen in the cases of Jacob and Peter. Various behavior problems, sexual deviations, and marital difficulties are also seen as deriving from a state characterized by lack of love.

Many of my clergy patients entered the ministry seeking a good father in God. Traumatized by an inadequate or too angry human father they have tried to become their own fathers. Frequently only children or the lost child in a large family, they identify with Christ, the only beloved Son of the good Father. The impact of later identifications with both good and bad father figures in their pastors and superiors is shown repeatedly as, for example, in the cases of James and Samson.

When we begin to open the Pandora's box of the unconscious repressed needs, strivings, the still-operative traumatic memories with all their distorted meanings, we are reminded that sometimes a captain sets sail with a scurvy-ridden crew and on the high seas has a mutiny to quell. Some of the crew are put in irons, and some of the crew are confined to quarters. But no matter how well-fashioned the irons, or how sturdy the locks, or how unwearied the watch, the mutinous men find their way back on deck, disguised, hidden, in many shapes and forms. Yet the master of the vessel never is aware that each time he suppresses a mutiny, he is suppressing the same mutiny, and not a new one. We call this, analytically, the return of the repressed.

An early experience with the death of or abandonment by a parent figure is an important unconscious dynamic in choosing religious work as vocation. Such an experience will often result in a loss of trust in human relationships by the child and cause him to seek magical, omnipotent identification with God as his minister, as in the cases of Peter and James. It can be said with sufficient assurance that a death or abandonment experience in early childhood, as in the case of John, tends to be an unconscious motivation and that its presence in the history of religious personnel is an important indication in favor of therapeutic intervention. Unfortunately, the history may lack this material because of repression, as in the cases of Jerome and Patience.

Samson's delinquency following the death of his beloved bishop is another instance of the traumatic effect of the death experience, even in so-called adult life.

In James we have the case of a man whose basic emotional security became inadequate as a result of the immaturity of his mother. Due to her psychological illness she imposed upon a constitutionally healthy and aggressive child a passivity, a feminine identification and a withdrawal from playmates of his own age. Lacking a basic emotional development of his religious sense, he found in his grandfather a masculine identification in the only relationship in which he felt loved. His vocation seems to have begun in this identification with a man who was a dedicated churchman, and who taught him a good concept of God. In response to the badly handled grief reaction to the death of this beloved parent figure, James endured the overwhelmingly angry reaction of the infant whose total security is lost when his mother leaves him. In this unexpressed and later entirely repressed temper tantrum James identified himself with his fantasy of the omnipotent all-powerful cruel magician perceived in the role of the minister at the funeral service. This in itself was solely the projection of his own unacceptable destructive wishes for everyone in the situation. This is the usual angry reaction of the infantile person unable to accept the death of a loved and needed person, who cries out, "Why did God do this to me? I hate God." Some react with a denial—"There is no God," others with, "God is an angry cruel God." James tried to master this by identifying himself with the role of priest as the omnipotent angry destructive one and then tried to repress it. In the repression of his angry bewilderment he emerged more shallow and passive. Two years later he again began to identify with a good parish priest so that he developed a good learned concept of religion and of the ministry.

Without therapy he would have continued to be more and more depressed. His homosexual needs would have gradually overcome his weaker heterosexual identifications. One wonders if he would have been able to defend against his homosexuality in time, or if the developing schizophrenic process would have become overt as his last defense?

The therapeutic value of releasing his aggression from the encapsulated death experience is probably the core of the successful outcome. This enabled him to be able to realize his masculinity and his ability to love and be loved. Gradually the omnipotent angry baby grew up. Fortunately he himself realized the danger of his becoming a sorrowful self-righteous unconsciously cruel person.

The basic import of the case of Abel lies in his personal distortion of the Eucharist as a reliving as well as an attempt at mastery of the traumatic death and funeral of his sister. This emphasis on the commemoration of the death and not the resurrection of Jesus is not uncommon in my experience, but in no other case have the dynamics been so clearly demonstrated. The death of Abel's sister reinforced his traumatic reaction to the death of his grandmother in his infancy, which had been followed by night terrors for several years.

The death of his sister was further deeply traumatic because of the unspoken self-accusation, his previous death wishes toward her, the repression of his grief as well as his guilt, and his intense feelings of isolation because of the silence and the pathological composure of the family. As a result he felt himself to be a pariah, ostracized and unclean.

His need to go into the Episcopal Church was the need for the obsessive-compulsive safeguards of liturgy and ritual, the need for the frequency with which the Eucharist is celebrated by the minister as compared to the infrequent, informal communion service of the Congregational Church where the service is usually conducted by the elders while the minister sits by, having no function except to preach. In his need to master the funeral experience he needed to be an active and not a passive participant. This is usually the case in our attempts to master a traumatic incident by its reenactment.

Although the cases of Phillip, Andrew, Jerome, and Matthew are much the same in the distortion of the sacrifice of Holy Communion as "kill or be killed," yet each has come to this syndrome in a different manner. Phillip was first overwhelmed by his misunderstanding of his father's work as a pathologist, and was apparently fixated in his fear of his mother's murderous aggression when she nearly drowned him. For him, like Andrew, the angry God was not really a father but an implacable Mother God. It was safer to be angry with an angry man so it was not until he worked through this that he could get down to the more terrible mother.

I still cannot tell where Phillip's religious vocation began, but early he so mistrusted human relationships and human intervention that all the love he had experienced in childhood was transferred onto his God-idea. This was later covered over and distorted as his twisted, unhappy life developed. Like Andrew he found his devotion through the nonverbal communication of music.

Freud had fears that he would die before his parents and they would be alone and desolate in their old age. Phillip had fantasies of comforting his dying parents. There is little difference between the wish and the fear, as Freud himself made clear.

The pressure of unfulfilled unconscious needs may also result in distortions of logical thinking. In the area that concerns us such distortions may manifest themselves in deviations from doctrine. Similarly, the pressure of unconscious needs may distort primary-process thinking. Primary-process thinking relates to the instincts and to the unconscious rather than to outer reality and manifests itself in the picture-language thinking of children and in the creative mentation of artists, poets, and mystics. Errors in primary-process thinking—which, in our field of concern, may result in the unconscious distortion of the concept of God, for example—are not subject to correction by logical thought but can be corrected by psychotherapeutic techniques that provide channels of communication between primary-process and logical thinking. This was illustrated in the case of Stephen as well as many others.

Only the psychiatrist and the psychologist who have studied the differences between the repressed distorted primary-process thinking of neurotics and the schizophrenic thinking disorders will understand the real import of these cases. One could discount to a great extent the problem of the unconscious distortions of religion in the clergy if one saw them all as schizophrenic. In the cases presented, Jacob, Martin, Samson, Abel, Jerome, and John are neurotics by the most severe Rorschach standards. James, Andrew, and Matthew were borderlines who would have been considered neurotics by most clinical psychiatrists. Probably only Stephen and Patience would have been considered overt schizophrenics by the average clinical diagnostic standards.

How Jerome's need for treatment could have been discovered by our usual psychological screening I do not know. He showed no signs or symptoms that I could discern until he was ordained priest and began to celebrate the Eucharist. This phobic situation he could repress and master until he was overwhelmed by his father's illness which he felt as a "death."

Until such a time as our seminaries are more aware of the need of the clergy to have personal psychoanalytic therapy for the same reasons as the student analyst, not because they seem to need it or not for their personal lives but in order to make them fuller and deeper, more understanding, more mature people, such well-compensated men as Jerome and Jacob will go on suffering with crippling conflicts and psychosomatic illnesses.

The phobic defense is that means by which we try to confine our anxieties to a situational condition. We only develop the anxiety in the presence of the phobic situation. We are no longer afraid of father, but we are deathly afraid of dogs. Isaac was bound on the altar of his sacrifice. He could not become a mature man in his religious thinking, but his rationale was not that he was afraid of God. Rather, he was afraid of the rituals and the places of ritual observance where his God was found. He could only worship from a distance, even at the cost of cutting himself off from so much of himself he could not be really comfortable at any time.

Andrew also reveals the problem of the man whose phobic fear is in his distorted symbolization of the work of a religionist. Without treatment we can be very sure that he would never have gone on to ordination. How many other such valuable men exclude themselves from their vocation we cannot know. I feel that the reason so many of my clergy patients find their vocations to be real in treatment is because, as in the case of Andrew, I try to help them face their fears, their doubts, their distorted unconscious symbolization. I no more consider it good therapy to help a man to run away from his fears at the altar than to let him run away from his fears of sexuality or aggression.

There are many obsessive-compulsive clergymen who cannot enjoy performing any ritual service. Their anxiety centers in the need that every word be read correctly and every gesture made properly. In this they betray the underlying feelings of magical omnipotence, for the effectiveness of all magical incantations depends upon this very meticulousness.

Jacob presented the clinical picture of an obsessive compulsive neurotic whose first line of defense was his compulsive cheerfulness and verbosity. His core problem was in severe early infantile dependent needs which resulted in his psychosomatic symptoms. In reaction to these unfulfilled infantile needs he had developed a great deal of anger which he tried to hold in check by his obsessive-compulsive defenses.

In searching out his lack of devotion we uncovered these deeply buried needs to be fed and loved. We then provoked intense transference reactions which, when resolved, enabled him to utilize his anger to open his repressed inner world and find his childhood devotion. This childhood devotion, once it was integrated with his total personality, quickly grew into a mature and healthy devotion. As he realized this devotion he felt more self-esteem and no longer needed to hide behind the guise of a phony which he had felt himself to be. He then reached out for love and, in return, was loved.

Conflicts in self-image are common. When personal devotion is lacking, or when the patient's personal behavior is deviant, his self-image is in conflict with his concept of himself as a clergyman. This may result in a sense of being "phony," and is expressed in feelings of personal failure, inadequacy, and guilt. Only when his idealized self-image is a reasonable one and is congruent with the perception of the self in reality can the clergyman feel fulfilled in his vocation.

The pathologic demands of the idealized self-image are often quite terrible. I once asked Andrew what he felt was demanded of a priest. In his agony he said, "Perfection. If I become ordained, I will have to become like Jesus—perfect. That means I would have to be utterly alone, completely isolated in my perfection."

Now we can begin to understand Andrew's defense of isolation, the isolation of the goldfish bowl, in his own inner world of fantasy. He was sure that he did not know as a child that in the early Christian church the fish was a frequently used symbol for the Christ figure. To him the church symbolized, in the perfection of its stonework and in the massive strength of its high walls and in its windows high above the heads of the people, a building in which he would be isolated and protected, so that even if the whole community approached he would be protected from killing and destroying them. I begin to wonder how many of the people who make up our omnipotent professions—that is, all those professions concerned with life and death, such as medicine, the ministry, law, teaching, psychoanalysis—how many of these are not isolating themselves in their self-made prison walls in order to protect their loved ones and their communities from the danger of their destructive powers. This is a frequent occurrence with the severe schizophrenic who goes out of contact with outer reality and withdraws deep inside his body in order to protect outer reality from the destructive power of his destructive wishes. He commits a symbolic suicide in order to keep from killing the environment—and his mother.

It is my feeling that when these set-apart people, these lonely ones, are criticized as being arrogant, of being too good to associate with people, of being able to relate to people only in a very structured situation, the people who criticize are doing them a grave injustice. There was no one quite so arrogant as Andrew in his dreams. No bishop ever had more amethysts and one cannot find an altar higher in all the world than the high altar at St. Peter's, nor communicants higher than the Pope and his cardinals. And yet, this man was unconsciously seeking in his isolation only to protect the world from the scourge of his dreaded destructiveness. He was like a leper who, realizing the danger and the contagiousness of his illness, retreats far from the world and dies a hermit.

Andrew is only one of many in my experience who has had this conflict. One wonders why this man became an Episcopalian. Of course there was something in the identification with his mother and in the rebellion against his father; but on deeper insight, there was the utter barrenness of his emotional and devotional life until the beauty and structure of the liturgical music of the Episcopal Church made the first chink in the armor of his defended isolation. Here was the beginning of a nonverbal devotion in the music. He also began to find in the tradition of the Church a feeling of the historical sweep of the centuries, and somehow in coming into a church whose tradition extended back into history for two thousand years, or more if we include our Hebrew heritage, he could feel identified and have a semblance of participation in the immortality which he sensed in the Church and in the eternity of the Divine, an immortality which somehow began to give him some reassurance against the terrible threat of killing and being killed.

The repeated problem of my clergy patients has been the displacement of all that has been evil and cruel in personal life experience onto the God-idea. The theme of sacrifice in atonement to this angry God has occurred again and again.

Yet there are a number of ways in which the individual responds to the religion of despair which Jonathan Edwards preached. For instance, financial success through hard work and frugality often operates as a continual reassurance that one is good and one is saved. Conversely a period of financial depression may be a sign of God's wrath, just as the ancient Hebrews accepted defeats in battle as punishment for the sins of the nation. Some are unable to use success as a sign of God's approval but instead react with depressive feelings of futility because the longed-for conversion experience does not occur, until another endeavor is launched and the cycle is repeated. For example, Samson used primarily the mechanisms of compulsively cheerful denial of any possibility of personal damnation, and of magical coercion of God both in his priestly functions and in the testing operation of his "acting out" the behavior problems which resulted in his deposition.

As months and years went by Samson was seemingly successful in proving that his rituals were effective and that God loved him. No matter what he did he got away with it. The more he got away with, the less reality testing he was able to bring to bear on the situation. Thus he came to believe in his magic and his omnipotence. Yet he desperately wanted God and man to do what his old, beloved bishop had done to stop him. He wanted to be told that his rebelliousness would not be tolerated. Underneath there was a severe conscience which expressed itself in more and more hostility toward his environment as his unconscious guilt increased. That both God and man failed to stop him, failed to control him, was a continuously nagging source of doubt to him. Perhaps he was damned after all; perhaps God just did not care how black his record might be on Judgment Day. Perhaps God really hated him and had predestined him to a life of sin and eternal damnation. To reassure himself that this was not true he would again test the situation compulsively, and then he would cheerfully try to force himself to believe that his success proved God's love.

In Samson's change to a more ritualistic religious observance there was an attempt to develop obsessive-compulsive defenses in order to control his hostility and his acting out. Included in the liturgical rigidities of his Anglo-Catholicism was the scrupulous daily recitation of the morning and evening offices of the Prayer Book. Throughout the period of his suspension he continued to read these offices. At one point after his deposition I challenged this: Was it a denial of his deposition? Was there any inherent devotional fulfillment in it? For two months he ceased all prayer, but then he found himself repeating the "Jesus prayer": "Lord Jesus Christ have mercy on me."

This he found himself chanting silently in coordination with his footsteps as he walked. He became aware of his anger with me for "taking his prayer life away," and returned to the saying of the offices. He also found himself using very orderly, methodical, compulsive patterns of behavior in everyday life in his very conscious attempts to restrain himself from further acting out. As the years have gone on these defenses have become more functional and less obsessive. His body tensions show a similar change. In the beginning he was overweight; his muscles were somewhat flabby; he slouched. Now his body is hard and lean, his muscles in excellent tonus and responsive to the slightest change of word or intensity. To this is added the characteristic flavor of masculinity in gesture and general habitus.

He had used ritual and ceremony to dominate and thereby control his hostility to women, who were all either Mama or Grandmother Hecate, and likewise to control Mother Church. This has been a common finding among my patients with religious problems. As would be expected, the more severe the feminine component in the priest the less effective is this defense, and the greater is the need for outside control.

In this case there were danger signals all along the way which should have been noted by those who were his ecclesiastical superiors. Similar symptoms ought always to be examined with care by those who are concerned with the evaluating of candidates for the ministry, and by the pastors and therapists of clergy and laity.

1. His inadequate psychosexual development, which was so severe in his late thirties, would have been equally obvious in his early twenties. Intellectually he was far above average; emotionally he was a child.

2. His search for a father provoked his sudden conversion within months after he lost his own father. This was the first point where his history showed plain evidence of pathology, but apparently it was not noticed at this point. Immediately thereafter

he was accepted as a postulant for Holy Orders without psychological screening. This practice had not become a canonical requirement in the Episcopal Church, and his first bishop had not availed himself of the new tools. When he found a father in the old bishop, he stabilized; when he lost this father his behavior problems began.

3. The sudden development of extremes in seminary should have further alerted ecclesiastical authority. The change from the orientation of a severe fundamentalist to that of the ritualistic, sacrament-centered Anglo-Catholic implied a serious attempt to reorganize his personality structure. Had he simply converted from the liberal Presbyterian Church to ordinary broad or low Episcopal Church, the event would more than likely not have been so indicative of religious conflict. But there was clearly the need to have a wider scope to coerce God by magical omnipotence, as well as to have more rigidly defined obsessive-compulsive defenses.

4. He first defended against severe feminine identifications, his very deep dependent need of women, and the resultant anger toward them by planning to be a celibate priest. As such he could enjoy his unconscious femininity, control women, and keep away from them. This defense broke down and resulted in behavioral symptoms of a homosexual sort, so that he was urged by his superiors into the equally inadequate defense of marriage, where he began his heterosexual promiscuity.

Perhaps the factor that most blinded his ecclesiastical superiors was, in addition to his outstanding capabilities in certain areas, his very real devotion, his dedication, and his vocation. As distorted as these were by his magical thinking, they were still real and projected. Devout persons always feel that a man who is devout and who prays will be led by God to a good life. Unfortunately this is too often a snare and a delusion. Methods of assaying the childish and adolescent distortions of a man's personal perception of his God must be found. Ways of evaluating his transference distortions, as well as the general primary-process distortions of his God and his church have to be worked out.

The tragedy of this case is that a brilliant, capable, and devout man has been cut off from his life work, where his leadership is needed, because of his severe illness and the ignorance of his superiors. The church is left with the challenge of rectifying those things in her which contributed to the tragedy or of continuing in her failure and guilt.

Still another unconscious dynamic lies in the sexual area. Exhibitionism, for example, may, when sublimated, become a source of deep fulfillment for religious personnel but will cause problems and conflicts when sublimation has not taken place. It is the function of psychotherapy to bring about successful sublimation in such cases. Serious sexual problems respond more favorably to psychotherapy among the clergy than they do among laymen, because religious personnel are more forcefully motivated to make a socially acceptable adjustment. On the other hand, defects in the formation of object relationships require longer treatment periods and present greater difficulties because they are less responsive to motivational dynamics. Working with marital problems also has practical difficulties in a church where divorce for the clergy is not acceptable. But, as in the case of Patience, there is greater motivation for working through the problems within the marriage when divorce and remarriage are so difficult.

Patience is a good example of a clergyman's sick wife, but she does not reveal the problem of a woman with a religious vocation who marries a minister for a vicarious existence or who goes into the work of a religionist for herself. Patience, except for her family tradition and the accident of her fiance finding his vocation after they were engaged, might very well be a lay person, but a lay person whose religious conflicts would still have required analysis. Without going into her personal religious life, I do not feel we could have been able to help her; so much of her anger and her guilt was projected onto her personal God-idea.

Her defense was primarily in her silence. She had never confided in her mother, her friends, or her husband. This same silent withdrawal had occurred in her relationship to God. She could no longer pray. It came out repeatedly in her negative transference reactions to the individuals in the group but especially toward the therapist.

She typifies the Judeo-Christian distortion of suffering as atonement to appease her angry God-idea. She had the same angry

God, the Patriarchal Father of the Primal Horde as Freud did.

Like Freud, Patience had reacted throughout her life in response to the operative but repressed successful death wishes toward a younger sibling. Before the sibling died she had learned to use illness as a means of coercing love. After the death she developed masochistic behavior which was both an atonement and a means of coercing love.

Yet on a deeper level she had an even more destructive self-concept. She struggled within herself to keep in check her destructive, castrating death wishes toward men and the Father God. Out of their own masochism her father and her husband reinforced her fears of her own magical powers that were so hidden and proved in the death of her sibling. So, back of the angry Father God was an even more vicious White Goddess.

Andrew's fear of killing as well as his unwillingness to be the sacrificial victim as he symbolized it in the breaking of the Host in the celebration of the Eucharist kept him from going on to ordination. His intense sexualization of pain and suffering was expressed both in his masturbation fantasies and his distortions of theology, as were typified in the fantasy of torturing the Christ figure and in the symbolization of the meaning of the divine Liturgy.

This seems to stem from his first sexual awareness that occurred when, at age twelve after his circumcision, his father held his hand with tender concern when the doctor took out the stitches. Here tender fatherly love and exquisite castration pain merged and fixated.

Perhaps we can also understand more deeply Andrew's early dream of being vested and bedecked with amethysts, his mother's and a bishop's stones. A woman had emasculated him and a woman and a Mother God would make it possible for him to have his masculinity again in balls of amethysts dangling from his ear lobes so that all could see and admire. This symbolization of permission and right to be a man carries with it the right to be ambitious, and powerful, as did his enjoyment of the cardinal's robes at the masquerade party. He expresses the exhibitionism in his love of beautiful vestments and his pleasure in ritual and preaching. He is also the unseen organist, for the organist is always unseen but whose presence is deeply felt by all those whose devotion is expressed in and through music. He could never have been a fulfilled minister in the Church he was brought up in, where there is no instrumental music, no ritual, no vestments, and where the occasional communion service is blessed by the spontaneous prayers of the elders and given to the congregation by the deacons while the minister twiddles his thumbs until it is time to begin preaching. For some people this primitive simplicity is fulfillment but for Andrew it represents utter desolation and deprivation. He is a convert who has found in his adopted church an expression of his devotion and an expression of his unconscious and conscious needs that spells fulfillment.

We should also concern ourselves here with the problem of Christianity and homosexuality. Does Christianity actively promote the development of homosexuality, and does the church give the homosexual a place in which he can hope to sublimate his homosexuality?

Many of my clergy patients, such as Andrew, were brought up in a sternly Protestant environment where the concept of a man and a minister is that of a married man with a family. In the case of Andrew, his mother imbued him with a strong negative feeling toward sex. She convinced him that he should be faithful to her and thereby be her "sacrifice." She also impressed upon him the sinful destructive effect of man's sexuality and anger upon helpless fragile woman.

The Protestant tradition permits and even encourages a man in his anger toward women. The "Blessed Virgin" can be degraded as "that woman." The "Mother of God" can be thought of as the mother of other children and is reduced to human proportions. But in making God into a Patriarchal Father God the submissiveness and passivity of the son is also pathologically intensified. It is the problem of the religionist to find the healthy middle ground somewhere in between the Mother God, the White Goddess with her castrated priesthood and the equally implacable Father of the Primal Horde God which Freud struggled with.

The problem of homosexuality among clergy is a problem that one does not talk about. More than half of my male clergy population have suffered this crippling behavior symptom. This tells us nothing about our clergy population as a whole, for more than half of my nonclergy patients have also been homosexuals. I am interested in the problem and enjoy working with it and have had rewarding results from the treatment of the homosexual. As a result I tend to receive such referrals more than the analyst who prefers other problems.

This is not the place to go into the problem and therapy of homosexuality. But it may be well to state my position. I consider it a symptom which expresses deeper core problems. With the lay homosexual who does not wish to change I can be content to help him live in the world without disturbing the anxiety of the majority of the latent population and to develop good and fulfilling relationships. With the clergy I must insist ultimately on their working through the necessary period of disciplined discretion to a time of comfortable acceptance of a celibate life or to go on to working through the problem to the ability to make a good marriage. I encourage them in marriage as a goal when they desire it, but I do require that sufficient and successful therapy be done so that we are reasonably sure that a good marirage occurs. I also insist that they remain in therapy for at least the first year of marriage.

In my experience and that of my associate, a man, there has been a significant difference in the recovery rate of the clerical homosexual as compared to the layman. Of 16 exclusively homosexual ministers who remained in treatment more than one year, six or 37 per cent became exclusively heterosexual after two to three years of psychotherapy; two more became exclusively heterosexual after three to five years of therapy. Five are continuing in treatment, so that the 50 per cent recovery is only indicative and not final. Of 12 laymen exclusively homosexual who have remained in therapy more than one year, one has become exclusively heterosexual. This man, a deeply religious person, went through all the severe conscience upheavals in relation to both homosexuality and heterosexuality which we usually find only in the minister patient.

The startling difference in results in the clergy and the nonclergy series would seem to indicate that ministers are less liable to settle for homosexuality as a way of life. To the clergyman, homosexuality presents a serious problem of conscience as well as a professional problem. In general, they are more inhibited and tend to come into therapy younger and with less of the "acting out" characteristic of the homosexual. They generally feel a greater conscience demand to give up their homosexuality and a greater sense of sin and guilt in relation to it. In addition to all the other factors found in the genesis of homosexuality, the clerical patient suffers amazing feelings of sin and guilt in relation to his first stirrings of heterosexual attraction and is in great torment of conscience when he first engages in heterosexual activity.

Severe dependency needs, as in the case of Stephen, are more easily coped with in those whose personal religious devotion has been so deepened that fulfillment in personal prayer life results. When dependency needs are transferred to a God who has been cleansed of the pathological transferences of his life experience, and when magical coercive ideas of intercessory prayer have been worked through, the patient then finds in his devotion a source of strength and self-acceptance which permits a better than expected rate of recovery.

To this question of why some homosexual males respond better in therapy Arieti has suggested that the process of "imprinting" which is called "neotony" in mammals may be a factor. He says:

> The primitive response may have not only a negative aim—avoidance of unpleasantness—but also a positive one, such as quick attainment of pleasure. For instance, if a gosling can obtain quick mothering from a man he may be "imprinted" to respond to every man as to a goose. If a boy at an early level of his sexual development receives strong stimulation and gratification from another boy or man, he may learn to respond at a homosexual level, instead of overcoming this fixation and moving toward heterosexuality. Additional factors in the family constellation may facilitate this fixation.[1]

In other words, how very real is the need for good mothering by women for little boys and good fathering by men for little girls.

[1] *The Microgeny of Thought and Perception* by Silvano Arieti, M.D. The Archives of General Psychiatry, June, 1962, Vol. 6, pp. 454–468. Used by permission.

The development of religious devotion is, in my opinion, related to this process of neotony in which imprinting is extended into the later life of the individual. The loving environment is experienced during the early months of infancy and is later remembered and perceived as devotion. The infant experiences the same sense of omnipotence, spacelessness, and timelessness as is experienced in profound religious mystical experience. The next phase in the development of religious devotion is the formation of the concept of God, which takes place during childhood. In the mature individual this concept is a changing and growing one, freeing itself step by step of the distortions of childhood.

When no religious indoctrination is experienced by the individual this wellspring of health may be perceived as a depth of "spirituality." This is seen in many creative people who in the moment of creative activity experience what the devout person realizes in the fulfillment of prayer.

Thus it may be found that the religious person has in his religious dedication a vital potential for psychological health which will become available when the pathological conditioning of later life experience is cleared away. I feel that even in the severe psychotic, who seems to have never experienced human love, the psychotic religious experience, even though distorted, is nevertheless a religious one and when integrated into the life experience of the patient becomes a source of strength, as Anton Boisen has shown.

Based on these concepts, psychotherapy can help the religiously indoctrinated person achieve a state of personal devotion and fulfillment. These concepts also have important implications in the field of religious education both in the religious education of the child and the seminarian. "Dry spells" and the "dark night of the soul," periodically experienced by religious personnel, may be considered as depressive phenomena and are amenable to the proper psychotherapeutic approach.

Patience is an example of the failure of adult religious education to undo the distortions of childhood, for her conversion to the Episcopal Church was not one of convenience. She had become a convert in college, largely owing to long hours of talking throughout adolescence with her fiance who did not at that time know that he intended to go into the work of a religionist. She was a convert because she was searching for the mature ideal of a good God-idea which both she and her husband found in the Episcopal Church. Had he not been brought up in that denomination she might have found her needs met in liberal Methodism.

Except for the fact that Jacob and Isaac stayed within their own religious group I would classify them as converts. In one way they actually are both converts because they changed from the religion absorbed by them in childhood to a religion they could intellectually approve of in adult life. In each case the acceptance of the newer religion was accomplished without any integration of the previous faith, thus running counter to the normal process of growth. By their use of repression and phobic defense both Jacob and Isaac demonstrate the same mechanisms of defense as those used by converts. In this sense everyone whose repressed and distorted childhood religion is still operative is, in his conscious adult religion, a convert.

It is not enough to say that every convert needs therapy. They do, but there are so many who, like James and John, were brought up in the church in which they were ordained. Their conflicts were in the unresolved childhood religion so that they too were essentially converts to their adult religion.

As in all good psychotherapy, constant watchfulness and interpretation of the transference attitude is essential. It is not enough, in my experience, to analyze the transference attitudes to the therapist. One must also analyze the transference attitudes to God, His Son, the Bible, and the Church. Jacob, ordinarily the most rational of men, at one time perceived God no longer in relation to His natural law but in the guise of his mother and father who were poor managers of the home and business. Patience experienced God as an angry parent and at those times she could not talk to me or pray to God. The freedom to experience anger in relation to God as well as to me was vital to Jacob and Phillip. Patience felt that only in suffering could she win human and divine love.

The tape-recorded session in the case of Patience illustrates the use and value of emotional intensity in the working through of the therapeutic process. A similar use of such intensity was experienced with Andrew in the Prayer of Consecration which, unfortunately, was not recorded. Such moments of intense emotional experience are extremely dangerous. There is always the hazard that the patient cannot synthesize after the shattering effect of the impact of such an emotional upheaval. This is like major surgery. One has to have the judgment to know when it is safe and good and when it is not. This ability to know intuitively that this is the moment and follow through skillfully can only come with long years of experience. It is not a technique for the student analyst to use. One condition I feel is certain and that is an atmosphere of positive transference and countertransference and the willingness to stay with the situation until it is resolved. This type of intensity usually requires freedom to continue the session to its logical conclusion regardless of the time involved. A group session is like a good analytic session. It has a beginning, associations and emotional interactions between group members, an interpretation, and a summation.

The value of the intensity is in its breaking through resistances and repressions. Also, within the group relationship, its experiencing of a living vital situation where a new and healthier pattern of reaction to an old conflict is first realized, not just intellectually but emotionally. The neurotic breaks through his barriers and regains and egotizes his inner world. The schizophrenic does the same in the extension of the feeling of self into the outer world thereby bringing new life and vitality, new relationships, into the self. This allows for a broad and full integration of the inner and outer world.

Why Patience, so seriously disturbed, could respond with ego synthesis to such seriously shattering experiences as in the recorded group therapy session is impossible for me to explain. In her masochistic reaction to previous therapists she became sicker with every session. Here she was able to plunge into the free experiencing of her unconscious conflicts and emerge stronger and healthier.

In the case of Andrew, whose defenses were so facile and evasive, the direct confrontation as in the Prayer of Consecration and the Funeral Service saved much time and effort. One might well say that it enabled us to cut through a tangled mass of red tape and get to the heart of the matter.

The core of Andrew's sadomasochism was broken in the confrontation of the acting out in the therapy group of the Prayer of Consecration. The spontaneous use of a Sacrament as an acting-out, of impulsive use of psychodrama with intense emotional involvement is a technique which many therapists and many religionists, too, might well disapprove. I feel that if the problem itself is understood the individual therapist with his own individual patient can find his own method of resolving it. With a number of the clergy, such as Phillip and Jerome, the similar problem of what they experienced in their actual performance of their work as priests at the altar was worked through by means of interpretation in therapy. As Phillip explained, it is perhaps harder that way since one is alone with one's fears during therapeutic situations instead of being in the bosom of one's family. Jerome was afraid that he would need to take sick leave for it was such an ordeal that he could not be certain from one moment to the next whether or not he would be able to go through each service. Several other priests have had to leave the sanctuary, vomit, and return. Others have had moments of uncontrollable weeping either in the sanctuary or in the pulpit. This is always interpreted by the congregation as "overfatigue."

The seminarian often suffers from a dread of what will happen when he is ordained. In two cases, reading the Communion Service in the group has resolved these doubts of vocation and led to deeper insight. This is such a serious use of the Sacrament and causes so much anxiety because it is canonically illegal that we have permitted it very rarely, and only when the circumstances clearly indicated that there was a valid emotional need and when the entire group agreed to participate. In each case it has been a most rewarding therapeutic and devotional experience.

One cannot help wondering how much more our seminaries could do to help these men find their vocation or their crippling distortion if "dry runs," as rehearsals of services are called, were done in a deeply emotional and devotionally meaningful manner.

As more clergy are studied we shall undoubtedly find a whole range of possible human psychopathology which undermines the varied and wide human investment in religion, ritual, and doctrine. As our religionists can be cleansed and healed we can look forward to a time when God's healing Grace will be even more abundantly available to mankind, for only the mature individual can be truly righteous.